D1612332

AZTECS

AZTECS

Edited by Doris Kurella, Martin Berger and Inés
de Castro in cooperation with the Instituto
Nacional de Antropología e Historia (INAH),
Mexico

LINDEN-MUSEUM STUTTGART
Staatliches Museum für Völkerkunde

welt
museum
wien

MUSEUM
VOLKENKUNDE

HIRMER

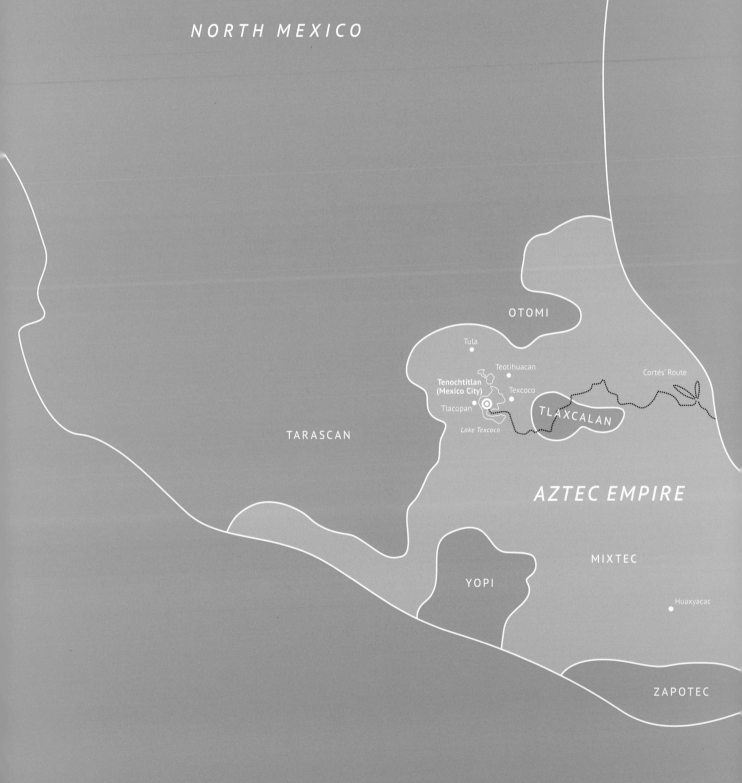

NORTH MEXICO

OTOMI

Tula

Teotihuacan

Tenochtitlan
(Mexico City)

Texcoco

Cortés' Route

Tlacopan

TLAXCALAN

Lake Texcoco

TARASCAN

AZTEC EMPIRE

MIXTEC

YOPI

Huaxyacac

ZAPOTEC

Pacific Ocean

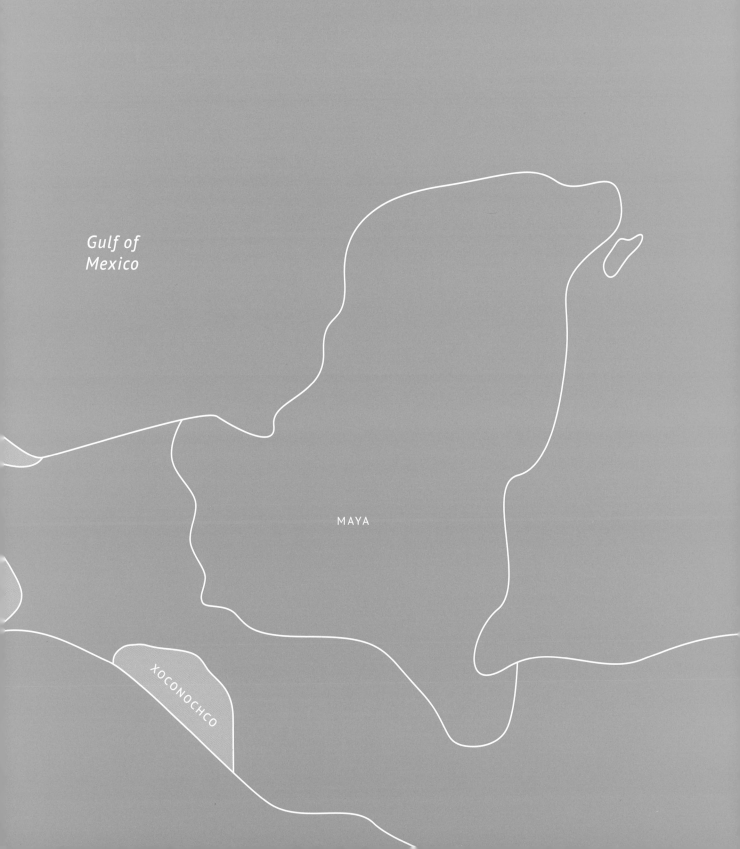

Gulf of
Mexico

MAYA

XOCONOCHCO

Contents

Words of Welcome

The Aztecs and the life and culture of their civilisation have long been a source of great fascination. Their artistic and artisanal forms of expression, the rich legacy of this Meso-American culture which blossomed between the fourteenth and the beginning of the sixteenth centuries, can be marvelled at between 12 October 2019 and 3 May 2020 at the Linden-Museum in Stuttgart. This unique exhibition which was developed in cooperation with the Nationaal Museum van Wereldculturen in the Netherlands will then be shown in Vienna and subsequently in Leiden.

The landing of the Spanish Conquistador Hernán Cortés in the Gulf of Mexico in the year 1519 signalled the beginning of the intermingling of indigenous and European culture. 500 years later, the exhibition "Aztecs" makes it possible to experience and follow Cortés on his journey through the provinces to the Sacred Precinct of the capital city Tenochtitlan. With around 250 precious items on loan from Mexican and European museums, the visitor is treated to a unique glimpse into the art and culture of the Aztecs. Articles of everyday use as well as ritual objects, funerary items and jewellery are included in this exhibition and allow for a better understanding of the culture. The detailed and lifelike depictions of the Aztec people can be seen in the exceptional featherwork shields – there are only four of these objects in the world, and here we are proud to display two of them – and the valuable greenstone carvings, which form the nucleus of this exhibition. Working in close cooperation with the state of Mexico, and especially, with the famous Mexican archaeologists Eduardo Matos Moctezuma, Leonardo López Luján and Raúl Barrera Rodríguez, we are able to present for the first time recently excavated objects found in the vicinity of the Templo Mayor, as well as the latest results of research and archaeological excavations.

I would like to thank all those who were involved in the development and realisation of this exhibition concept. Without your hard work and involvement, it would not be possible to keep the memories of the richness of the past alive, and to elicit the interest of the public, and bring them closer to the subject through the attractive curatorial design. I hope the large-scale state exhibition "The Aztecs" will be well received by both the public and the experts. I wish all the visitors to this exhibition fascinating insights as they experience the spellbinding history of the Aztecs!

Winfried Kretschmann
Prime Minister of the State of Baden-Württemberg

Words of Welcome

The government of Mexico and the Ministry of Culture are honoured to be involved in the exhibition "Aztecs". We are grateful for the efforts of the Instituto Nacional de Antropología e Historia (INAH) and all other institutions, museums and individuals who have contributed to this exhibition with their knowledge and expertise and who have thus made it possible. It will show selected pieces from European collections together with exhibits from the stocks of Mexican museums including the Museo Templo Mayor and the Museo Nacional de Antropología. They include objects which have never previously been shown in public and which open up a new perspective on Aztec culture.

The exhibition is accompanied by a catalogue which is co-published by INAH and which assembles a series of articles by international experts, especially Mexican researchers who are specialists in this field. Together they give us a better understanding of Aztec culture by basing their observations on the latest archaeological finds and results.

Five hundred years after the Europeans arrived on the coast of what is now Mexico, we welcome this magnificent exhibition on the Aztec people which will be shown in countries which have a particular interest in our diverse cultural manifestations. Visitors to the exhibition and readers of this catalogue will understand the profound meaning of the words of Hernán Cortés, addressed in his *Segunda Carta de Relación* to Emperor Charles V when he set eyes on the magnificent capital of Mexico-Tenochtitlan:

"[…] For in order to present an account of the size, the strange and wonderful things in this great city […] and the rites and customs which its people practise […], I know full well that they will be so admired that we can scarcely believe it, because those who have seen them here with their own eyes cannot comprehend them with their understanding. […]"

For Mexican society an artist, known as *toltecatl*, was someone who "entered into a dialogue with his heart". It must have been a turbulent dialogue at times, because today many Aztec sculptures evoke feelings of fear and amazement. The countenance of life and death, the realistic representations of real and mythical animals, gods, maize and life cycles are the accents which determine an aesthetic whose roots lie in concepts of victory, power and pride.

Seen through present-day eyes there is no doubt that we view these sculptures differently today, because we see in them a certain beauty which appears to appeal to our modern perception, a perception which recognises in the symbolic and meaningful the representation of poetic beauty.

All in all, Aztec art is a cry of victory: it is Ehecatl who thrills us. It is Coyolxauhqui, hacked to pieces but unconquered. Tenochtitlan is the voice of a victorious, confident people. Five hundred years have passed since their culture was carved in stone but it is still alive today. "Aztecs" is, quite simply, an exhibition which permits us to share in the grandeur of this empire. Welcome!

Alejandra Frausto Guerrero
Minister of Culture, Mexico

Preface and Acknowledgements

The Linden-Museum Stuttgart is proud to present for the second time a Baden-Württemberg State Exhibition and accompanying catalogue devoted to one of the great cultures of pre-Columbian America under the expert curatorial direction of Dr. Doris Kurella. Following on from the 2013 exhibition "Inca – Kings of the Andes", we now present the exhibition "Aztecs" as a special acknowledgement of this civilisation, 500 years after Hernán Cortés' landing in Mexico.

The main reason for this exhibition in Stuttgart are the two unique feather shields and a precious figure made of green stone, which are currently part of the Landesmuseum Württemberg's collections, but belonged in former times to the Linden-Museum's founding inventory. It was very important to me to be able to present these objects for the first time in their cultural context and I would like to thank the director of the Landesmuseum Württemberg, Prof. Dr. Cornelia Ewigleben, for making this possible.

Despite intensive ongoing scientific research over many years, our knowledge regarding the Aztec culture is still incomplete. Our understanding of the subject is mainly derived from two sources. Firstly, the accounts of the Spanish conquerors, which, based on the individual intentions of each author, differ in their emphasis or depiction of events and circumstances. Secondly, archaeological investigations, particularly in the centre of Mexico City, in the Templo Mayor and its immediate surroundings, continue to unearth objects successfully and deepen our knowledge. The archaeological results of the last decade have been especially fruitful, contributing to a new insight into the Aztec culture.

In contrast to earlier Aztec exhibitions, "Aztecs" will present art and everyday objects in the context of the civilisation's culture and society; this will allow for a better understanding of the subject.

Essential to the realisation of the exhibition as well as for this accompanying catalogue was the close cooperation with Mexico's National Archaeological Institution, the Instituto Nacional de Antropología e Historia (INAH). Thanks to this support we are able to share precious objects from Mexico – in some cases newly excavated and never before exhibited – in addition to artefacts specially selected from European collections. I was glad to carry out negotiations with the Mexican government and the relevant administrative bodies.

This exhibition came into being through close cooperation with the Netherlands' Nationaal Museum van Wereldculturen. I would like to extend special thanks to its director Dr. Stijn Schoonderwoerd and his team, especially the co-curator Dr. Martin Berger, for the excellent collaboration. For the future transfer of this exhibition to the Museum of Ethnology in Vienna, where it will be presented in 2020, I would like to thank its director Dr. Christian Schicklgruber, as well as the KHM-Museumsverband Wien under the direction of its general manager Dr. Sabine Haag.

It was only with the generous financial assistance of the State of Baden-Württemberg and its Prime Minister Winfried Kretschmann that this exhibition was made possible. Without this support such an important and significant project would not have been possible. Special thanks as well to Minister Theresia Bauer, State Secretary Petra Olschowski, and to the museum department at the Ministry for Science, Research and Art, Baden-Württemberg.

We are also indebted to the Mexican Minister of Culture, Alejandra Frausto Guerrero, as well as to the numerous ministry officials who assisted us in reaching our objective. The generous provision of loans from Mexico was made possible largely through the efforts of Alejandra Barajas Moreno and Itzia Villicaña Gerónimo from the INAH. Special thanks to the Mexican directors Patricia Ledesma Bouchan from the Museo Templo Mayor, as well as to Antonio Saborit from the Museo Nacional de Antropología. For their assistance throughout the negotiation process we would like to thank the Ambassador of the Republic of Mexico Rogelio Granguillhome Morfín, as well as the director of the Mexican Cultural Institute in Germany, Susana Garduño-Arana.

The generosity of our kind lenders has contributed greatly to the realisation of our exhibition. We would like to thank them sincerely for their efforts. We are also grateful to the many sponsors who have supported this project financially.

We would also like to express our thanks to our professional colleagues here in Germany as well as abroad, who, in sharing their knowledge with us, have made a very important contribution to the success of this exhibition. Special thanks to the Mexican archaeologists Eduardo Matos Moctezuma, official consultant to this exhibition project, as well as Leonardo López Luján and Raúl Barrera Rodriguez.

I would also like to praise the exhibition's chief curator, Dr. Doris Kurella, head of the Department of North and Latin America at the Linden-Museum Stuttgart, for her expert and tireless efforts and commitment in making this exhibition a success.

Exhibition teams from both the Linden-Museum Stuttgart and the Nationaal Museum van Wereldculturen deserve praise for their intensive collaboration over the past years. In the name of all those involved, I would like to thank Ivonne Athie Islas, Julisa van Beek, Myriam Berrich, Rik Herder, Isabel Klotz, Rosalie Möller, Margrit Reuss, Katja Scharff and Floortje Timmerman.

Notes on Terminology and Spelling

"Aztecs", as a term is largely European in origin, dating back to the 18th and 19th centuries, and derives from Aztlán, their mythical place of origin. They referred to themselves as "Mexica", the term from which the present-day Republic of Mexico takes its name. In the exhibition, we have decided to use the term "Aztecs" because of its familiarity in Europe; in the context of this catalogue, each individual author could decide which terminology they wished to employ.

Research into the Aztecs is still a relatively new discipline in which there are a number of different approaches and interpretations. This is especially true in the interpretation of written colonial sources. The reader of this catalogue will encounter a variety of approaches, name designations or different versions of myths drawn from the oral tradition. Human sacrifice is also a subject of controversy; it is indisputable that this practice took place, but was it as prevalent as the Spanish accounts describe? Experts will be given space in this publication to weigh in with their own interpretations of this phenomenon.

Prof. Dr. Inés de Castro
Director Linden-Museum Stuttgart

Introduction

Eduardo Matos Moctezuma

Introduction

In February 1519, Hernán Cortés landed on the coast of the island of Cozumel. Days before, he had left Cuba in defiance of the orders of Governor Diego Velázquez, setting sail with ten ships and four hundred men of war. It was in Cozumel that an encounter that would have enormous importance for the conquest of Mexico took place. The Spanish captain knew that, years earlier, a number of Spanish ships had capsized and that some of the survivors had managed to save themselves and reach land, only to be captured by the Maya who lived there. Some were sacrificed to the Maya gods; two of them, Jerónimo de Aguilar and Gonzalo Guerrero, survived. They had very different destinies: the latter immediately adapted, found a wife and from this union the first mestizos were born in Meso-American lands. The other, Jerónimo, was never able to integrate as his companion had done. On the contrary, as Bernal Díaz del Castillo tells us in his account *The True History of the Conquest of New Spain* (1943), he would read his "book of hours" as a refuge from that unexpected sojourn in foreign lands. We can imagine that, unlike Gonzalo, Jerónimo would keep his eyes glued to the sacred book when a well-formed young Mayan woman walked by. Here we can see two very different perspectives: Gonzalo, who made the new world that was opening up before his eyes his own, and Jerónimo, who was there physically but whose mind was still in Spain. These were two different ways of facing their destiny.

At the invitation of Cortés, Jerónimo de Aguilar joined the Peninsular forces. The fleet continued sailing along the coast of the Yucatán peninsula and, as they were passing through what is now the State of Tabasco, Cortés was presented with several native women as a gift. One of them, whose name was Malintzin (Malinche), was of noble birth and spoke several languages, including Nahuatl and Maya. Together with Jerónimo de Aguilar, who spoke Spanish and Maya, they would be enormously useful for the venture of the Conquest. When Cortés and his troops reached what is now the State of Veracruz, they observed that the attitude of the inhabitants changed radically: they were

Fig. 1 ◄
Portrait of Hernán Cortés

Real Academia de Bellas Artes de San Fernando, Madrid

17

well-received and given provisions and support. The Totonac people complained that they lived under the yoke of the Lord Moctezuma and had to send tribute to the Aztec city of Tenochtitlan. Cortés immediately took stock of the situation and told them that they would no longer have to pay tribute to Moctezuma, which gained him their full support since they saw this as a way to be freed from Aztec oppression. Cortés then decided to run his ships aground (not to burn them, as is commonly thought) and begin the advance to Tenochtitlan, capital of the Aztec empire.

Aztec (Mexica) society

Following a series of events, the Spanish forces finally reached the outskirts of the Mexica city of Tenochtitlan. The admiration they felt upon seeing that city in the middle of a lake gave way to great astonishment. Bernal Díaz del Castillo recounts what their eyes beheld in these words:

> "From the moment we saw such admirable things, we did not know what to say, or if what appeared before us could be believed, because on one side, on land, there were great cities, and many more on the lake, crowded with canoes, and in the causeway were many bridges at intervals and before us stood the great city of Mexico" (Díaz del Castillo 1943).

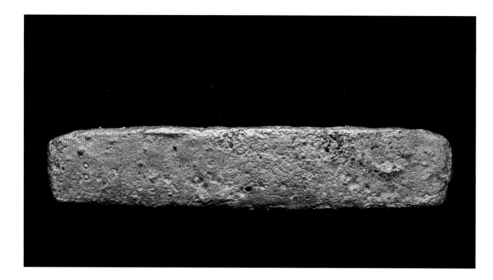

Fig. 3
Gold ingot made from Aztec
gold which had been melted
down. It was probably lost by
a soldier fleeing during the
"Noche Triste".

Museo Nacional de Antro-
pologia, Mexico City, D.R.
Secretaría de Cultura – INAH
(cat. 5)

Who were the Mexica, or Aztecs? According to ancient chronicles, this
people had left their native land, Aztlan ("The Place of Whiteness"), guided
by their god of the sun and war, Huitzilopochtli ("Left-handed Hummingbird"). After many years during which they would establish themselves
somewhere and then continue on their way, the Aztecs reached the Basin
of Mexico, where they finally settled in the middle of Lake Texcoco. It is
here that history and myth intertwine. History indicates how the Lord of
Azcapotzalco, who at that time had gained control over a large part of the
valley, allowed them to settle on small islands in the lake so that they would
have to pay him tribute. This actually occurred and, according to several
historical sources, the city of Tenochtitlan was founded in the year 1325 AD.
On the other hand, the myth states that they settled on the islands where
they saw the symbol of an eagle perched on a prickly pear cactus. This did not
actually happen, but it was a way of indicating that their city was founded by
the mandate of their god (the eagle represents the sun and Huitzilopochtli is
the warrior god of the sun).

They immediately divided the city into four quadrants or districts, with the
temple to the god in the centre. Thus, construction began on the main
building occupying the centre of the universe. Four causeways extended from
the large main square of the city, symbolising the four cardinal directions of
the universe and leading to the mainland. The *Templo Mayor* ("Great Temple") faces west and consists of a great platform upon which four superimposed pyramids were erected. One of the two shrines on top of the pyramid is
dedicated to Tlaloc, the god of rain and fertility and, therefore, of agricultural

production, while the other is dedicated to Huitzilopochtli, the god of war and the sun, who represents military expansion and control over other peoples, whom they subjected to tribute. Thus, water and war were present in the main building of Tenochtitlan and represented the Mexica economy, supported precisely by agriculture and war. Twin staircases led to the top of the pyramid to reach these two shrines.

An important aspect concerning the presence of these shrines dedicated to two of their main gods was that they represented the duality of life and death. This duality was of the utmost importance to Meso-American peoples because many of their actions involved complementary dualities or opposites. Thus we find life and death; cold and hot; night and day; masculine and feminine; heaven and the underworld, and many more. The Great Temple, considered

Fig. 4
Head of Tlaloc

Museo Nacional de Antropologia, Mexico City, D.R. Secretaría de Cultura – INAH (cat. 130)

the centre of the universe, was the most sacred place in the empire: through it, it was possible to reach the celestial levels or descend to the underworld. In the Mexica worldview, the universe was believed to be comprised of three fundamental levels: one was the Earth, where man lived; from there upwards were the 13 heavens, with the highest level reserved for the creator couple representing duality: Tonacatecuhtli and Tonacacíhuatl; and below the Earth lay the nine strata of the underworld, of which the ninth and deepest was Mictlan, the place inhabited by Mictlantecuhtli and his wife Mictlancíhuatl, the skeletal couple that lived in the world of the dead. This vertical idea of the universe was linked to the horizontal concept, with the four cardinal directions of the universe, each ruled by a god, a colour, a bird and a plant.

The Nahuatl calendar marked the festivals and celebrations dedicated to the gods. It consisted of 18 months of 20 days each, totaling 360 days, plus an additional five days, which were considered fateful. An analysis of the distribution of the days of the calendar reveals a significant presence of water-related gods. Deities related to war or the mother goddesses who gave birth to warriors also figure prominently. It is important to note how the gods were a significant presence in all the events of the lives of men. From birth to death, individuals were subject to the designs of the deities. This is why man had to make offerings to the gods in a series of ceremonies and oblations, so that the positive side of the deities would predominate. One example of this is the cult of Tlaloc. The rain god had both a positive and a negative side: he could send enough rain for plants to germinate but could also send hail that would kill them. This is the origin of the enormous number of ceremonies and offerings dedicated to the gods.

So how was Aztec society structured? It was comprised of two groups: on the one hand the *pillis*, or nobles, and on the other, the *macehualtin*, the common people. The former included the head of the government called *tlatoani*, which means "He who Speaks". The *tlatoani* was elected by a council; by custom, he was not necessarily the son of the previous ruler but could be a brother or any other person, as long as he was a member of the Royal House. High-level heads of the empire, priests and high-ranking warriors formed part of the nobility. Nobles were not required to pay internal tribute and were educated in a school called the *calmecac*. One way to obtain a high social standing was to distinguish oneself as a great warrior in battle. On the other hand, we have the merchants, who enjoyed certain privileges, such as having their own militia to support them in the journeys they had to make to distant places and carry their merchandise; they also had their own judges at the market, who settled the disputes that could arise in the exchange of products. Some authors maintain that the merchants, or *pochtecas*, were a class located in between the *pillis* and the *macehuales*. The latter accounted for most of the population and consisted of specialists in different areas of work, such as stonecutters, weavers, potters, architects, masons, labourers, physicians and various types of artists, such as sculptors and painters. They had their own school, the *telpochcalli*, and had to pay tribute in the form of products crafted for the *tlatoani*. A considerable number of this group consisted of rural workers involved in agricultural production. To do this work, they used an instrument known as the *coa*, or planting rod, to cultivate crops on the *chinampas*, an agricultural system that involved taking advantage of the wetlands by opening channels around them and piling on moist soil, allowing them to obtain good harvests every year.

This was the society encountered by the Spaniards and their indigenous allies, the enemies of the Mexica. The tribute system, which the Mexica or Aztecs had imposed on the peoples they had conquered by force of arms, led to the ill will of those conquered, who saw the possibility of no longer having to pay tribute to Tenochtitlan if they joined the Spaniards. Ultimately, many thousands of indigenous contingents supported the *conquistadores*. The siege of the Mexica cities neighbouring Tenochtitlan and Tlatelolco came to an end on 13 August 1521, when the Mexica *tlatoani* Cuauhtémoc was captured and brought before the Spanish captain Hernán Cortés. Today, there is a plaque on view in the archaeological remains of Tlatelolco, the last bastion of indigenous resistance, that reads:

> On 13 August 1521,
> heroically defended by Cuauhtémoc,
> Tlatelolco fell to Hernán Cortés.
> It was neither a victory nor a defeat,
> it was the painful birth
> of the mestizo nation
> that is Mexico today.

Ivonne Athie Islas

Meso-America

For thousands of years, Meso-America was the scene of the development of an extraordinary cultural tradition. In this region of great geographic and ethnic diversity, human groups created and shared a unique lifestyle based on the agriculture of maize.

Meso-America covered a vast area that included part of northern Mexico, all of central and southern Mexico, as well as the whole of present-day Guatemala, Belize and El Salvador. The region also encompassed the west of Honduras, the western coast of Nicaragua, and north-western Costa Rica. This extensive territory comprised diverse and contrasting environments, from mountain highlands to tropical lowlands, and from semiarid regions to lake and river areas. Its boundaries were not fixed, but fluctuated throughout Meso-American history.

The temporal limits of Meso-America are defined by two landmarks. The appearance of sedentary agriculturalists marks the beginning of the cultural tradition around 2,500 B.C., while the end of Meso-America is set in A.D. 1521 following the Spanish conquest. However, the tradition did not disappear; in fact, many beliefs and practices are still present in the area today (Carrasco 2014).

The unique cultural tradition shared by the inhabitants of a large part of Mexico and Central America has been noted since the colonial period. In 1943, the philosopher and anthropologist Paul Kirchhoff (1943) designated this geographical and cultural area as Meso-America, describing the extension of its territory and the diverse ethnic groups who inhabited this region. In addition, he identified cultural traits and practices that unified the area, such as writing systems, intensive agriculture, the construction of stepped pyramids, the manufacture of obsidian-edged tools and weapons, the production of elaborate pottery, the use of two unique calendars, the long-distance trade within the territory and beyond its borders, and the practice of ritual human sacrifice.

Derived from Kirchoff's study, multiple models and theoretical frameworks have been proposed to define the extraordinary cultural tradition established

Fig. 2
Doña Isabel disperses smoke
across the sacrificial altar

Photo: Raul Macuil Martinez

in this region. However, scholars agree that Meso-American societies were diverse in many aspects, yet were still able to create and share a cultural tradition because of the constant complex and heterogeneous interactions they had throughout their history.

The study of the Meso-American tradition is a complex endeavour because of the diversity of the societies that lived in the area, their different paths of development, the astonishing social and political transformation, the extensive territory, and the long history of Meso-America (López Austin and López Luján 2001). López Austin and López Luján identify three interwoven elements which define Meso-America: the cultivation of maize as the principal means of subsistence, the existence of a shared tradition created by these cultivators of maize, and a shared history that enabled the creation of a joint tradition.

Meso-American societies belonged to 16 different linguistic families. Some of them were represented by only one language, while others included several. Although the language families were independent of each other, some of the languages shared a number of linguistic features that are evidence of the intensive relationships among Meso-American speakers of different languages. This can be noticed in the use of specific metaphors composed by pairs of couplets in formal speech. In addition, Meso-American languages use number systems based on 20 units, derived from the use of a shared calendar and mathematics system (Joyce 2003).

Meso-Americans relied for subsistence on the agriculture of maize, beans, squash, chilli, and other fruits and tubers. They settled in small villages close to sources of water and gradually developed irrigation systems. The agricultural labour was carried out by peasants themselves because the only domesticated animals were turkeys and dogs.

Trade and commerce networks were an integral part of Meso-American life. The diverse environments provided a wide variety of resources that were exploited by societies. For example, on the mountainous ranges, volcanic activity resulted in the formation of obsidian, a natural volcanic glass that was essential for making cutting instruments and weapons, while in the humid tropical forests Meso-Americans obtained valuable animal and plant resources. The varied products were traded all over the Meso-American area, locally, regionally, and beyond the boundaries of the area. The interactions that resulted from exchanging goods were fundamental in the creation of the Meso-American tradition.

Meso-Americans imagined the universe as three superposed bodies: one was composed by the upper heavens which was dry, luminous, and masculine; another was composed by the underworld that was dark, humid, and feminine; and in the middle lay the world of humans which comprised the surface of the earth and the lower heavens. The two opposite regions of the universe were separated by five posts or trees. There were four trees on each corner of the cosmos, and through them, the two opposite elements converged and caused time to flow on the surface of the earth. The fifth tree located in the middle of the universe was the *axis mundi*. Time flowed in a cyclical motion

which was recorded in a complex calendrical system. In this way, the universe was composed of a space-time that belonged exclusively to the gods and another space-time which the gods created for humans. In the human space-time, divinity infiltrated all creatures, giving them their particular characteristics. Creation myths explain the origin of the mundane creatures, which were created from divine elements. In mythical times, the gods had all sorts of adventures which ended with their transformation into earthly creatures (López Austin 1994).

In consequence, Meso-Americans believed they were in debt to the gods and felt obligated to reciprocate through ritual practices. The rituals were periodically performed based on calendrical and astronomical information (López Austin and López Luján 2008). Ceremonial centres were built to provide stages for rituals; they comprised temples, ball courts, and astronomical observatories. These complex ritual practices constituted the language in which humans communicated with the gods, and therefore they were strictly regulated. Rituals included music, dance, offerings, ritual bloodletting, ritual human sacrifice, prayers, and penitence. By performing these ceremonies, Meso-Americans sought to please the gods in order to obtain benefits and to avoid negative actions and through them they ensured the continuity and stability of the world. ⏎

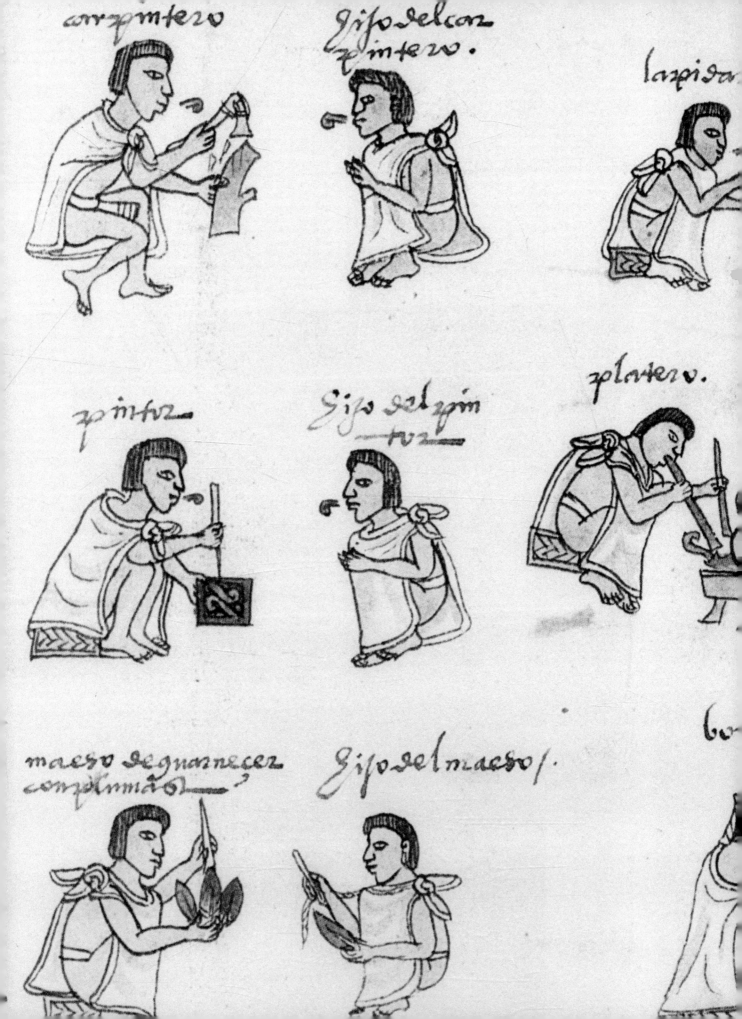

carpintero

hijo del carpintero

lapida[rio]

pintor

hijo del pintor

platero

maestro de guarnecer con plumas

hijo del maestro

gijo dell a
pidarp

Giciv8o de mala
lenguas

gijo del zpla
terbf.

borrachos, que del vicio de la bo
rrachera podim de venir
a ser ladrones

⌧ **The Sources**

Martin Berger

The Sources

Our knowledge of Aztec history, culture and daily life comes from multiple sources: indigenous pictorial documents, often called codices; colonial European accounts, mostly referred to as chronicles; archaeological science, and contemporary indigenous culture in modern-day Mexico. This last element sets research on the Aztecs apart from that on many other ancient civilisations outside Meso-America. Despite centuries of cultural assimilation and discrimination, indigenous cultures and languages still thrive in Mexico (Bonfil Batalla 1987). The cultural continuity that exists between pre-Conquest and modern-day cultures is not only a testament to the resilience of indigenous peoples, but also an important key to understanding ancient Aztec life.

Examples of this continuity are seen in many aspects of contemporary indigenous culture, including daily life, gastronomy, religion, ritual and dress. Naturally, there is no one-to-one correspondence between the indigenous cultures of today and those of Aztec times. Five centuries of globalisation, Christianisation and cultural assimilation have had their undeniable impact on the way people lead their lives. Nonetheless, many central tenets of the Meso-American way of life link today's indigenous culture with that of the Aztecs and their predecessors: the importance of mountains as sacred spaces (López Austin and López Luján 2009), the centrality of maize for sustenance and in ritual, the many indigenous languages still spoken in Mexico today, and designs in weavings and dress are but a few of these links between past and present.

The knowledge and traditions of contemporary indigenous peoples complement other ways of knowing the Aztecs, all of which are employed by academics who attempt to better understand the Aztec Empire. At the basis of many studies of Aztec life lie the European accounts of indigenous religion and culture that were compiled by clerics and conquerors in the sixteenth century. Friars like Bernardino de Sahagún, Diego Durán and Toribio de Benavente Motolinia, and conquerors like Hernán Cortés and Bernal Díaz del Castillo, as well as many others, documented indigenous life as they saw it shortly after the Conquest, or as it was later described to them by their native informants. In the past, these sources were sometimes treated uncritically as

eyewitness accounts of indigenous culture. However, nowadays, an awareness has taken root of the fact that many of these accounts were part of a Colonial and missionary endeavour, the main aim of which was to better understand indigenous religion and culture, in order to eradicate and replace them with Christian customs.

While many of the sixteenth-century chronicles were written by Spanish friars, they were always based on the information supplied to them by their native informants. Likewise, the drawings and illustrations that accompany these texts were frequently created by native artisans, who were often trained in the ancient tradition, creating hybrid documents that combine European and indigenous artistic codes. The skill of these native draughtsmen is evident not only in colonial documents, but also in the few pre-colonial codices that survive to this day. Alongside the myriad examples of Aztec religious art found in museums around the world, these codices form our most direct insight into ancient religious practices and constitute the precious few primary sources at our disposal (Jansen, Lladó-Buisán and Snijders 2018).

Together, the codices, chronicles and contemporary indigenous culture help archaeologists understand the structures, objects and features that they excavate. As a result, the archaeological study of the Aztecs is by definition an exciting multidisciplinary and multi-vocal undertaking, including a rich variety of sources that enliven archaeological interpretation and enable us to sketch a picture of what life in the Aztec Empire may have been like. ⌐

Fig. 2 ▲
Maize was and still is the basic staple crop in Meso-America. This can be seen not only in the diet, but also in rituals like this ceremony for the first maize harvest in Chicontepec, Veracruz.

Photo: Eduardo de la Cruz

Fig. 3 ▶
Greenstone figure with calendar signs

Museum am Rothenbaum Hamburg (cat. 7)

Leonardo López Luján

The Archaeology of Tenochtitlan

An urban palimpsest

Archaeologists who work on the ruins of Tenochtitlan – the insular capital of the Mexicas – have much in common with their counterparts who explore the vestiges of ancient Rome, Constantinople (present-day Istanbul), Lutetia (Paris) and Colonia Claudia Ara Agrippinensium (Cologne): they study legendary ancient settlements buried under bustling modern metropolises. For these persistent researchers, Mexico City, like modern-day Rome, Istanbul, Paris and Cologne represent almost insurmountable barriers in the form of all manner of buildings and thick layers of asphalt that allow them only to open tiny windows into the past (Matos Moctezuma 1988; López Luján and Levin 2006; López Luján 2015, 2017).

Without a doubt, the archaeologists of Tenochtitlan work in less than romantic surroundings, especially when compared to their colleagues who excavate hunter-gatherer camps in the wide expanse of northern Mexico's deserts, or who exhume Mayan palaces in the dense jungles of the country's south. In Mexico City, in contrast, scholars of the pre-Hispanic world spend the best part of their days inside dark, damp and foul-smelling trenches within the midst of a bustling and chaotic city which today is home to 20 million inhabitants, and a city centre that prides itself on having the highest concentration of historical and artistic monuments on the American continent. In such circumstances, archaeologists take every opportunity to penetrate the subsoil: the resurfacing of streets, the building of a Metro line, the installation of an underground electrical transformer, the replacement of an old building's foundations or the repair of drinking water and drainage networks. They invest immeasurable efforts and considerable sums of money in this venture, knowing that the best outcome they can hope for is the discovery in record time of just part of a Mexica temple, a canal, a house or a rubbish dump. But no matter how small these vestiges may be, bringing to light a fraction of Meso-America's most famous city always gives them enormous satisfaction and the feeling that one more mission has been accomplished.

Fig. 1 ◀
The excavations
by Eduardo Matos
Moctezuma and the
complete exposure
of the Templo Mayor
in 1978.

With the kind permission
of Proyecto Templo Mayor
Photo: Anonymous

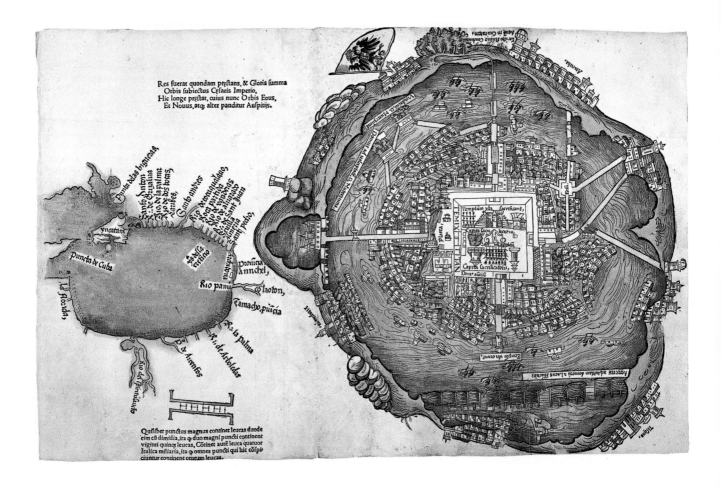

Fig. 2
The island city of Tenochtitlan on a map attributed to Hernán Cortés. It was published for the first time in 1524 in Nuremberg.

Obviously, there are certain advantages to excavating in an urban environment such as this. For example, archaeologists have regular access to a range of specialists, libraries, archives, comparative collections and laboratories with scientific instruments that are generally not available in the desert or the jungle. In addition, in the case of the archaeological zones of the Templo Mayor and Tlatelolco, which are protected areas and therefore exempt from the frenzied construction that characterises the modern city, it is possible to carry out exploration projects that last as long as necessary. This simple factor enables the detailed recording of information and effective conservation of the materials uncovered.

Ruins on ruins

Whenever an archaeological exploration is
undertaken in the historic centre of Mexico
City, it is important to bear in mind that the
ground layers are technically difficult to penetrate given the concrete foundations and stone
fillings dissected by unruly water networks,
electrical wiring and fibre optics. As if this were
not enough, immediately beneath these ground
layers lies unstable clay subsoil, through which
groundwater, often contaminated by sewage,
soon makes an appearance. This is where the
levels of the capital of New Spain, which dates
from the period between 1521 and 1821, are
located (López Luján 2018). These layers are
marked by the abundance of cultural artefacts
that attest to the opulent life of the European
conquerors and their descendants: the floors
and walls of sumptuous mansions, fragments
of Chinese porcelain and Spanish and Italian
majolica, as well as an exorbitant number of
pitchers used to transport wine, vinegar, oil, olives and other fine preserves
from far-off Andalusia. These extravagant consumption habits are under-
standable in a city that, within a matter of decades, had established itself as
the fastest-growing Hispanic colony. Mexico City at the time was a true
economic emporium, where the wealth originating from agriculture, cattle-
rearing *haciendas* and mining regions was concentrated and which profited
from strong trade relationships with Spain and the Philippines, the latter
effectively a province of New Spain. The city was also the most influential
cultural centre in the New World. America's first printing press and second
university were established there.

Fig. 3
The Aztec Sun Stone when
it was still embedded in the
west tower of the Cathedral
of Mexico City

With the kind permission of
Proyecto Templo Mayor
Photo: Anonymous, ca. 1870

If you dig beyond the colonial layers, you will find the ruins of a Tenochtitlan devastated by the clashes of 1521 and by the systematic demolition of its buildings undertaken after the Conquest. Naturally, it is rare that archaeologists reach this far deep. For this reason, little has been discovered through archaeology about the structure and functioning of the ancient city. Perhaps the only exception is the ceremonial ground, known as the Sacred Precinct, located in the heart of the Mexica capital. This was a majestic and sacred space that was built and renovated tirelessly between 1325 and 1521. It was separated from the secular ground by a quadrangular platform, inside which the most illustrious religious buildings of the empire were erected, included the Huei Teocalli or "Templo Mayor".

Fig. 4 ▾
The complex stratigraphy of the historic centre of Mexico City: the modern, Colonial-era and pre-Hispanic layers

With the kind permission of Proyecto Templo Mayor
Drawing: Michelle De Anda

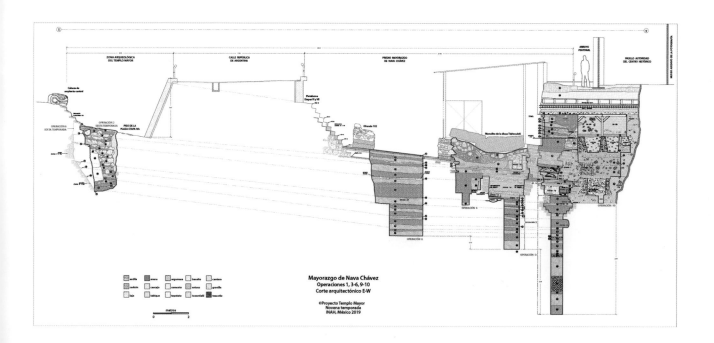

In search of times gone by

The unexpected discovery of the monolith of the lunar goddess, Coyolxauh-qui, on 21 February 1978 triggered a series of events that transformed the face of Mexico City and revolutionised our knowledge of the ancient Mexica civilization (Boone 1978; Broda et al. 1987). In this unique turn of events, the National Institute of Anthropology and History managed to implement one of the most ambitious and enduring archaeological enterprises of recent times: The Templo Mayor Project. Founded forty-one years ago by Professor Eduardo Matos Moctezuma, this scientific research project has since been charged with exhuming a good part of the Sacred Precinct of Tenochtitlan, with the express objective of reconstructing the religious, socio-political and economic life of the imperial capital. To date, eight long periods of excavation have been carried out, the first three of which were directed by Matos

Fig. 5 ▲
The excavations by Manuel Gamio and the discovery of the Templo Mayor in 1914

With the kind permission of Proyecto Templo Mayor
Photo: Anonymous

Moctezuma himself and the remaining five by Leonardo López Luján (Matos Moctezuma 1988; López Luján 2005, 2006, 2015, 2017). During this period, an area of 1.29 hectares has been explored, which is equivalent to no less than 10.5 percent of the 12.24 hectares that the Sacred Precinct would have covered, and 0.1 percent of the 13.5 square kilometres that the island would have spanned at the beginning of the sixteenth century.

Another decisive moment came in 1991 with the creation of the Urban Archaeology Programme which is currently coordinated by archaeologist Raúl Barrera Rodríguez. This programme is responsible for rescue and recovery operations in the heart of Mexico City and is complementary in many ways to the Templo Mayor Project. The key to success for the two teams involved, a research team and a rescue archaeology team, is continuity. Successive generations of specialists have compiled their efforts, gradually adding "pieces" to a gigantic "archaeological puzzle", which they know will never be completed. Such "pieces" include the Templo Mayor (a double pyramid in honour of the sun god, Huitzilopochtli, and the rain god, Tlaloc), the Casa de las Águilas ("House of Eagles"), the Templos Rojos, the Huei Tlachco or main ball game court, the Calmecac or temple-school where nobles were trained in all fields of knowledge, the Temple of Ehecatl (the god of wind) and the Huei Tzompantli or palisade where the skulls of the sacrificed were exhibited. Along with these constructions, which are now

Fig. 8
Mexica Chacmool figure, representing the rain god Tlaloc.

Museo Nacional de Antropología, Mexico City, D.R. Secretaría de Cultura – INAH (cat. 120) in ruins, a multitude of worship shrines, sculptures, mural paintings and altars have appeared, enriching the heritage of the Mexican people.

Over the years, the work of the Templo Mayor Project has resulted in the conservation, refurbishment and opening of an archaeological site that is visited by hundreds of thousands of people each year; the construction of the Templo Mayor Museum, a modern building whose eight rooms exhibit the treasures found during the excavations; and the creation of a research centre that has produced more than 1,200 publications on all manner of subjects (López Luján and Chávez Balderas 2019). The impact of these achieve-ments has been such that the Archaeological Zone of the Templo Mayor and the rest of Mexico City's historic centre were declared World Heritage Sites by UNESCO in 1987. ⌐

Fig. 9
Almena, roof ornamentation of the elite school *calmecac*

Museo Nacional de Antro-pología, Mexico City, D.R. Secretaria de Cultura – INAH (cat. 114)

contar y musico que tiene
bidados, y les da musica

Ha conocesca suhijo que
plique a todo sutid y no
ande Sego balgaminido

mancebo

balgaminido

Jugador de pelota

mancebo

cat

cat

ladron

Jugador de
patol

ne

Maarten E.R.G.N. Jansen and Gabina Aurora Pérez Jiménez

Mexican Codices: An Introduction

The use of writing is a hallmark of the ancient Meso-American civilisation. We may distinguish two main writing systems or modalities. One is the representation of phonetic units (syllables, words) through specific signs: hieroglyphic writing, which was prominently practised by the Maya (Eastern Meso-America). The other system consisted of communicating information directly through iconic images: picture writing (pictography), used by the Nahua (Aztec), Mixtec and other peoples in Central and Southern Mexico.

The two systems were not mutually exclusive. Pictography may include phonetic signs, especially for names of persons and places, while hieroglyphic texts may be combined with figurative scenes. Both developed simultaneously from ± 800 B.C and were optimised during the Classic period (± A.D. 200 – 900). No books have survived from those early times, but we can identify elements of writing in frescos, sculptures, decorated ceramics etc.

The wall paintings of the Classic metropolis Teotihuacan show a fully developed system of pictographic conventions. It seems likely that the preference for pictography in this culture was related to the fact that its realm or influence sphere involved many different languages, which were often tonal in character, with tones changing under the influence of sentence melody. The communication of meanings directly through a sophisticated but easily recognisable system of iconic images was certainly easier, more efficient, and more generally understood than a register of such meanings through hieroglyphic signs which referred to words in a specific language and were therefore not readable in other languages.

Less then twenty books have survived from the time before the Spanish conquest (A.D. 1521). They consist of folded strips of deerskin or bark paper, covered with a white plaster (gypsum) layer on which diverse types of colourful figures and signs were painted. There must have been (many) thousands of such pre-colonial books, but the Spanish conquistadors and missionaries destroyed most of them in an attempt to eradicate indigenous knowledge, religion, memory, and art, which they considered pagan and diabolical. A few examples escaped because they were sent to Europe as "curiosities of the New World".

Fig. 1 ◀
Codex Mendoza, Fol. 70r

Bodleian Library, Oxford

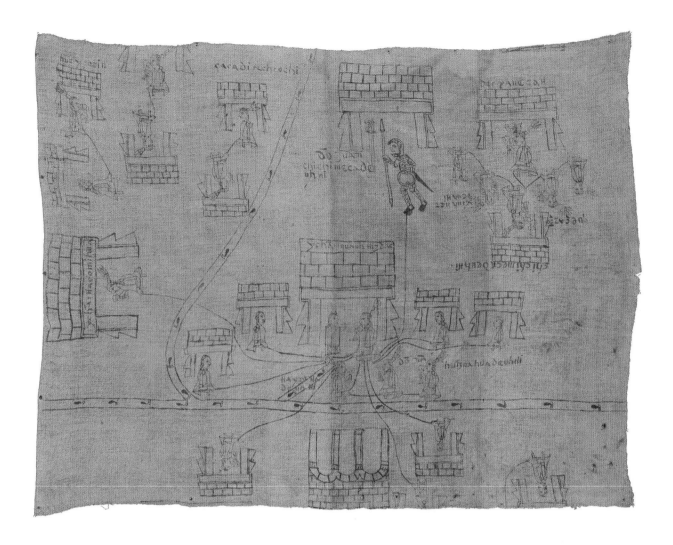

Ancient literacy did not immediately come to an end with the conquest, however. During the early colonial period, books in ancient style continued to be produced, often with annotations in Spanish or in indigenous languages written using the European alphabet. There are hundreds of such later manuscripts, which – precisely because of those annotations and other comments – offer crucial insights into the pre-colonial art of writing.

This corpus of books, now called codices, was produced by speakers of diverse languages. A prime source of information about the ancient history of indigenous peoples, these artworks are nowadays preserved as delicate treasures in museums, libraries, or other collections in different countries. As most information about provenance, original context, and meaning was lost during their diaspora, the documents were named after the libraries, owners, or researchers with which they became associated. In recent years new names have been proposed, more in accordance with their contents and cultural-linguistic affiliation (Jansen and Pérez 2004).

The surviving codices may be classified into two main categories. The first is the historical and administrative genre: it registers genealogies and historical acts of rulers (e.g. wars and conquests but also origin narratives and ritual events), as well as tributes, land holdings and communitarian customs. Colonial examples are often related to lawsuits and other conflicts in which the indigenous dynasties and communities tried to maintain their rights in the face of colonial domination.

Codex Bodley, preserved in the Bodleian Library, Oxford, is a pre-colonial example of the historical genre. We have renamed it *Codex* Ñuu *Tnoo – Ndisi Nuu* or "Book of Tilantongo and Tlaxiaco" after the Mixtec towns it refers to. One section deals with the dramatic biography of Lord 8 Deer 'Jaguar Claw'. The first part of this Mixtec ruler's name (8 Deer) is a "calendar name", i.e. the day on which he was born, while the second part ('Jaguar Claw') is a more poetic "given name". In the codex (page 7-V), his figure is shown with an umbilical cord connected to the day 8 Deer (his birthday) of the year 12 Reed. The following signs clarify that this was the 18th day in the "month" of the Rain God (the month called Etzalcualiztli in the Aztec calendar). Most likely this was 15 June 1064 in the Julian calendar (= 21 June 1064 in the Gregorian calendar), the day of the summer solstice. An upward-looking eagle probably represents the hour of daybreak, called *tonatiuh quauhtleoanitl*, "the sun (as) soaring eagle" by the Aztecs.

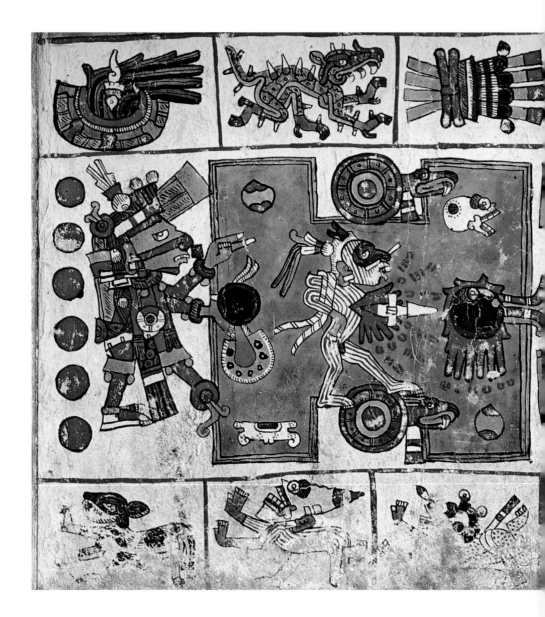

The second genre is religious in character, presenting divinatory symbolism and diverse ritual practices in accordance with the ancient calendar. The early colonial examples were generally produced under the supervision of Spanish missionaries, who wanted to document the native beliefs in order to combat and extirpate them.

Codex Borgia, renamed *Codex Yoalli Ehecatl*, the "Book of Night and Wind" is one of the most spectacular pre-colonial religious manuscripts. Most likely, it was painted for (and in) the ceremonial centre of Cholula in Central Mexico; nowadays it is in the Vatican Library. The painted symbols express the

Fig. 4
Codex Borgia, Ball Game
(Inv. Nr. Borg p 21 inf)

Biblioteca Apostolica
Vaticana

influence of specific deities on subdivisions of the calendar and indicate the care that humans should take during those times. A series of eight images (pages 18–21), for example, lists threats and challenges for the ruler, the priest, the woman who carries water, the ball player, the traveller, the farmer, the logger, and the married couple. The scene of the ball player may be read as follows (from right to left):

"The ball player is under the patronage of the Black Tezcatlipoca ("Smoking Mirror"), the numen of obsidian, the deity of the mysterious powers of the universe.

Fig. 5 ▶

Paintings in the style of
the codices also appear
as decoration on ceramic
vessels which were probably
used for ceremonies in
honour of the gods or
ancestors

Nationaal Museum van
Wereldculturen (cat. 88)

In this period ball players should be careful and take precautions:
their initiative (the ball) may be affected by the danger (serpent) of vices,
ruptures, and bloodshed.
In the playfield of life (hearts) and death (skull, bone), there may be violence
and killing.
Dangers surround the rings of the ball game: the goals and aims.
The adversary is under the patronage of the Red Tezcatlipoca, the numen of
metal:
though being smaller, he holds the ballgame implements, i.e. he controls the
game."

In-depth study and interpretation show that ancient Mexican pictography was
a highly sophisticated system, capable of registering data in a precise manner
and of producing impressive, elaborated readings through declamation and
performance in accordance with the conventions of ceremonial discourse and
other forms of oral literature. Contemporary indigenous tradition (cultural
continuity) holds a valuable key for further decipherment.

Fig. 6
Model of a ball court

Museum am Rothen-
baum Hamburg
(cat. 108)

Setunda Relaçion

En la otra rrelaçion muy exçelentisymo prinçipe dixe a vra
magestad las çibdades y villas que hasta entonçes a su rreal
serviçio se avian ofresçido: E yo al tienpo subjeta y conquis-
tadas. E dixe al rrey mismo que tenya notiçia de un gran
señor. que se llamava mutezuma. que los naturales d'esta
tierra me avian dicho que en ella avia que estava segund ellos
señalavan las jornadas hasta noventa o çient leguas dela
costa y puerto donde yo desenbarque. y que confiando en
la grandeza de dios. y con esfuerço del rreal nombre de vra alteza. pensava yrle aver. a do quiera que estuviese. y aun me
acuerdo que me ofresçi en quanto a la demanda d'este señor. a mu-
cho mas. de lo que me era posible. porque çertifique a vra alteza que
lo avria preso o muerto. o subdito a la corona rreal de vra magestad. y con este proposyto y demanda me party de la çibdad
de çenpoal. que yo yntitule Sevilla. a diez y seys de agosto
con quinze de cavallo y trezientos peones lo mejor adereça-
dos de guerra que yo pude y el tienpo dio lugar. dexe en la
en la villa de la vera cruz çiento y çinquenta hombres con dos
de cavallo haziendo una fortaleza que ya tengo casy acabada
y dexe toda aquella provinçia de çenpoal y toda la sierra
comarcana a la dicha villa que seran hasta çinquenta mill hombres de guerra y çinquenta villas y fortalezas muy seguros y
paçificos y por çiertos y leales vasallos de vra magestad como
hasta agora lo an estado y estan. porque ellos heran subditos
de aquel señor mutezuma y segund fuy ynformado lo heran
por fuerça y de poco tienpo aca. Y como por my tuvieron notiçia de vra alteza y de su muy grande y rreal poder / dixeron
que querian ser vasallos de vra magestad y mis amigos y que me
rrogavan que los defendiese de aquel grande señor que los tenya
por fuerça y tirania e que les tomava sus fijos para los ma-
tar y sacrificar a sus ydolos y me dixeron otras muchas
quexas d'el. E con esto an estado y estan muy çiertos y leales
en el serviçio de vra alteza y creo lo estaran syenpre por ser

Felix Hinz

The Written Sources on the Aztec Culture and the Spanish Conquest

The indigenous sources

The investigation of ancient Mexico faces the problem that written pre-Hispanic sources of purely historical content about the Aztecs unfortunately did not survive. What we have left, in the best of cases, are Aztec Codices (Anders and Jansen 1988) that were elaborated when Mexico was already under Spanish rule. Even what was first considered "Aztec" by European eyes, when analysed in more detail, was often marked by Christian aspects. In the *Codex Boturini* (between 1530 and 1541), for example, the Aztecs set out from a certain "Aztlán" and finally arrive at their Promised Land, guided by their god Huitzilopochtli, recalling Moses and after passing through many stations that strengthen their group identity. It is a legend that has aroused scepticism as to the assumption that it was a pre-Christian foundational myth. This also applies especially since the said land is marked by an eagle (which also devours a serpent), which could also be interpreted perfectly as an animal symbol of the Roman Empire or as a Christian metaphor for light – or as Christ's victory over Satan.

Christian and colonial refractions of this nature should be considered in all present sources, such as the *Codex Mendoza* (approx. 1541). As historians, we have to admit that, unfortunately, we know almost nothing with *certainty* about Old Mexico or Ancient America. The more one delves into the existing sources, the more doubtful they appear. This applies in particular to texts explicitly identified as European.

The stories of the conquerors as eyewitnesses

The conquerors, especially Hernán Cortés and his men, wrote the history of their conquests themselves. They moved in a world in which the experiences of the famous authors of antiquity could not be referred to. Even the authority of the Bible could not be applied, because it does not mention the New World. As never before, the eyewitness gained the power of interpretation.

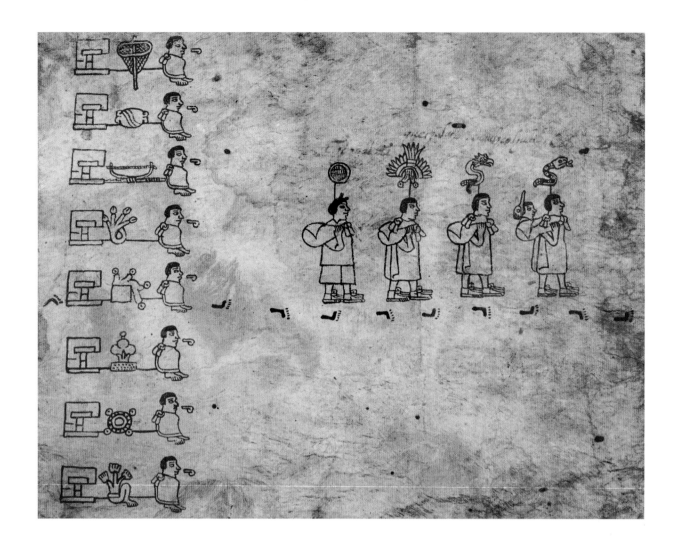

Fig. 2
Codex Boturini (Tira de la peregrinación): The Aztecs move from Aztlán to the Mexican highlands to establish their dominance there. On the back of the first figure: the Sacred Bundle of the god Huitzilopochtli.

Museo Nacional de Antropología, Mexico City, D.R. Secretaría de Cultura – INAH (cat. 68)

No one else could confirm the conquerors' reports, but neither could they contradict them. The fact that essentially everyone relates similar things does not necessarily mean that the accounts are accurate.

Among the stories of eyewitnesses, the "letters of report" (*cartas de relación*) of Hernán Cortés "to the Emperor Charles V" occupy a special place. From the beginning they were written, in fact, for a wider European public. Cortés rightly assumed that his reports would attract general interest. Although we know little about his years of study in Salamanca, there is no doubt that he could write well and was familiar with Julius Caesar's *Commentarii de bello gallico* (The Gallic War), as he used it as a literary model. (It should be noted that Julius Caesar was also in a position to interpret the history of the conquest of Gaul himself without waiting for protests.) Was it true that in Cholula an Aztec conspiracy occurred against the Spaniards, that Motecuhzoma wanted to cede control to Cortés and was then killed by a stone thrown by his disappointed subjects? We doubt it (Rozat Dupeyron 1993, Hinz 2005). Another extraordinary thing about the *cartas de relación* is that they were written in parallel to the events, that is, the first two letters were written in 1519 and 1520, before the author knew how the historical development he was describing would end in 1521. The mood swings that are reflected in them give the stories their particular tension. The other conquerors, who wrote shorter accounts at certain intervals to emphasise their performance, agree most of the time with their Captain General in the decisive points. None of them had the linguistic talent of Cortés, with one exception. The author of the chronicle *Historia verdadera de la conquista de la Nueva España* was (at least allegedly) a certain Bernal Díaz del Castillo. His description of the Aztec world and its conquest is so graphic and exciting, that it has influenced decisively the way the history of these events has been narrated since it was found in the seventeenth century. It is a very detailed and extremely moving text, which was presumably written in 1568 when all the other conquerors of Mexico had already died. This being the case, it could have occupied the powerful position of offering the last valid interpretation of the events if it had been published then. It is a story rich in anecdotes which make it seem highly credible; as a result, however, there is a tendency for readers not to recognise that the chronicle displays a number of peculiarities. How is it that the author, who claims to have been a foot soldier, could write so well? Why did someone with his obvious intelligence never receive a command? How could it be that he was always present, that he enjoyed the confidence of both Cortés and Motecuhzoma, but is not mentioned in any other eyewitness account? In 2012, Christian Duverger raised the highly controversial thesis that Bernal Díaz never existed and that the man behind the name is none other than Cortés himself, who continued to work on his posthumous fame under a pseudonym after he had failed to be granted the political power over Mexico he had expected to receive from the crown. Duverger, however, fails to resolve all the incongruities in his argument (Duverger 2015).

As for the Aztecs, it remains to be said that the Spanish conquerors admired them, except for their religion. In their writings, however, they often simply lacked points of comparison. They called the pyramids "mosques" and when faced with the size and complexity of Tenochtitlan, they were compelled to have recourse to the popular novels of those times, such as the *Amadis de Gaula* of the late fourteenth century. However, the more the subjection of the Aztecs became a brutal conflict, the more abrupt was the religious and cultural rejection of this culture on the part of the Spaniards.

The *Anales de Tlatelolco* and the *Lienzo de Tlaxcala* should also be considered eyewitness accounts. The first ones, written from 1528, describe the conquest

from the point of view of the Tlatelolcas, who were also subdued, but were traditionally at odds with the Tenochcas. Although it was written in Nahuatl, albeit using Latin characters, the authors are under Christian rule. The *Lienzo de Tlaxcala* (ca. 1550) is a graphic account of the conquest from the perspective of the Tlaxcalans allied to Cortes. In this very interesting representation, it is evident that the war over Tenochtitlan at times had the features of an indigenous war that the Spaniards in no way always determined alone.

The chronicles of the missionaries

The Spanish conquerors were followed in 1524 by Christian missionaries. The friars who wrote the records, mainly Toribio "Motolinía" Benavente (written from about 1528–1569), Bernardino de Sahagún (written from around 1530–1590) and Diego Durán (*Durán Codex*, 1579–81), understood that the Aztec religion permeated the entire culture and, therefore, confiscated all the Aztec codices. Most of them were destroyed, but some were also read, interpreted with the help of Aztec witnesses and transcribed with Latin characters.

This also applies to the historical transmissions and memories that the missionaries reinterpreted in Nahuatl according to Salvation history. This is where we find the interpretation (unmasked as a colonial legend in 1980 by Werner Stenzel), that the Indians thought that the Spaniards were the returning god Quetzalcoatl and the insinuation that the Christian God announced his coming to Motecuhzoma by unequivocal omens. From this comes the image of the fearful, doubtful, and melancholic *huey tlatoani* (Great Speaker). While the historical Aztec ruler had probably clearly dismissed the Spaniards, this Motecuhzoma of apocalyptic interpretation knew that he would have no chance against the conquerors, who as envoys of God in a way, would overcome the Aztec paganism that practised human sacrifices and was consequently the work of the devil.

Long before the Spaniards arrived, the Aztecs themselves, upon assuming power, had rewritten the history of the Mexican highlands and destroyed older sources. The missionaries proceeded in the same way and imposed their new interpretation as obligatory for all converted Christians. ⌐

The Political Economy

Doris Kurella

The Political Economy in the Basin of Mexico

Upon reaching the shore of what is today the east coast of Mexico, and as they journeyed towards the Aztec capital of Tenochtitlan, Hernán Cortés and his companions were immensely impressed with the economic life and prosperity enjoyed by the populace of the Aztec Empire. They were especially fascinated by the large and well-organised marketplaces and the sheer variety of goods that were on display. The density and proximity of diverse ecological zones and the demand for products from one zone to another led to the development of a closely-knit trade network that, for lack of pack animals, vehicles and waterways, was served by human carriers, the *tlameme* (Hassig 1985). Canoes were also used on small lakes, and most of all, on Lake Texcoco, surrounding the capital Tenochtitlan (Hirth 2016).

Prior to its conquest by the Aztec Empire, densely populated, highly urbanised Pre-Columbian Central Mexico was a mosaic of diverse ethnic groups that were politically independent but interlinked by economic relationships. During the time of the Aztec Empire, the population of the highland Basin of Mexico was estimated to be roughly 3 million (Smith 2000). Today it is currently assumed that this area was home to approximately 40 different languages. The population was organised in city states (Hodge 1984) similar to the system used in the Mayan region in its Classical Period (3rd to 9th century CE). A typical city state, known as an *altepetl* in the Aztec language Nahuatl, was ruled by a local elite, who received tribute from their subjects and possessed the land rights (Berdan 1996). At most, these elites comprised 5% of the population.

The Basin of Mexico was subdivided into 50 city states of varying sizes, whose principal settlement was the only one to have reached the size of a city. It was here that the *tlatoani*, the ruler of the *altepetl*, resided. The elites of the various city states were interconnected through marriage alliances, the exchange of luxury goods, through their privileged access to writing and the calendar, and also by common rituals (Berdan and Smith 1996). Nevertheless, they were often open to expanding their power at the expense of neighbouring city states or to appropriating trade routes. This was a system that was characterised by a high level of competition among the elites. Then again,

Fig. 2
Two carriers

KHM-Museumsverband,
Weltmuseum Wien (cat. 52)

this could explain why many of these *altepeme* were so willing to submit to the Aztecs. The city state elite were absorbed into the Aztec Empire's ruling middle class and were assured some level of rule (Berdan 2005; Berdan 2006a). *Tlatoani* who were once subject to other *altepeme* hoped that their integration into the Aztec Empire would allow them to move upwards in the social structure.

The economic system consisted chiefly of two components: domestic production in the family, and institutional production. Domestic production formed the basis of Meso-American society. The overwhelming majority of the population consisted of farmers, who, alongside their agricultural work, also worked in trades (Nichols 2017). Women were responsible for the weaving of cotton textiles, which were used as a currency in much the same way as cacao beans and copper axes. Surplus production could be sold at the many markets, predominantly by the producer himself (Hirth 2016). Healers, fortune tellers, singers and dancers, as well as scribes, would also offer their services at the marketplace. Moreover, there were also specialised markets such as, for example, in Otumba, where obsidian and high quality ceramics could be acquired, or in Santa Mara Acxotla, where goldsmiths, feather artists and paper manufacturers offered their wares (Filloy Nadal 2017; Hirth et al. 2017).

Fig. 3
Plan of the Aztec capital of Tenochtitlan, known as the "Uppsala Map".
It dates from the early Colonial period
and shows the lively traffic on Lake
Texcoco. Recent research has shown
that the plan was drawn during the
early 16th century by a citizen of
Tenochtitlan.

University Library, Uppsala

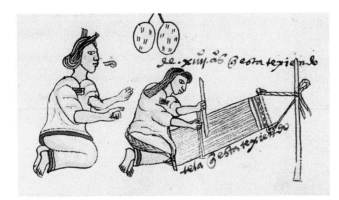

These important markets were at once a meeting place for members of different ethnic groups, the abode of merchants, and the contact points for long-distance traders, *pochteca*. These traders did not just travel to remote corners as far afield as what is now Guatemala, looking to acquire luxury goods such as quetzal feathers; they also maintained factories which manufactured products for the Aztec Empire.

The highland Basin of Mexico, and thus the Aztec Empire itself, formed part of what is called the "Mesoamerican World System", a network of markets and trade relationships which allowed for a wide-ranging exchange of not just goods, but also ideas and values across political borders (Blanton and Feinman 1984; Smith 2000). The Aztec Empire adapted this system and indirectly altered it through the addition of tributary demands. Places that once had to ship a reasonable amount of cotton textiles to its local elite were now faced with a demand for thousands of these goods as tribute. This led to regional specialisation as well as to the emergence of commercial centres, because either considerably more textiles had to be manufactured or they would need to be brought in through inter-regional exchange. The Aztec Empire can be described as a tributary empire as essentially the Aztec elite demanded tribute not just for their luxurious lifestyle in Tenochtitlan, but also for the carrying out of large-scale state rituals (Carrasco 1996; Hinz 2014). The dissemination of an ideology and the implementation of certain economic principles – aspects that were of great importance for the Inca in South America – were ultimately secondary to the aims of the Aztecs (Carrasco 1982). ⌐

Ehrentraud Bayer

Geography, Ecology, Cultivated Plants and Nutritional Crops

At the time of the arrival of the Spanish, the surface area of the territorial dominion of the Aztecs had reached its greatest extent in its 200-year history. Centred on what is now Mexico, it sprawled out from the central plateau with its capital, Tenochtitlan, to the Atlantic and Pacific coasts. The frontiers of Aztec influence extended 250 kilometres from Tenochtitlan towards the north and northwest, and 400 kilometres towards the east. The Xoconochco region on the eastern edge of the Pacific coast, more than 850 kilometres away, represented the furthermost region ever reached by the Aztecs (Prem 2011).

The territory covered tropical, warm, temperate and cold climatic zones, and ranged from coastal lowlands through enormous mountain ranges and structured high plains all the way up to snow-capped volcanoes over 5,000 metres high. The variety of the landscape provided the population with a variety of natural resources since it was rich in flora and fauna as a result of its geomorphic and climactic diversity.

The highland Basin of Mexico was originally a basin with no outlet lying at the southern end of the central high plateau. This irregular elliptically-shaped basin is 130 kilometres long and has a maximum width of 90 kilometres (Rzedowski 2010). It is situated some 2,250 metres above sea level and extends across 7,500 square kilometres with a flat base measuring approximately 2,000 square kilometres. It is bound by the Sierra de las Cruces to the west, which are almost 3,900 metres high, and to the south by the volcanic belt of the Sierra Neovolcanica. This belt continues up the eastern side of the basin in the Sierra Nevada, a mountain chain, whose southern end boasts Mexico's second and third-highest mountains, the permanently snow-covered volcanoes Popocatépetl and Iztaccihuatl. These impressive peaks rise almost 3,000 metres above the basin floor to an altitude of 5,426 and 5,230 metres respectively.

The climate of the basin is temperate, with an average annual temperature of between 14° and 17° C. Determining factors include the moist trade winds from the northeast; the dry wind from the northwest; the intense exposure to the sun arising from the high altitude and the low humidity, low atmospheric pressure, and the thinness of the air. Typical for the basin are extreme

Fig. 1 ◄
Marigolds (*Tagetes*) were frequently used in rituals during pre-Hispanic times, and some statues of deities were decorated with wreaths of marigolds. Today they play an important role on the altars on the Day of the Dead (Día de los Muertos).

Photo: tunedin/stock. adobe.com

fluctuations in temperature which are larger than the seasonal fluctuations and which range between 15° and 18° C (Rzedowski 2010). Mornings and evenings are cooler, but starting from midday and depending on the month, the temperature can rise to between 18° and 35° C. The coldest months are December and January, although frost is rare; the highest precipitation falls in the warm season, between May and October, typically with torrential rain during the afternoon (Rzedowski 2010).

When the Aztecs reached the basin, they discovered an ecosystem with a variety of water surfaces, characterised by great differences in water quality. There were areas no deeper than 10 metres by the bulrush-lined shores of lakes where they more or less flowed into one another, depending on the amount of precipitation. The Aztecs founded Tenochtitlan on an island in the largest lake, the Lago de Texcoco. The surrounding slopes were wooded with oaks, pines and other trees, which were later heavily deforested to accommodate the construction of aqueducts and dams. This practice led to erosion and flooding.

The Aztecs had at their disposal a great variety of wild and cultivated plant species, partially provided by local subsistence farming and partially procured as tribute from afar, brought by carriers or acquired from traders. Plants served as the most important foodstuffs, spices, construction and work materials, and allowed for the production of clothing, writing and the dyeing of fabrics. They also fulfilled medical, ritual and religious functions, and were

Fig. 3
Cactus flower

Photo: Andreas Gross

used as currency and to decorate gardens. In the context of this paper and for the sake of brevity, only a few of these plants can be listed.

As with other Meso-American cultures, maize (*Zea mays*, *centli*, also known as corn), easily identifiable by its cob-shaped ear, was the basic staple of the Aztec diet. The importance of this crop is evidenced by the Meso-American calendar, which orientates itself to the phases of growth in maize production (Staller and Carrasco 2010). The enormous significance of the maize plant is also reflected in the number of deities associated with it. Among others there was the maize god Cinteotl and the goddess Chicomecoatl, who appeared in various forms depending on the growth cycle of the maize. The moniker of Xilonen, "the hairy one", references the fibrous hair-like corn silk, and he was associated with the early stage of maize growth. Ilmatecutli, on the other hand, took the form of an old woman, symbolising the mature and ripe maize. One of the codified obligations of all women over 13 was the grinding of the corn; this was done with the aid of a smooth stone that crushed the maize on a rectangular millstone, the *metate*. Additionally, the women were required to prepare tortillas and corn flatbreads, as well as tamales, cooked corn dough wrapped in a maize husk (Hinz 1982).

Maize was traditionally planted together with haricot beans (*Phaseolus vulgaris*) and gourds (cucurbits) in a crop-growing system known as *milpa*. This mixed field cultivation approach provides better yield and soil quality than planting only one type of crop. This is mostly due to the bean plants, whose root systems are populated by *rhizobiaceae*, bacteria that fix nitrogen, effectively fertilising the soil. The corn plants, whose growth is fostered by the enriched soil, provide physical support for the growing beanstalks. The low-lying and sprawling gourd plants provide shade for the soil with their large leaves, and prevent erosion, desiccation and hinder weed growth. Haricot beans are important protein sources and are food plants that occur only in cultivation. They were first domesticated in Mexico some time between 9,000-10,000 BCE and rank as one of the oldest food crops in the Americas, together with corn and gourds (Kistler et al; Staller 2010; Sitzer and Ibarra 2018).

However, the farmland located on terra firma was not sufficient for the nutritional demands of a growing population. New agricultural land was created using a system that was adapted from the Chichimeca, whereby artificial islands, *chinampas*, were constructed. Their construction necessitated the driving of rows of piles into the shallow lakebed until a defined rectangular space was staked out. This space would be filled with alternating layers of earth and mud drawn from the lakebed or recovered from old *chinampas*, and piles of water plants and bulrushes (*Schoenoplectus acutus*) until an island arose (Thurston and Fisher 2006). The edges were secured with Bonpland willow (*Salix bonplandiana*). These islands provided not just land to cultivate the classical *milpa* plants, but were also used to plant amaranth, tomatoes and chilli (*Capsicum frutescens*) (Hinz 1982). The Aztecs also discovered *tecuitlatl* (Parson 2005) in Lake Texcoco, an edible and nutritious green foam consisting of green algae and the protein and mineral-rich cyanobacterium *spirulina*. Interwoven with the life of the populace were the agaves (*metl*), plants that were adapted to a dry climate and known for their rosette of leaves that blooms only once during their lifespan, often after decades. Their long, stiff, spike-edged leaves contain tough fibres, known as *ixtle*. They were worked into rope, mats, sandals and articles of clothing (Gentry 1982), and a spike attached to some fibres provided a natural sewing needle. The spikes were also used to punish disobedient children and were necessary for the evening blood offering in the priest school (Hinz 1982). By cutting back the young flower bud and some nearby leaves, the plant also provided a drink, where the sweet syrup dripped down and formed pools.

Fig. 5
Ceramic depicting Chalchit-
licue, the goddess of waters

Museo Nacional de Antro-
pología, Mexico City, D.R.
Secretaría de Cultura – INAH
(cat. 22)

Fig. 6
Milpa, traditional
field of maize beans and
squash. Obtained by
slash-and-burn agriculture

Photo: Fabian Hanneforth

Fig. 7
Pumpkin
(*Cucurbita moschata*)

Photo: imageBROKER/
stockadobe.com

Consumed fresh, it was nutritious and refreshing; fermented, it turned into a milky white slightly alcoholic beverage that was once known as *octli*, and today as *pulque*. This drink was sacred to the Aztecs and closely connected to the goddess Mayahuel. The enjoyment of *octli* was only allowed at certain festivities, while three cups of *pulque* daily were allowed for the sick, those over 52, and the privileged (Gentry 1982).

Fig. 8
Cultivated *chinampas*

Photo: Peter Vogel

Cacti are the plants best adapted to an arid climate, and in no other country in the world are they present in such diversity than in Mexico. Tenochtitlan's name can be translated as "cactus (*nochtli*) growing among the rocks" (Yetman 2011), and the prickly pear (*Opuntiaficus indica*) or *nopal*, is heavily anchored in both the foundation myth and everyday life of the Aztecs. Its fruits could be enjoyed and its offshoots could be consumed as vegetables. Cochineals lived parasitically off opuntias; these insects were important for the red pigment that they provided, which proved to have many uses (Schweppe 1992).

For the Aztecs, one of the most important plants was the cacao tree (*Theobroma cacao*). Since the tree could not thrive in the cool climate of the Basin of Mexico, its highly-prized seed, the cacao bean, had to acquired as tribute payment or through trade. The cacao bean provided the basis for the preparation of *cacahuatl* or *xocolatl*, which translates roughly as "bitter water". The drink was prepared in a variety of ways but it was basically seasoned with chili, *pulque*, vanilla, and the orange-red colourant annato from the achiote shrub (*Bixa orellana*). As Fray Sahagún reported: "It was then that the ruler was served his cacao in his house...: green chocolate made from unripe cacao, honey-chocolate with dried flower petals and green vanilla, light red chocolate, orange-coloured chocolate, pink chocolate, black chocolate and white chocolate. The chocolate was served in a painted bowl made from a gourd. " (Riese 2010). Cacao beans were also used as a currency, and were saved and stored in great numbers in much the same way that money is used today (Homborg 2019). At the market, a turkey would cost roughly 200 cacao beans, a cottontail rabbit 100.

Other plants were also demanded as tribute, including raw cotton, calabashes, oil-bearing seeds, copal (*copalli*), a resin with uses similar to frankincense, as well as amate (*amatl*), a bark paper that was made from the fig tree (Ficus varieties), and agaves (Gierloff-Emden 1970). This paper was used to make

Fig. 9
Cocoa pods

Photo: Andreas Gross

representations of deities, as sacrificial offerings, and as a surface for writing the codices (López Binnqüist et al. 2012, Gierloff-Emden 1970).

Today many of the plants used by the Aztecs, particularly corn, are planted and traded across the globe (Viola and Magolis 1991). Many of these foodstuffs retain an Aztec root in their very names. One has to only think about cacao, chocolate, avocado, tomato, chilli or chia seeds. There are also some well-established garden plants that hark back to the Aztecs, who loved flowers and their scents, and who honoured their rulers and gods with blooming garlands and flower sacrifices. In the grand gardens which the kings set up for themselves, decorative plants were cultivated next to medicinal herbs and vegetables (Heyden 2003, Riese 2011). Among these ornamental plants are the "Aztec marigold", the *cempoalxochitl*, from the genus *Tagetes*; the cultivated "four o'clock flower", the *Mirabilis jalapa* (PBS 2015); and the *acocotli*, known widely as the dahlia (DFGG 2019). At least in a botanical sense, in one way or another, we are reminded of the Aztecs practically every day.

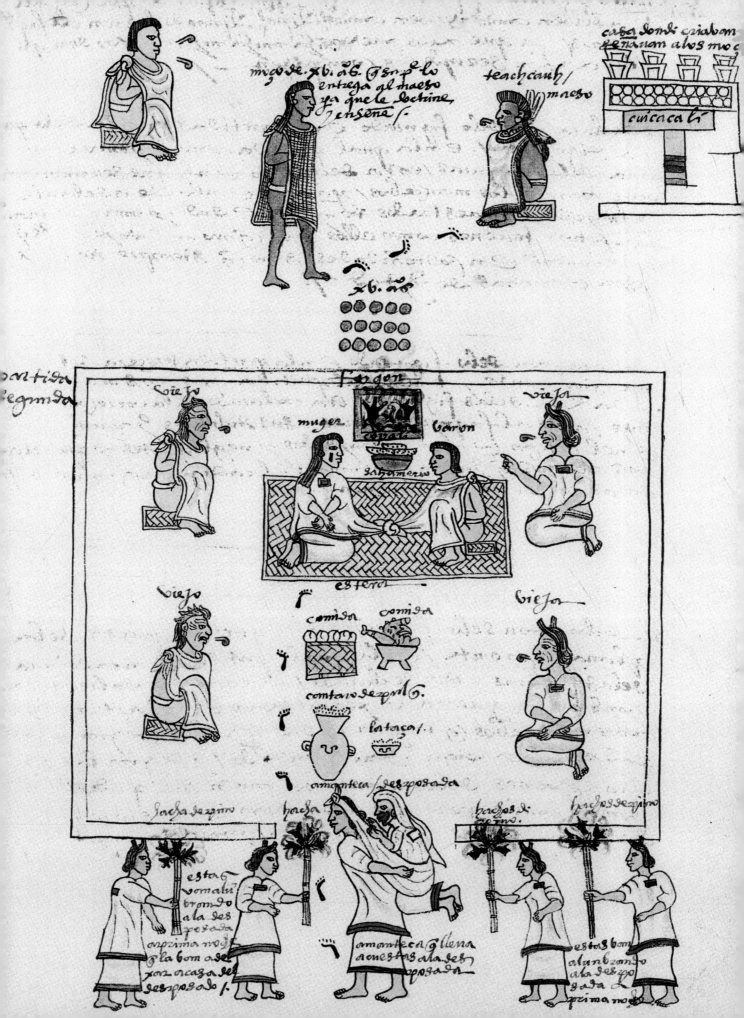

mço de xb. a̅ɡ. q̃ ɛnp̃ lo
entrega al maeʃo
ya que le doctrine
y enʃeñe ʃ

teachcauh/
maeʃo

caʃa Jondi criabam
ʃenauam a los moç
cuicacali

xb. a̅o̅

Fogon
ʃacaleʃ

muger
ʃahumerio
varon

viejo

viejo

viejo
comida
comida

comanos de papel ɡ

viejo

contano de papl ɡ
Jataca/

amonteca ʃ deʃpoʃada

Jacha de ocino
hacha

hachos de
ocino
hachos de ocino

eʃtaʃ
vomalũ
brom̃do
a la deʃ
poʃada
oprima noͤ
y la bon a deᵉ
yon oncaza del
deʃpoʃado ʃ

amonteca ɡ llena
a eneʃtaʃ a la deʃ
poʃada

eʃtaʃ bom̄
a lanbrondo
a la deʃpo
ʃada ᵉ
oprima noͤ

Manuel Aguilar-Moreno

Mexica-Aztec Society and Government

The *altepetl*

Early Mexica-Aztec history and mythology preserve the story of a people originally coming from a place called Aztlan in the "north" and eventually migrating to the central Basin of Mexico, where they founded their city Tenochtitlan in about 1325 AD. Their city would eventually become the capital of the Aztec Empire. During this migration, the wandering Mexica-Aztec are said to have stopped for a time at the sacred mountain of Culhuacan, which contained the sacred womb-like caves of Chicomoztoc ("Seven Caves") (Alvarado Tezozomoc 1975; Carrasco and Matos Moctezuma 1992; Chimalpahin Quauhtlehuanitzin 1997; Day 1992; Horcasitas, 1979; Lockhart 1992). Once again the sacred mountain acts as a source of life where water is found in abundance, and the caves represent the womb of the mountain giving birth to humanity. In the next stage of the journey, the Mexica stopped at a mountain they named Coatepec, where they participated in rites of regeneration and rededication. This was where the story of the birth of the god Huitzilopochtli began. Centuries later at Tenochtitlan, the Aztecs would build a Great Pyramid with Huitzilopochtli's shrine on top, commemorating a mythic mountaintop battle between Huitzilopochtli and his siblings (see chapter on Migration by Martin Berger in this volume). Thus the ideas of sacred mountain, mother earth, the birth of the people, and the battle of the god Huitzilopochtli would all be manifested and commemorated in the building of a similar man-made mountain-shrine at the Great Temple in their capital of Tenochtitlan. After all, the Nahuatl word for city is *altepetl* (water-mountain or water-producing mountain), and it is easy to see how the sun, the water, the mountains and the earth were linked with historical myths and religious beliefs and incorporated into daily life. A city (*altepetl*) was therefore a copy of the natural environment. Since the Mexica-Aztec believed that the landscape was bound by the four cardinal directions, they divided their cities into four quarters (*campan*) and they raised a two-temple pyramid at the heart of each city. This pyramid represented the womb of the pregnant earth reaching out to the heavens, and the two temples represented the belief that the universe was ruled by a force that had a male and a female aspect. Therefore, duality and the four directions were an integral part of the institutions, plan and architecture of Tenochtitlan and later Mexico City. In the

Fig. 1 ◄
A marriage ceremony,
Codex Mendoza, Fol. 61r
Bodleian Library, Oxford

sixteenth century the Spanish built the City of Mexico on top of Tenochtitlan. They are not different cities. Tenochtitlan formed the foundation and the cultural base for Mexico City.

The *altepetl* was not simply the physical space of a town or city. According to the missionary friar Toribio "Motolinia" de Benavente (ca. 1487–1569), the term referred to both the town and its people. It was a community connected to a particular geographic environment and was the source of identity. The *altepetl* (or city) of Tenochtitlan was ruled by the *tlatoani* (speaker, or he who speaks) and the *Cihuacoatl* (woman-serpent) (Blythin 1990). This dual leadership reflected how the Aztecs believed that every institution from families to cities should be represented by the male and female forces that governed the universe. The *tlatoani,* by speaking for the city and controlling the military forces, represented the father who worked outside, harvesting, trading, and fighting; the *Cihuacoatl* provided for the internal rule of the city just as a mother owned and directed the activities of the home. Eventually, as in Rome, the growth of the Aztec Empire led to a change in government and the office of *tlatoani* became king-like. The first of these independent kings was Itzcoatl (1427–1444 AD), who was chosen by a council of four people because he was related to the last *tlatoani* and he had military experience. Subsequent leaders were chosen for the same reasons. Tenochtitlan, like most Aztec cities, had four *campan* (quarters), and it is possible that at one time the council that selected the *tlatoani* also represented each quarter of the city.

People in the Aztec world defined themselves by their *altepetl*, so the people of Tenochtitlan saw themselves as Tenochca. The altepetl had four *campan*, but there was also a smaller unit of organisation called the *calpulli* (group of houses) that represented a clan and a neighbourhood. Usually, the *calpulli* was made up of a group of *macehualtin* (commoners) families led by *pipiltin* (nobles). According to laws passed by Motecuhzoma II, each *calpulli* had to have a school (*telpochcalli*). The *calpulli* also served as the basis for the squadrons of the Aztec army, for maintaining small temples to the god of the *calpulli* and for other such needs of everyday life.

The *calpulli*

A *calpulli* was a group of families who lived near one another. *Calpulli*, in urban settings, were comprised of neighbourhoods. In our modern categories, a *calpulli* can be understood as a district, quarter, or neighbourhood of a town. Some *calpulli* encompassed a single profession while others were home to a mixture of farmers, craftsmen and traders. The craftsmen *calpulli* might consist of feather workers, goldsmiths, precious stone workers or other artisans. But for the most part, the *macehualtin* (commoners) were grouped within the *calpulli*. The city of Tenochtitlan was composed of four *campan* (territorial divisions organised according to the cardinal points), and each *campan* was composed of several *calpulli*.

In rural areas, some of the *calpulli* wards formed a territory, spread out over a large area, while some were clustered together to form rural towns. A small *calpulli* could consist of a cluster of 10 to 20 houses, while a larger *calpulli* could be composed of several wards under a common *tecuhtli* lord. Those serving the *tecuhtli* directly lived in a *teccalli* (noble house). Urban wards generally consisted of noble dwellings, while those who lived in the rural wards were peasants.

All *calpulli* wards contained a temple to which the members of the community dedicated themselves. The temple was administered by a priest, or *quacuilli,* who played a role equivalent to the parish priests of today. The citizens worked and maintained plots to support themselves. A *telpochcalli* (young men's house) was attached to the temple within the *calpulli*. The distinguished and outstanding warriors of the *calpulli* were responsible for educating the students in martial arts at this school. The young men trained at the *telpochcalli* were then responsible for the upkeep of the school, and they provided daily fuel and provisions, made repairs to the building, and cultivated a field for the support of the school (Offner 1983; Prescott 1983).
The Aztecs identified themselves according to their *calpulli* or community. They did not consider themselves as a culture or as a collective whole. Each *calpulli,* and in a larger sense, each *altepetl* (town) had its own history with its own identity. People from Tenochtitlan would have identified themselves as Tenochca; those from Xochimilco (a southern lake region) would have identified themselves as Xochimilca (Boone 1994).
Although the *calpulli* was ultimately run by the *tlatoani* who appointed a *tecuhtli* to oversee the people, members of the *calpulli* elected within them a *calpullec* (headman) to distribute lands to them according to need. The *calpullec's* job was to maintain census maps of his *calpulli*. The maps showed all vacant and occupied lots in the land. Through these maps a current record

was known of all people that should be paying tribute to the state. At the death of a *calpulli* member, the name-glyph that represented the head of the household was erased and was replaced by his successor. The person to fill the position of *calpullec* was not necessarily part of the noble class, but they had to have held the office of a *principal* (elder). Members of the *calpulli* were responsible for cultivating land for the *calpullec* so that he could perform his job. He was required to meet with the members of the *calpulli* to discuss their needs, and he needed to present himself to the chief tribute collector of the state (*calpixque)* daily to receive orders.

In the eastern Nahua area of Puebla and Tlaxcala, nobles headed large *teccalli* (noble houses). Commoners were attached to them by obligations of service and tribute. In the Basin of Mexico, Morelos and the Toluca area, members of a *calpulli* were under the jurisdiction of a noble, and the local commoners were required to pay tribute to him. The nobles owned land apart from the *calpulli* in which some peasants were considered dependent upon their lord to work these lands. Within the conquered areas, the members of the equivalent of the *calpulli* were also required to provide services for the local ruler and the Aztec administrator.

Both the *teccalli* and the *calpulli* were territorial units, but not much is understood about their full organisation. In the *calpulli*, land was distributed among the members for their use, for example, for farming. If new land opened up, or if an existing plot was left abandoned, the *calpulli* council would reallocate the land. Land was not usually sold – it was passed down to heirs; however, in some *calpulli* lands were the privately owned by certain commoners and could be sold. But ultimately, the land remained under the general jurisdiction of the *calpulli* and the *altepetl* (city-state).

Social structure and class hierarchy

The social structure of the Mexica-Aztecs was divided into two classes and was determined by birth: the nobles (*pipiltin,* or singular *pilli*), and the commoners (*macehualtin,* or singular *macehualli*) (Townsend 2000; Velasco Piña 2001). Within this structure were different levels. The hierarchy of the nobles in descending order were the kings/rulers (*tlatoque,* or singular *tlatoani*), the *cihuacoatl* (second in command and ruler over internal affairs), *quetzalcoatl totec tlamacazqui* and the *quetzalcoatl tlaloc tlamacazqui* (two supreme priests), the high lords (*tetecuhtin* or singular *tecuhtli*), and the *pipiltin,* or the rest of the nobles.

Fig. 4
A child is held in the smoke
as a punishment, *Codex
Mendoza*, Fol. 60r

Bodleian Library, Oxford

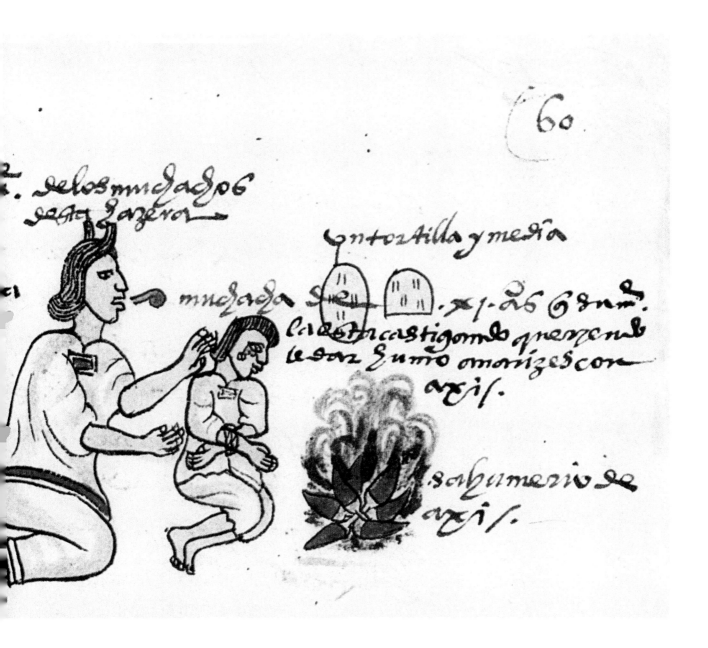

The *pipiltin*

The highest-ranking *tlatoani* was the Aztec emperor over Tenochtitlan, who was also a member of the Triple Alliance (the cities of Tenochtitlan, Tlacopan, and Tetzcoco). Other *tlatoque* ruled over smaller cities and towns. Each of the *Tetecuhtin* controlled a smaller area, or *calpulli* (neighbourhood).
Priests or *tlamacazqui* were people from noble and peasant backgrounds, but only the men of noble heritage could become the *quetzalcoatl totec tlamacazqui* and *quetzalcoatl tlaloc tlamacazqui* (high priests). The *quetzalcoatl totec*

tlamacazqui was associated with the cult of Huitzilopochtli, the god of war, while the *quetzalcoatl tlaloc tlamacazqui* was associated with Tlaloc, the rain god.

Despite these specific social distinctions, there were in a sense only two levels in the Aztec social structure, noble and non-noble. In Nahuatl, the word *pilli* means 'child' and is equivalent to the English word 'noble'. A person could only be considered a *pilli* if he or she was a child or a descendant of a king. The status of the *pilli* was transmitted through male and female lineages alike. If only one parent (either mother or father) was a *pilli*, then the child would acquire the status of a *pilli*. Also, if one of the parents was the *tlatoani*, the child still would have the status of a *pilli*.

Members of the nobility enjoyed certain privileges. They lived in impressive houses with many servants and possessed expensive luxuries such as fine food, elegant clothes, works of art and precious jewellery. Only the *pipiltin* males were allowed to be polygamous because they alone could afford more than one wife. The *Crónica Mexicayotl* lists twenty-two children of Axayacatl, twenty of Ahuitzotl, and nineteen of Motecuhzoma. Tlacaelel the *Cihuacoatl* (second in command) had five children from his principal wife, then a son or daughter from each of his twelve secondary wives.

Another privilege that the nobles received was tribute from the lower classes in the form of personal services, food and labour in order to build and maintain the temples, palaces and other public places of Tenochtitlan.

A benefit to further the nobility's standing was the privilege to enter their children into the *calmecac* (school of higher education) to be trained in the military arts, religion, law, history, the calendar, oral literature and writing.

Girls from a noble heritage also attended the *calmecac,* but they learned how to direct servants in household tasks, how to weave cotton textiles, and other concerns dealing with the home. The purpose of the nobility was to serve the ruler, another aspect of the *calmecac* education, and they were given jobs as ambassadors, tax collectors, provincial governors, teachers, scribes, judges, priests and army generals.

The *macehualtin*

In a general sense the Nahuatl word *macehualli* means commoner. This group encompassed merchants, artisans, peasant farmers and the rest of the free citizens who were not of noble birth. For the Aztecs, the commoners formed the backbone of society: they worked the fields, sold and traded goods and gathered tribute to give to the *tlatoani* as a tax. Those taxes would then go back to the community to maintain activities and services.

Macehualtin were subject to work for and serve the nobility. They worked on noble lands and palaces and were required to go to war if they were called upon to do so.

The *macehualtin* children went to school just as the *pilli* children did. However, rather than receiving instruction at the *calmecac*, the commoners attended the *telpochcalli* (youth house). If a child was exceptionally gifted, he would be allowed to attend the *calmecac*. At the *telpochcalli*, children learned how to become warriors or good housewives. The children also learned the basics of their ancestral history and religion.

Pochteca (merchants) and master craftsmen outranked any peasant farmer. These groups could accumulate great wealth through their trade, but they were never considered nobles because they usually did not have a royal blood heritage.

Below the commoners in social rank were the *mayeque* (landless commoners) and then the *tlacotin* (slaves). The *mayeque* were not part of a *calpulli* because they were bound to the land of the nobles they served. *Tlacotin* were also bound to a master's land but for different reasons. They had become slaves as a result of being punished for a crime, usually theft, or as a result of acquiring a gambling debt. Also, during times of famine or hardship, people sold their children into slavery, but individuals could buy their freedom back if situations improved. So slaves were bound to a master only as long as their debt was to be paid. The master was required to feed and clothe the slave, and the slave was required to work without pay. Slaves could marry whomever they chose and the children of slaves were born free.

The household

The Aztec home

Most of the *macehualtin* (commoners) houses were made of sun-dried brick and were L-shaped with a single storey. The number of rooms increased with the family's wealth, but the most modest homes had one main room. The entrance opened up to a patio in the centre, while the side facing the street was closed for privacy. The average house had a kitchen, a room where the entire family slept, and two altars. One altar was located near where they slept and the other was located near the door. The kitchen was a separate building in the courtyard and the *temazcalli* (bathroom) was also built separately from the house. Families and also their extended families occupied these houses.

Furnishings were simple and sparse in both elaborate and modest homes. *Petlatl* (mats), *petlacalli* (chests), and a few seats woven out of reeds or rushes provided the furniture in the houses of both rich and poor Aztec alike. Great lords and commoners both had mats for beds, but some mats might have a bed curtain over them, which was the case when the Spanish stayed in Axayacatl's palace. During the daytime the same *petlatl* (mat) for sleeping was

Fig. 6
A midwife at the naming ceremony for a child, *Codex Mendoza*, Fol. 57r

Bodleian Library, Oxford

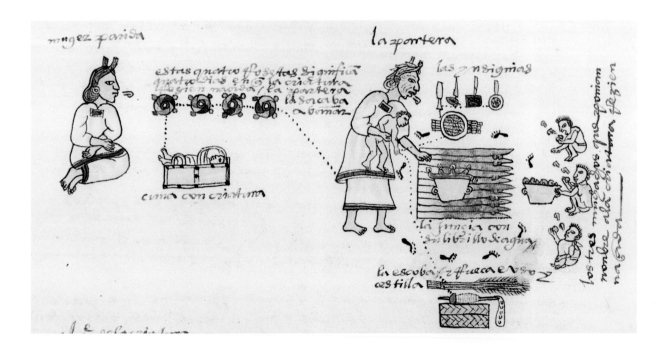

used as a seat. The mat was either set up on a mound of earth or on a wooden platform, regardless of whether it was in the private house or in the court-yard. A more elaborate chair, an *icpalli*, was a legless seat made of wood or wickerwork with a back slightly higher than the sitter's head. One would sit cross-legged on the ground on the *icpalli* and lean backward a little. This chair was common among the people but only the emperor's *icpalli* could be covered with cloth or skins and be adorned with gold.

A family's storage box or chest where clothes, pieces of cloth and jewels were kept was called a *petlacalli*. This same word also identifies the state treasure and is found in the name of the official, the *petlacalcatl*, who was in charge of the finances of the empire. But the household *petlacalli* was simply a fragile covered basket with easy access. Only a very strict law against theft kept people from stealing. Other chests found in the house contained their gods (small and large), small stones and flints, and books of paper made from the bark of a tree that contained the signs and dates of past events.

In the middle of every house lay the hearth and the image of Huehueteotl, the old god of fire. The hearth consisted of three stones on which the pots were placed, and logs were burned between the stones. The mystical power of the fire god was within the stones, and it was a superstitious belief that anyone who offended the fire by walking on the hearthstones would die.

Household populations

In Tenochtitlan, the number of individuals in a household cannot be known for sure, but authorities such as Soustelle (1979) suggest that four to seven people lived under the same roof. This estimate is thought to be modest, because servants also lived within the same dwelling. So if the average number of people in a household was seven, there were 80,000 to 100,000 households within Tenochtitlan and Tlatelolco, bringing the population up to more than 500,000 but below 1,000,000. Other scholars disagree with these calculations, and now Edward Calnek's suggestion that Tenochtitlan had a population of about 200,000 is widely accepted (Calnek 1976).

Family relationships

Aztec families were closely knit and supportive of each other. Parents, grandparents and neighbours helped rear the children in the neighbourhood. Aunts and uncles also helped raise and support the upbringing of children. If a member of a family refused to help look after the family children, they were considered bad people by other society members.

Ideally, the family was expected to behave properly, to work industriously and to treat each other and elders with respect. Elders played an important role in Aztec ceremonies, and although strict laws prohibited the rest of the Aztec society from being drunk in public, the elderly were allowed to drink alcoholic beverages in excess.

The roles of men and women

The father

According to Sahagún (1951–1969), an individual's father was the source of lineage, the beginning of lineage. The man was the head of the family. If he had more than one wife, he was to treat all of them as equals. The father was to amass wealth for himself and for his family, and he was to take care of his assets responsibly. He regulated family life, distributed his wealth with care, and established order in the home.

The mother

Sahagún (Edmonson 1974) writes that a woman's greatest duty was that of being a mother; she had children and nursed them. She was to be sincere, vigilant and an energetic worker. He further describes the good Aztec woman as an attentive teacher, willing to serve others and be mindful of their welfare. He emphasises that she was to be careful, thrifty, and constantly at work.

If a woman's husband died, she could either remain unmarried or remarry. She could become a secondary wife to one of the dead man's brothers, and it was not unknown for a widow to marry one of her husband's slaves and make him her steward.

Aztec women lived by an Aztec standard of beauty. Women were taught to wear make-up and paint their faces moderately; some Meso-American women wore red paint around their mouths. Only promiscuous women used make-up and face paint excessively. Aztec women were also taught to dress well, to wash themselves and their clothes everyday, and by these gestures, they would earn their husbands' love. Women got ready by looking into mirrors made of obsidian or pyrites, by cleaning their mouth, and by washing their face and hands. It is said that when they had finished preparing themselves, they looked like flowers.

Cleanliness was one of the most cherished virtues of Aztec society, for all citizens, not just women. The Aztecs used the fruit of the *copalxocotl* (called the soap tree by the Spaniards) and the root of the *saponaria americana* for soap. These soaps were used to wash the body and to clean the laundry. Most people bathed often, and some bathed every day. It has been documented that

Motecuhzoma bathed twice a day. However, not all of the people were very clean all of the time. Certain priests did not wash their hair so that the blood of sacrifices stayed in their long matted hair. Also merchants vowed not to bathe until they returned from a long, dangerous expedition. During the month *Atemoztli*, as penance, people did not use soap. Women wore their hair loosely and a few women also had their teeth dyed red with cochineal. They used a yellow cream called *axin* on their faces as make-up; promiscuous women, *auianime*, wore red colour on their faces and mouths. Then they applied perfume with an odoriferous censer.

The children

Children, especially newborn babies, were called "precious stones" or *quetzal*-feathers, and they were believed to be gifts from the gods. Midwives delivered children in the household, and welcomed them into the world while warning them about the uncertainty and sorrows of this life. A legitimate child was born to a man and wife who had been properly married; this usually meant the first marriage that underwent the appropriate marriage rites. A good son was expected to be obedient, humble, gracious, grateful and reverent. He was also expected to follow his parents' character and way of life. A good daughter was required to be obedient, honest, intelligent, discreet and with a good memory, respectful, prudent, modest, and chaste.
When a child was orphaned, his or her uncle and aunt provided support for their niece or nephew.

The midwife

Midwives helped with the birth of a child, and gave a long speech at the birth of a child to warn the infant of the dangers in life and also to give advice. The midwife also gave children their baptismal names after consulting the soothsayers.

Marriage

Most girls married at the age of 15, while most boys married at the age of 20, after they graduated from the *calmecac* (priest school) or the *telpochcalli* (warrior school). Boys had to ask permission to marry from their masters at school, and an elaborate banquet was given by the young man's family to facilitate the request (Aguilar-Moreno 2007).

A man could only marry one woman in the traditional marriage ceremony, and she would live as his legitimate wife. But he could have as many secondary wives as he could afford. Those who lived together without this ceremony were not recognised as married by society, and the children born of the union were not considered legitimate; therefore, they did not receive inheritances. Relatives of the young man chose whom he was to marry, but not before soothsayers had been consulted. The soothsayers considered the signs under which the bride and groom were born, and then determined what omens might befall them if they were to marry.

Before the day of the marriage a wedding feast was planned at the bride's home. Preparations for the feast could last approximately three days. The bride bathed and washed her hair. She then sat near the fire on a dais covered with mats and the elders of the young man's family came to offer her advice. She was told to leave childishness and to be most considerate, to speak well and tend to the sweeping. The advice of an elder was greatly encouraged.
On the night of the ceremony, a procession escorted the bride to the groom's home. Once all had arrived at the groom's home, he came forward to receive her. Both the bride and groom were seated on a mat in front of the hearth. The bride's mother gave presents to the groom, and the groom's mother gave the bride a blouse and a skirt. Finally, the *cihuatlanqui* (matchmaker) tied the groom's cape with the bride's blouse together, and this signalled that the marriage ceremony was complete.
The couple's first act together was sharing a dish of tamales by giving the other the little maize-cakes by hand. They were expected to live as husband and wife until old age unless illness, childbirth, warfare, or sacrifice killed one of them.
Couples who could not wait for permission for the marriage rites to be completed, as in the case of an unexpected pregnancy or an elopement, were married without permission. But to be socially accepted, the couple needed to carry out the traditional marriage ceremony. The young groom therefore apologised to the bride's parents for not gaining their consent before getting married. Then they proceeded with the ceremonies and festivities that their modest situation might allow. ⌐

Fig. 7 ▸
The "Old Fire God"
Huehueteotl-Xiuhtecuhtli

Museum der Kulturen Basel
(cat. 51)

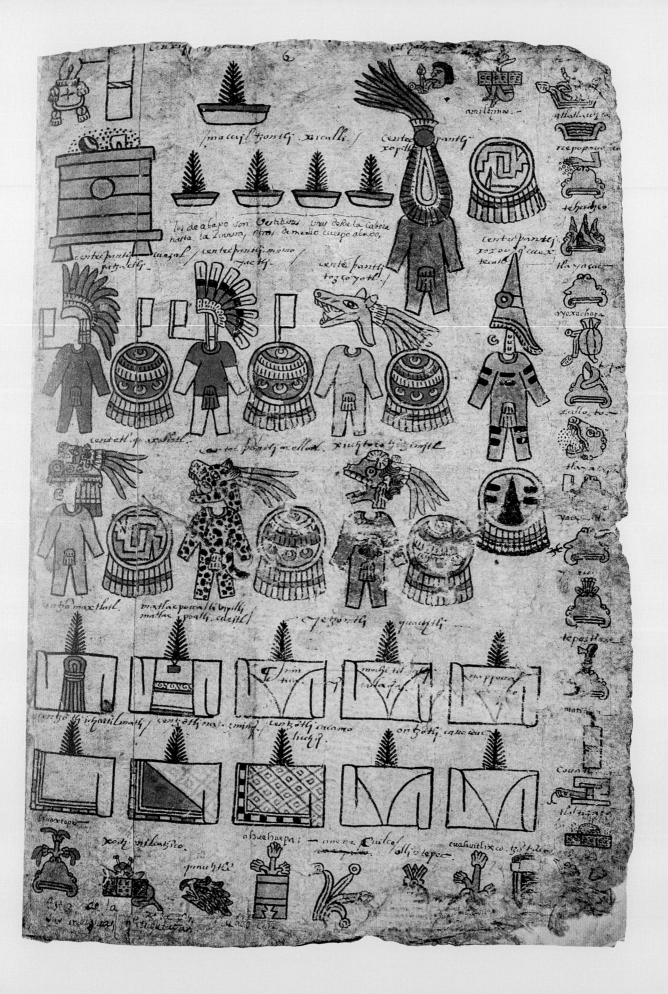

Frances F. Berdan

Markets, Merchants and Tribute in the Aztec Empire

In the year 1519 unprecedented quantities and varieties of material goods were available to the people living in the great city of Tenochtitlan. Even the poorest in the city would at some time observe the elaborately decorated cotton cloak flaunted by a noble as he strutted by on the street. They might gape at the bright shimmering feathers on warriors' banners in their ceremonial return from battle, and admire their battered feathered shields. They would glimpse intricate turquoise mosaics, greenstone jewels and gold ornaments (including gold earrings, as in this exhibition) on deities' images as they passed by in flamboyant processionals – and shining bells and shells and flowing feathered litters. If the ruler Motecuhzoma Xocoyotzin appeared in public, only his elegant sandals and perhaps his gold-bedecked calves could be glimpsed through the resident's downcast eyes. These individuals may also have imbibed small amounts of watered-down chocolate drink during special events, or enjoyed the taste of an unusual species of chile on market day.

Goods and objects like these were, however, daily fare for the elite in the city. Nobles, both men and women, were dressed elegantly in decorated cotton clothing and bedecked with gold adornments and fine stone jewels. They consumed a wide range of foods from both local and distant regions and used beautiful polychrome plates, bowls and cups (as seen in this exhibition) during their hearty meals. Some of these wares were produced locally, but others were imported – after all, the emperor Motecuhzoma Xocoyotzin (ruled 1502–1520) dined on ceramic wares from Cholula, across the volcanoes to the east.

Rich or poor, the residents of Tenochtitlan and the many other cities in the highland Basin of Mexico were only able to procure some of the goods they needed and desired locally or nearby – mostly foods and utilitarian goods such as pottery, stone tools and baskets. The raw materials from which most luxury objects were made (such as colourful feathers, turquoise, jadeite, gold, shells and jaguar pelts) came from afar, both within and beyond the bounds of the expansive Aztec Empire. Other products such as cotton, cacao and fine sea salt were produced only in temperate, lowland or coastal zones, beyond the highland Basin of Mexico. Conversely, some lowland or coastal areas lacked

Fig. 1 ◄
Tribute list for Tenochtitlan, *Matrícula de Tributos*, Fol. 4r

Biblioteca Nacional de Antropología e Historia, Mexiko-Stadt, D.R. Secretaria de Cultura – INAH

Fig. 2
Quetzal

Photo: ondrejprosicky/
stock.adobe.com

highly desired goods and materials such as maguey products and obsidian that were native to the highlands or other localised regions. This means that a great many raw materials and goods were moving about from region to region, from city to city and from household to household throughout the ecologically diverse empire and beyond its borders. These movements largely took place through exchanges at a multitude of markets, the activities of energetic merchants, and the imposition and payment of tribute.

Markets

The centres of the cities and towns in the Aztec realm characteristically contained three primary features: a temple or temples, a palace or palaces, and a plaza that hosted a market daily or periodically. The largest market in the land

was held at Tlatelolco, the sister-city of Tenochtitlan. On a tour of that marketplace shortly before the Spanish conquest, the *conquistador* Bernal Díaz del Castillo (1963) finally despaired of describing all the displays he saw by declaring, "If I describe everything in detail I shall never be done." That particular market was indeed impressive: unlike most other markets, it enjoyed its own dedicated plaza with permanent arcades, and it took place daily with bigger gatherings every five days. Reportedly, this exceptional marketplace drew an estimated 20,000–25,000 people every day and 40,000–50,000 every fifth day (Anonymous Conqueror 1963). Local as well as exotic goods were found in profusion. Most vendors hailed from nearby and were producers of their own products or wares: a farmer with some extra maize or beans; a potter with his pots and plates; an obsidian tool maker forming blades on the spot, and so on. Some of the objects of this type are seen in this exhibition, including obsidian core and blades, and polychrome plates and bowls. But professional merchants also participated in large numbers, selling exotic goods obtained in distant lands: shimmering tropical feathers, golden ornaments, graceful shells, precious stones such as jadeite, and despondent slaves. Cotton and cacao were also sold by traders, being brought to this highland market from lower elevations.

This metropolitan marketplace attained such prominence largely due to its strategic setting: it enjoyed a prominent location in the midst of a large lake (allowing efficient traffic and transport by canoe), as well as proximity to enormous concentrated urban populations. Therefore, a great many buyers and sellers had ready access to the marketplace on foot (via causeways) and in canoes. The people attending the market represented a variety of occupations, ethnicities and social statuses, contributing to the vast assortment of goods sought by consumers and displayed by vendors in response to those demands and desires.

The availability of different types of commodities in the markets fluctuated during the year. Some products flowed according to natural cycles such as agricultural harvests, and some goods responded to cultural cycles such as the elaborate and flamboyant ceremonies held on predictable schedules. The marketplace was sensitive to these rhythms, and everyone looked for fresh *elotes* (corn on the cob) near harvest time, and was assured that a profusion of little red feathers and glues would be available for decorating the arms and legs of women who danced at particular monthly ceremonies.

Barter (the exchange of goods for goods) was customary in the marketplaces, although different forms of money circulated widely. Cacao beans were the most common currencies, serving as "small change," while large white cotton cloaks (*quachtli*) provided standards of value for more expensive goods and services. Thin copper axes (seen in this exhibition) also reportedly served as a form of currency. Whether barter or currency (or a combination of these) was used, the value of each specific purchase was established through bargaining (haggling). This was facilitated by the aggregation of the same types of goods in specified areas of the plaza, and the fact that the marketplace was a bustling hub of information. People came to the market not only to buy and sell, but also to catch up on the news of the day, whether it be to confirm rumours of an impending war or to check up on the progress of a cousin's courtship. In short, the bustling, lively marketplace served as the local newspaper.

The Tlatelolco marketplace typifies markets elsewhere in the Aztec realm, albeit on an extraordinary scale. Markets big and small were held on known schedules throughout the realm, goods were organised in the marketplace by type, and marketers engaged in bargaining while using barter and money. In and around the Basin of Mexico, some markets were renowned for specialised offerings and everyone knew what they were. Acolman was known for its profusion of dogs; Texcoco for cloth, ceramics and fine cloth; Azcapotzalco and Itzocan for slaves; and Otompan and Tepepulco for turkeys (Berdan 2014). Farther afield, some large markets were also well known, such as the market at Coayxtlahuacan, whose rich goods may have been one incentive for Aztec

Fig. 7
Cocoa beans

Photo: Andreas Gross

conquest, and the market at Tepeacac which was required by its Aztec conquerors to assure regular supplies of exclusive luxuries. Most of these types of markets met on five-day cycles, although some, such as that at Tochpan on the Gulf Coast, met on a 20-day schedule; on that day, the market would have been marvellous indeed. And we must not forget that innumerable markets supplied the everyday needs of all households throughout the realm. The profusion of markets allowed elite and ordinary people access to a wide array of goods from near and far, regardless of their region or residence. Some of these goods entered markets through the commercial activities of professional merchants.

Merchants

Merchants were instrumental in moving goods and materials from city to city and market to market. Some of these individuals were full-time merchants (*pochteca*) who travelled long distances across difficult terrain and dealt in high-end luxury goods. Although these merchants could reside in almost any city, the *pochteca* who resided in twelve Basin of Mexico cities are particularly well documented. These merchants lived in exclusive districts in their cities, drawing support from their fellow merchants and strength from their collective resources. When *pochteca* headed out on their long and perilous expeditions, they typically carried goods from their associates who could not travel. They tended to specialise in goods of high value and low bulk such as tropical feathers, precious stones and golden ornaments, but they were not above carrying more ordinary goods such as needles and obsidian blades for exchange with the ordinary people in the markets they visited. They were private entrepreneurs in a commercial world, buying and selling to their advantage.

Some of these long-distance professional merchants, those in political favour, might also serve their city-state rulers. As such, they acted as state agents by delivering their own ruler's goods to rulers in distant lands and carrying the foreign ruler's goods back to their own ruler. These exchanges appear to have been diplomatic engagements rather than economic transactions. But these economic opportunists should not be underestimated, as they used these same state-sponsored journeys to engage in marketplace exchanges in these same and other outlying areas. Favoured by their rulers, *pochteca* also gained some political clout within their own city-states. For instance, the *pochteca* from Tenochtitlan and Tlatelolco were especially esteemed by the Tenochtitlan ruler, who installed them as market judges in the renowned Tlatelolco marketplace. Sitting haughtily in a corner of the market plaza, they presided over all market behaviour and laid down swift and severe punishments for any misconduct – powerful positions indeed.

Many of these merchants became very wealthy in the highly commercialised Aztec world, and one of their greatest concerns was jealousy on the part of established nobles. The merchants made a point of walking around in ordinary clothes and behaving humbly – basically keeping a low profile. But there were expectations for rich merchants to contribute tangibly to the broader social and religious life of their communities. They did this, when they were able, by sponsoring a feast and offering a slave for sacrifice at specified public ceremonies. This was extremely costly. While this seemingly selfless action demonstrated the merchant's willingness to contribute to the "broader good" and not just hoard his wealth, he essentially exchanged material wealth for social prestige, a less tangible form of wealth.

Fig. 8
Stone sculpture
representing a dog

Museum am Rothenbaum
Hamburg (cat. 53)

There were many other types of full-time or part-time merchants beyond the renowned *pochteca*. Particularly notable were the merchants who traded localised resources and goods across regions. These goods tended to be heavy, bulky, and of medium value. For instance, traders moved cotton and cacao from lowlands to highlands, carried fine salt from coastal to inland regions, and transported foods such as special types of chile that grew in localised areas. The commercial activities of these merchants inside and outside the imperial boundaries were instrumental in provisioning households with a wide range of raw materials and finished goods.

Tribute

Tributes streamed into Tenochtitlan from its conquered city-states on quarterly, semi-annual or annual schedules. Deliveries were spectacular occasions as almost-endless lines of porters laden with recognisable and exotic goods trudged along Tenochtitlan's causeways to the entrance of the ruler's palace. The bounty of the empire was on open display.

Tribute payments provided the ruler with materials and goods to support his extravagant lifestyle, including exquisite clothing, precious stones, golden ornaments, colourful tropical feathers, seashells, live eagles, reed seats and jaguar pelts to cover those royal seats. Tributes also included numerous feathered warrior costumes and shields (like the ones seen in this exhibition) that the ruler ceremonially bestowed on valiant warriors who had captured enemy warriors on the battlefield. Also among the tributes were items of clothing woven of plain cotton or coarser materials; some of these were used as a form of money (*quachtli*) and others were worn by less elite persons. There were also large quantities of staple foodstuffs: maize, beans, chia and amaranth, along with loads of chiles. And then, finally, were the numerous miscellaneous items such as wooden beams and carrying frames, gourd and pottery bowls, cochineal and yellow ochre dyes, paper, reed mats, lime, salt, honey, rubber, and much more (Berdan and Anawalt 1992). In addition to these regular tribute payments, tributes were also demanded by the imperial powers on special occasions, offsetting the extraordinary expenses of a royal coronation or funeral, or the expansion of a major temple.

These myriad materials and goods were demanded from conquered city-states according to local availabilities. Assessments were also responsive to the constraints of transport on human backs or in canoes. Staple foodstuffs, being heavy and bulky, were demanded from provinces close to the imperial capitals, even though virtually everyone throughout the empire produced these foods. Other goods hailed from more distant and localised areas – for instance, tropical feathers from the humid lowlands, seashells from both coasts, live eagles from the eastern empire, copper objects from the western empire, and gold from the southern empire. Paper came from temperate lands, and reeds from lakesides. Some goods assessed in tribute, such as amber, were available only beyond the empire's boundaries; such goods were most likely carried by merchants from outside the empire and sold in market-places within the empire, later to be paid in tribute by the empire's subjects.

Specific tribute payments were negotiated at the time of conquest, and were modified over time as the needs of the empire evolved and the empire's relations with its subjects changed: for instance, it was well known that payments would be vastly increased if the province revolted and was re-conquered. This occurred following the rebellion of Cuetlaxtlan, whose new tribute was increased in size and difficulty: from spotted jaguar skins to white ones, from green stones to red and white ones, from single-sized to double-sized cloths, and twice the amounts of cacao, gold, and feathers (Durán 1994). This was intimidating and probably a deterrent to future rebellions.

In the Aztec Empire every imaginable product, whether foods, utilitarian goods, or exotic luxuries, circulated across broad and diverse regions: shimmering feather devices were flaunted in the highlands, and at the same time pulque (a fermented beverage made from maguey syrup) was enjoyed in the lowlands. This was an energetic, commercial world where bustling markets were held on regular, known schedules; professional merchants travelled far and wide; and caravans of porters transported loads and loads of essential and luxury goods from myriad conquered subjects to imperial capitals. ⌐

Fig. 9
Little bell made of gold

Museo del Templo Mayor, Mexico City, D.R. Secretaría de Cultura – INAH (cat. 127)

Tenochtitlan

Martin Berger

The Migration of the Mexica and the Founding of Tenochtitlan

The capital city of Tenochtitlan was the beating heart of the Aztec empire. Founded on a swampy island in the waters of Lake Texcoco, this Aztec refuge grew to be one of the largest cities of the world in its time. The story of the foundation of this magnificent city is a classic tale of exodus, casting the Mexica/Aztecs as a chosen people who began as the underdogs but found a promised land in which they fulfilled their destiny as rulers of an empire. This story was doubtless re-written many times in the past by Aztec/Mexica rulers to suit the political and religious needs of the moment. All versions, however, served to affirm for the Aztecs their place as a chosen people.

The Aztec migration began at their ancestral home in Aztlan. While opinions differ on its location, and whether or not it was a mythical place, it is clear that it lay to the north of Tenochtitlan. According to the Spanish chronicler Durán (1964), the Aztec emperor Moctezuma I already attempted to locate the ancestral homeland in the fifteenth century. In the year 1 Flint (AD 1168) the Aztecs, following earlier migrants, set out from Aztlan (Martínez de Cuervo 1990; de Rojas 2012). Four priests carried on their back the sacred bundle that contained their patron god Huitzilopochtli. During their wanderings, Huitzilopochtli led the Aztecs by sharing his prophecies with these high priests.

The Aztec migration took them to and through countless places, where they settled by building a temple to their patron god and planting corn, beans, and other foodstuffs (Smith 2011). They would stay at these places for several years, and sometimes decades, until they were prompted by local events or their god Huitzilopochtli to continue their search. Among the locations that they visited, several stand out.

First among these is Chicomoztoc or "Seven Caves". Chicomoztoc was the second place of origin for the Aztecs after Aztlan. Here the Mexica branched off from the other peoples who had left Aztlan with or before them. After leaving Chicomoztoc, the Aztecs/Mexica established themselves at Malinalco. It was here that Malinalxochitl, a sister of Huitzilopochtli, created many problems for the wanderers. The Aztec priests consulted their god, who ordered his followers to secretly leave Malinalxochitl during the night. When

Fig. 1 ◄
Relief plate with the founding motif of Tenochtitlan

Museum der Kulturen Basel (cat. 65)

Malinalxochitl woke up, she and her followers found that they had been deserted and founded the city of Malinalco. While attempting to avenge his mother's disgrace, Malinalxochitl's son, Copil, would later play an important role in the founding of Tenochtitlan.

From Malinalco, the Mexica/Aztecs continued on to a place called Coatepec
– 'Snake Mountain'. Coatlicue, the earth goddess, lived nearby. One day when
she was sweeping a temple, a ball of feathers landed on her belly, miraculous-
ly impregnating her. This enraged her daughter Coyolxauhqui, who called

Fig. 3
Codex Boturini (Tira de la Peregrinación Azteca): In the year "1 Flint" the Aztecs leave Aztlan, their mythical original homeland, by canoe. Their first stop is Mount Colhuacan, where a priest speaks to Huitzilopochtli.

Museo Nacional de Antropología, Mexico City, D.R. Secretaría de Cultura – INAH (cat. 68)

Fig. 4
Stone sculpture in the
form of a locust

Museo Nacional de Antro-
pología, Mexico City, D.R.
Secretaría de Cultura – INAH
(cat. 15)

upon her brothers, the Centzon Huitznahua, to aid her in killing Coatlicue. Coatlicue fled to Coatepec, hoping to save herself. When the assailants reached the top of the mountain, Huitzilopochtli was born wearing his warrior costume and killed the attackers. He dismembered his sister Coyolxauhqui and threw her down the mountain. The Aztecs inscribed this episode from their saga of origin into the urban landscape as the Templo Mayor. At the foot of the main temple, which was surrounded by snakes to invoke the mythical Coatepec, lay the dismembered body of Coyolxauhqui, represented in a monolith.

From Coatepec, the Mexica travelled on to Chapultepec. Here, Copil, son of Huitzilopochtli's sister Malinalxochitl, incited the local lords against the newly arrived migrants. The locals attacked the Mexica but were quickly defeated. However, Huitzilopochtli's priests managed to kill Copil and, on the instructions of their god, threw his heart into the reeds on the borders of Lake Texcoco.

After their defeat at Chapultepec, the Aztecs settled at Tizaapan, a snake-infested marshland in the lake. From here, however, they were eventually expelled as well and were forced to wander the swamps around the edges of the lake. Their god told them not to despair, since they were finally close to their destiny and their destination. Huitzilopochtli told the priests that they

Fig. 5
Gold jewellery in the
form of a heart

Museo del Templo Mayor,
Mexico City, D.R. Secretaría
de Cultura – INAH (cat. 123)

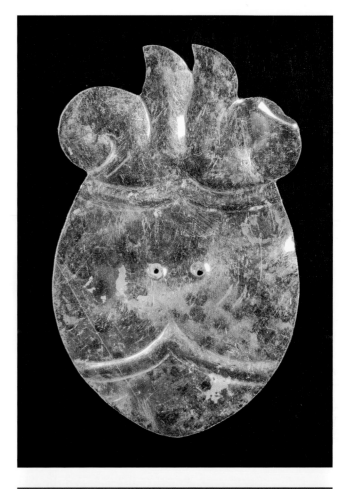

Fig. 6
Heart made of greenstone,
probably a pendant

Museum am Rothenbaum
Hamburg (cat. 125)

should look for a place where an eagle sat perched atop a prickly pear cactus. This cactus had sprouted from the heart of Copil, that had been thrown into the swamp some time before. Finally, in the year 2 House (AD 1325), the Mexica found the sight they were looking for – an eagle perched upon a cactus on an island in the lake. Here they built their first temple, and laid the foundation for what would become Tenochtitlan, the sprawling capital of Mexico's largest empire. ⌐

Fig. 7
The coat of arms of the Republic of Mexico

Barbara E. Mundy

Tenochtitlan:
Layout, Planning and Urban Life

The great island city of Tenochtitlan was built up over generations, as city residents piled up the sediment from the shallow bed of the surrounding lake, gradually transforming a series of small islands into a great metropolis (Carballal Staedtler and Flores Hernández 2006). By the year 1515, during the reign of Moteuczoma II, the city may have been home to 150,000 people. Gibson (1964) estimates the number of all inhabitants of the Basin of Mexico to have approached about 325 000 up to 350 000 people. When the Spanish conquistadors first glimpsed the city in 1519, they compared it to Seville and Venice, but it was, in fact, about three times more populous than the former, and closer in number to Venice, one of Europe's larger cities.

While large in population, Tenochtitlan was small in area. The Aztecs solved the problems that confronted any dense urban population through careful planning and urban management. The genius of Aztec city planners is evident in the map that was made to accompany the published version of a letter that conquistador Hernán Cortés sent to Charles V, seen among the objects in the exhibition (Mundy 1998) (see p. 32, image 2) .The city dominated the centre of the lake, appearing far larger than it actually was in relation to the surrounding water. And in the centre of the city was the enormous ceremonial precinct, defined by a rectangular wall, with four entrances to the west (the top of the map), east, north and south. Three of these led to the causeways, the main raised roads that connected the city to other cities in the basin. The causeway at top, to the west, held an ingenious two-duct aqueduct that carried freshwater to provision the city from the springs of Chapultepec, seen in the grove of trees at the top of the map. When the duct needed cleaning, the double design meant there was no interruption in the flow of water. The map shows breaks in the causeways that were spanned with bridges, allowing passage to foot traffic above and canoe traffic below. The artist shows us only thirteen boats, but since most of the city's provisions arrived via canoes, there was heavy traffic on the lake. Most market-bound journeys happened at night, when rowers in the agricultural zones around the lake, like those pictured in the map showing the floating gardens or *chinampas* loaded up food and produce and travelled in the cool darkness to arrive at the city's markets by sunrise (Conway 2012). By daybreak, market vendors were

Fig. 1 ◄
Plano en papel de Maguey

Biblioteca Nacional de Antropología y Historia, Mexico City, D.R. Secretaria de Cultura – INAH

117

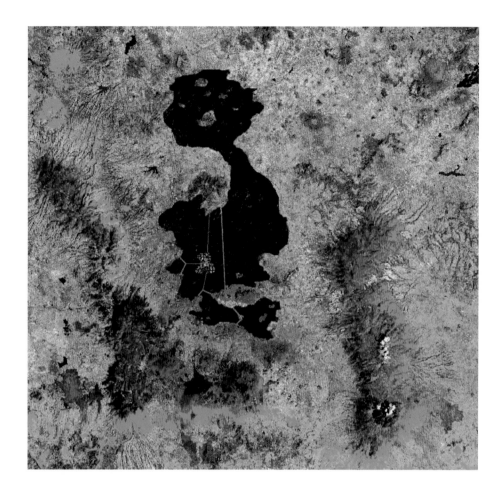

gathering to prepare for the thousands of buyers who would stream into the two main markets over the course of the day as described in the essay of Frances Berdan. Such open-air markets allowed the residents of the city to mingle, and see and smell the exotic goods that flowed into the city via vast networks. Some goods were brought by long-distance traders who connected the city to distant parts of Mexico and Central America, and others probably the tribute yielded by Tenochtitlan's aggressive conquests and recorded in the Matrícula de Tributos (Berdan and de Durand-Forest 1980).

Many of Tenochtitlan's commoners helped build the city's infrastructure as part of their tribute obligations to the city's lords (Zorita 1963). They were thus well aware of the effort and knowledge that it took for the island city to coexist with the surrounding lake. The great expanse of water around the city was actually an inland sea, with no natural drainage, and water levels fluctuated dramatically according to season. During the dry season, deeper canals cut into the lake bed allowed canoe traffic and provisions to reach the city. During the rainy season, the breaks in the causeways could be opened or

Fig. 3
Façade sculpture in the
form of a snake's head

Rautenstrauch-Joest-
Museum, Cologne, donation
of Peter and Irene Ludwig
(cat. 67)

closed to protect the city from flooding (Carballal Staedtler and Flores
Hernández 1989; Palerm 1973). Over the course of the fifteenth century,
two enormous dikes of stone and packed earth were raised from the lake bed
to the east of the city to further protect the city from seasonal fluctuations,
one of them 16 kilometres long and 5 metres wide (Carballal Staedtler and
Flores Hernández 2006). In the map of Tenochtitlan, this great dike below
the city looks like a thin wicker fence, but it was actually much more
substantial.

While there were practical reasons for the modifications of the surrounding
environment, the Mexica were also driven to position their urban capital as a
sacred centre, an idea that also animated the construction of the Sacred
Precinct, as Eduardo Matos Moctezuma has explored (Matos Moctezuma
2014). The integration of disparate phenomena into a holistic worldview, be
they the change in the level of a lake or the orientation of a shrine at the top of
a temple, has been termed "cosmovision" by Alfredo López Austin, and is a
feature of Meso-American thought across the millennia (López Austin 2016).

Fig. 4
Chinampas: the floating gardens of Xochimilco

Photo: Andreas Gross

Fig. 5 ⌃
The ruins of Tlatelolco

Photo: Inés de Castro

For instance, even though the roads and causeways seen in the 1524 map link the city to the shore at irregular intervals, they were carefully planned to align to the north, west and south, and east as they led out from the great ceremonial precinct (Aveni 1988). Together, these axes divided the city into quadrants and created the shape of a great quincunx, a sacred diagram of long-standing across Meso-America. Oriented along the solar axis and lying at the end of the western causeway, the twin sanctuaries of the Templo Mayor stood at the middle of the ceremonial precinct. During the winter dry season, a viewer standing on the main western causeway would witness the sun rising from behind the shrine of the solar deity Huitzilopochtli at the top of the temple. During the summer rainy season, the rising sun appeared behind the shrine dedicated to the rain deity Tlaloc. Thus, with every sunrise, the Templo Mayor showed itself to be in harmony with the agricultural and aquatic cycles of the surrounding city and larger valley. Sculpture, like the Throne of Moteuczoma / Teocalli of Sacred Warfare, commemorated the taming of the surrounding lakes in showing the deity of rivers and lakes, Chalchiuhtlicue, on her back and helpless at the bottom register of the sculpture, with an eagle, associated with the sun and Huitzilopochtli, perching on a cactus rising from the defeated deity's navel (Mundy 2015). Water, be it the life-giving rainfall or threat of flood, was a constant concern in the city, and thus many

Fig. 6 ◂
Relief plate, the water
god Tlaloc

Museo Nacional de Antro-
pología, Mexico City D.R.
Secretaría de Cultura – INAH
(cat. 21)

of the offerings cached in the great Templo Mayor and excavated by Matos Moctezuma and Leonardo López Lujan, contain ceramics painted with images of Tlaloc, like the one on view. Chalchiuhtlicue, sculpted in clay and stone was also frequently depicted (López Luján 1993).

Despite the devastating siege of the city between May and August of 1521, and the subsequent sack of the city by the Spaniards and allied indigenous warriors, Tenochtitlan endured (Mundy 2015). By 1524 it had been chosen as the site of the new Spanish capital by Hernán Cortés and became known as Mexico City. While Cortés and other Spaniards took over the houses and palaces of the Mexica lords, the majority of the population was indigenous through most of the sixteenth century. The four divisions of the city were recast as Catholic parishes, but retained their indigenous names, attached to the names of Christian saints: San Juan Moyotlan, Santa Maria Cuepopan, San Sebastian Atzacoalco, San Pablo Teopan (Moreno de los Arcos 1982). Indigenous elites, many members of the Mexica royal family, were crucial in the rebuilding of the city, and in organising the city's workforce. Despite the efforts of indigenous elites in maintaining the city's carefully calibrated relationship to the surrounding water, the new Spanish-led government had little understanding of the role of the causeways and dikes, and invested little in their upkeep. Chalchiuhtlicue found her vengeance in 1555, when a catastrophic flood swept through the city, and led a panicked Viceroy to consult with indigenous lords before deciding to rebuild one of the neglected dikes. But over time, European rather than indigenous technologies were favoured, and floods and droughts continue to plague the city, today one of the largest urban agglomerations in the world (López Luján 2012). ⌐

Fig. 7
Ceramic vessel with the image of the rain god Tlaloc

Museo del Templo Mayor, Mexico City D.R. Secretaría de Cultura – INAH (cat. 129)

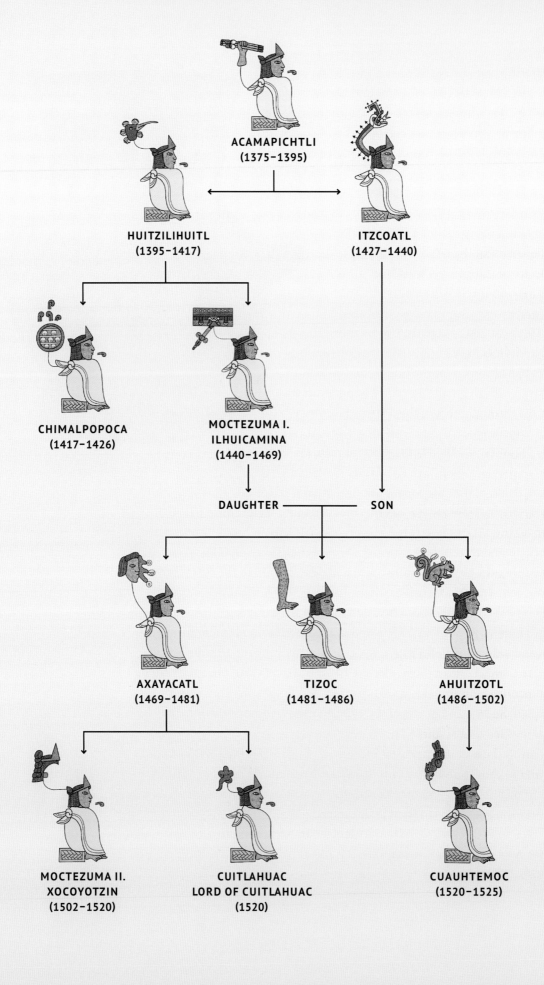

ACAMAPICHTLI
(1375–1395)

HUITZILIHUITL
(1395–1417)

ITZCOATL
(1427–1440)

CHIMALPOPOCA
(1417–1426)

MOCTEZUMA I.
ILHUICAMINA
(1440–1469)

DAUGHTER ——— SON

AXAYACATL
(1469–1481)

TIZOC
(1481–1486)

AHUITZOTL
(1486–1502)

MOCTEZUMA II.
XOCOYOTZIN
(1502–1520)

CUITLAHUAC
LORD OF CUITLAHUAC
(1520)

CUAUHTEMOC
(1520–1525)

Susan Toby Evans

The Aztec Palace

From November of 1519 to June of 1520, Hernán Cortés and his entourage lived in one of the great palaces of the Aztec empire, on the main plaza of the capital city Tenochtitlan. These administrative palaces were the essential nodes in the political framework of the Aztec empire (Evans 2004). In the few centuries that saw the rise of the Aztecs (1250 to 1519 AD), palaces proliferated across the landscape, representing territorial expansion and the consolidation of existing states together with the demands of administering a population that doubled in size twice during that period (Márquez-Morfín et.al. 2017).

Fig. 1 ◄
Genealogy of the
Aztec rulers

Diagram: OPERA
Amsterdam

Aztec royal administrative-residential compounds were imposing structures – Motecuzoma's New Palace, built after he became ruler in 1502, was later rebuilt and is now the Palacio Nacional of Mexico (Evans 2005). It covered somewhat more ground than the Alcazar Palace in Seville, although its façade was lower. Aztec buildings, even monumental ones, were single-storey constructions. Palaces achieved an impressive height, perhaps 6 metres, from the combination of a high solid platform, the exterior wall of the rooms it supported, and a rooftop parapet with merlons. Inside, groups of rooms on platforms surrounded open courtyards, the largest being the main entry courtyard, a spatial link between the public plaza and the ruler's dais room.

These three elements – plaza, courtyard and dais room – signal telescoping inclusion, characteristic of the Aztec political system (Evans 2013). While by no means a democracy, the Aztec hierarchy of power operated from the ground up, with commoner household heads meeting in the palaces of their local lords, who in turn congregated in the main courtyard of the ruler's palace in the city-state capital. Such lords themselves gathered in the imperial capitals. In all these contexts rulers spoke to their constituents, and in fact the Aztec ruler's name, *tlatoani*, means "speaker" or "orator"; mastery of rhetoric was as important a criterion of ability to rule as was military leadership. Rulers gave long sermons to their people, urging them to lead moderate and dutiful lives and avoid such perils as laziness, gambling and intoxicants. These periodic lectures in the main courtyards of palaces inspired the Spanish proselytiser Pedro de Gante, who lived in the Texcoco palace in 1524, to design open-air chapels for Christian worship by the converted natives.

Cortés quickly recognised that the Aztec tribute empire bore striking similarities to other archaic agrarian states like those on the Iberian Peninsula, in north Africa and throughout the Old World. Across many cultures, rulers cobbled together confederations of towns that drew on the tributes of local farmer-artisan commoners. In each capital the central focus of political and social activity was the ruling family's palace.

The Latin root, *palatium*, pertains to the name of a hill in Rome. In contrast, the Aztec (Nahuatl) term, *técpan calli* says exactly what it means: "lord-place house." It would attract a "court" for formal occasions such as ceremonies and festivals, and for informal daily hospitality with its gossip and food. When the emperor travelled, so did the *técpan* concept. In addition to their administrative palaces, Aztec lords also ruled from wherever they resided, be it a hay-bale shelter on a military campaign or pilgrimage, a lodge in a royal game park or horticultural nursery, or a pleasure palace on an island near Tenochtitlan (Evans 2000). Each was a *técpan*, and the glyph for *técpan* is that of a house surmounted by the mitre of rulership.

The greatest *técpans* in the Aztec empire were in the imperial capitals. Ten-ochtitlan's two imperial *técpans* were destroyed during the conquest while Texcoco's fell into ruin more gradually. However, we have good descriptions of several Aztec palaces and a few excavations of smaller ones. Ironically,

some of the best ethnohistorical accounts come from the letters and memoirs of the Spaniards who razed these buildings in the siege of Tenochtitlan after having lived for
months in Motecuzoma's Old Palace (aka Axayacatl's
Palace), as part of a hybrid court led by Cortés.

The establishment of Cortés's court began with his enthronement (as he describes it in his own words; Cortés
1986 [1519–1526]) in the Old Palace by Motecuzoma. Soon
after their initial meeting, Motecuzoma led Cortés to the
Old Palace, crossing the main courtyard to the dais room
where he seated Cortés, making him the palace lord. Within
a few days Motecuzoma was under house arrest in the Old
Palace. He had his own suite of lords and servants, and his
accommodations offered enough privacy for an efficient
espionage system: he was the first to know about Cortés'
own uncertain situation, threatened by other ambitious
Spaniards down on the Gulf Coast.

His entourage and that of Cortés lived together in reasonable harmony
because courtly customs in both cultures relied on feasting, watching enter-
tainers like acrobats and dancers, hunting at the game reserves and gambling
(Sahagún 1969, see also 1963, 1979 [1569]). Motecuzoma was such a
generous host that when a Spaniard was caught cheating, he covered the bet.
That was a minor expense compared with Aztec support of the Old Palace as a
burgeoning foreign colony embedded in their capital. Hundreds of alien
people and dozens of alien animals needed supplies (requiring complicated
logistics) and maintenance, all diverting resources and labour to the care of
the usurpers taking over the flow of tribute.

Fig. 4 ▾
Palace of Nezahualcoyotl,
the ruler of Texcoco, Mapa
Quinantzin

Bibliotheque nationale
de France, fonds mexicain,
collection Goupil-Aubin,
no. 12

While the Old Palace's residents comprised an
exceptionally varied household, to the Aztecs, "palace
people" (técpan pouhqui) traditionally included all
the people who frequented a palace: the ruling family,
their close advisors and courtiers, the visitors who
enjoyed special pleasures like chocolate and tobacco,
the servants who lived there and those rural commoners who worked there as part of their tribute
requirements. All maintained respect for the palace
patron deity Xochipilli/Macuilxochitl, whose special

interests were hallucinogenic intoxication (mushrooms, jimson weed, pulque beer), feasting, and gambling.

The Aztec palace was itself an important component of the economy because it constituted a weaving workshop in a society in which lengths of cloth were an established medium of exchange; every Aztec woman had learned textile production tasks since childhood. Every Aztec man – noble or wealthy commoner – took as many wives as he could afford in order to increase his household's affluence. Palaces also produced elite goods such as ornaments and sculpture. The palace of the Texcocan king Nezahualcoyotl is said to have covered a square kilometre and included teaching workshops where master artisans instructed apprentices. "*Tecpan*," still in use today in the country-side, now refers to the "comunidad" town hall, like its most common usage five hundred years ago, an administrative-residential building at the heart of its community.

Justyna Olko

Aztec Rule and Insignia

When the Spaniards arrived in Central Mexico, they discovered a highly multi-ethnic area dominated by speakers of the Nahuatl language, and – on the political level – by the Aztec empire. Aztec is a conventional term adopted in modern historiography; in reality, each *altepetl* or indigenous state had its own ethnonym, like the Mexicah, Tlatelolcah, Ahcolhuahqueh, Tepanecah or Xochimilcah. Its complex sociopolitical organisation and administrative apparatus were organised around ethnic states, called *altepetl* in Nahuatl, that varied in size, rank and ethnic composition. The head of each *altepetl* was a dynastic ruler called a *tlahtoani* ("he who speaks"; pl. *tlahtohqueh*), who received tribute and labour duties from the entire state. In some cases a given polity could be ruled by separate *tlahtohqueh* who represented its different, usually symmetrical parts. The *tlahtoani* was one of *teteuctin*, or "lords". Such lords were heads of "noble houses" where noble families lived and which had specific rights to land and commoners working on them. Although heads of local states sat at the top of the regional political hierarchy, they could be subordinated to other *tlahtohqueh*. This was the case with the domains subjugated by the Aztec empire based on the alliance of Tenochtitlan, Texcoco and Tlacopan. Indeed, while many of the Nahua states and their rulers accumulated considerable power, land and other resources, Tenochtitlan and its monarchs held quite an unusual position in this regard. Dominating within the Triple Alliance or *excan tlahtoloyan* ("triple place of rule"), the rank of the sovereign of Tenochtitlan was highlighted by his title of *huei tlahtoani* ("great speaker"), claiming superiority over other *tlahtohqueh*. The ruler of empire had jurisdiction over almost every branch of government, including the military, civil, judicial, legislative and religious aspects, as well as the economic domains. By the time of the Spanish conquest he enjoyed incomparably high status in the Nahua world, expressed by elaborate ceremonies, sophisticated courtly etiquette and precious insignia.

The enormous variety of status items used by the Nahuas before the Spanish conquest included numerous categories of apparel, incorporating also foreign objects and styles. While the same basic costume types could be worn by members of distinct social groups, their position was often indicated by the kind of material and decoration. Among the highest-ranking objects were head adornments as well as jewellery including nose rods, earplugs,

Fig. 1 ◄
Gold jewellery, pendant with little eagle's head

Ministerie van de Vlaamse Gemeenschap, Collectie Paul en Dora Janssen-Arts, MAS, Antwerp (cat. 78)

Fig. 2 ▶
Stone chest, probably
belonging to the ruler
Moteuccoma II.

Museum am Rothenbaum,
Hamburg (cat. 72)

necklaces, bracelets and armbands. Male dress code included cotton capes (*tilmahtli*) tied over one arm and loincloths, while jackets and tunics were worn in priestly and military contexts. Special-function garments included body-encasing battle suits (*tlahuiztli*), usually accompanied by lavish back insignia and shields. Considerable importance was attached to sandals and objects held in the hands, as well as to different kinds of seats appropriate for rulers, lords, judges or military leaders. While the entire Aztec nobility enjoyed the right to wear and exhibit elaborate clothing and paraphernalia, the royal dress code was particularly sophisticated. Early post-contact sources extol the richness of the attire of the *huei tlahtohqueh,* mentioning, for example, that "Moteucçoma Ilhuicamina . . . changed his clothes and precious stones each day, except for the capes, which he put on only once and would not wear again" (Tezozomoc 2001). Serving as an important marker of nobility, certain categories of garments and adornments were restricted by sumptuary laws. One of the most detailed descriptions of Aztec sumptuary laws was given by Fray Diego Durán (1984). In addition to mentioning regulations on the use of the royal headdress and sandals in the royal palace, he states that some of the precious capes were restricted to rulers, whereas other prestigious garments were appropriately assigned to various dignitaries, nobles and warriors, according to their rank. In much the same way, only rulers, including those of conquered provinces, and "great lords" were permitted to display jewellery and adornments of precious feathers. The commoners were reportedly forbidden, on pain of death, to wear cotton capes and, in the case of males, garments reaching below the knee.

The position of *huei tlahtoani* was enhanced by elaborate ceremonies, courtly protocol, precious insignia and rich metaphoric language that referred to him. Used in public displays and rituals, his apparel served as an essential marker in the social hierarchy and communicated a variety of messages, both reli-

gious and political ones. Thus, on numerous occasions, Aztec rulers donned costumes and insignia of their divine patrons. Enjoying a special relationship with powerful Tezcatlipoca, the *huei tlatoani* was called his lips, jaws, tongue, eyes and ears, as well as a mouth through which this deity spoke (Sahagún 1950–1982, vol. 6). He was also strongly associated with Xiuhteuctli, the god of fire and time. The most prestigious royal insignia were in fact those made of turquoise, decorated with turquoise mosaic or with designs imitating that stone. These attributes of the Mexicah were believed to derive from the Toltecs, the glorified predecessors of the Aztecs. Indeed, as shown in sculptural monuments, most of them appear to have been used since at least 800–900 AD, the time of the emergence of the Toltec state with its capital in Tula, Hidalgo. The origin of the turquoise diadem goes back to the time of powerful Teotihuacan (more than one thousand years before the Aztecs), whose rulers wore the so-called Year Sign headdress, a possible antecedent of the *xiuhhuitzolli* (Olko 2014; Nielsen and Helmke 2019). An early form of the diadem could have been related also to the Classic-period war or fire serpent, the ancestor of the Aztec fire god. Since these remote times (ca. 150/250–900 AD) it was closely associated with creation and legitimate power. Its wearing by the monarchs of Tenochtitlan and other rulers who emulated royal insignia of the Mexicah, linked them to their patron, the fire deity. It also highlighted their inheritance of the ancient tradition of Meso-American rulership.

The embellishment with the turquoise insignia was crucial for the royal transformation in accession and coronation rites (Olko 2014). The regalia embraced the turquoise nose-rod, the royal diadem with turquoise mosaic (*xiuhhuitzolli*), the cape with the turquoise-mosaic design (*xiuhtlalpilli tilmahtli*), and a similarly decorated loincloth and sandals. However, before the monarch was seated on the jaguar-skin mat and throne, one of the paramount symbols of royalty among the pre-conquest Nahuas, the future *tlahtoani* appeared at the beginning of his metamorphosis clad in the priestly fasting costume, signalling the rituals of purification and sacrifice. In it he went through a painful phase of ritual death in order to be reborn to

the entirely new role of the royal person (Olivier 2006). The transformation was marked by the perforation of his septum and insertion of a nose rod made of turquoise and then receiving other turquoise regalia. In accordance with this symbolism, coronation rites in Tenochtitlan involved the direct participation of Xiuhteuctli, implying that the acquisition of celestial fire made up the nucleus of the ceremony. For example, according to an account that accompanies the investiture scene in the *Codex Tudela* (fol. 54r–v), "they went to the house of him whom they had elected or who was to be the lord and put before him a costume, and this happened before the fire god. ... And they took him with a great dance before Xutecle, the fire god". Thus, transformations of a ruler were equated with the increase of the divine fire and personal "heat" resulting from an extraordinary accumulation of his spiritual essence, *tonalli*. In an oration directed to the monarch, he was said to be no longer an ordinary human being, for he communicated in an incomprehensible language directly with the creator god, who gave him fangs and claws (Sahagún 1950–1982, vol. 6). In another speech preceding the royal accession and directed to Tezcatlipoca, a priest asked the deity to fill a *tlahtoani* with fire, transforming him into a fierce animal (Sahagún 1950–1982, vol. 6).

In fact, the association of kings with the divine fire was an inherent part of the concept of the nobility. This is expressed by the verb *tleyotia*, literally "to fill someone with fire", but meaning "to ennoble someone". Seen in this light, the turquoise insignia were much more than just symbolic links with the fire god: they were conceived as physical forms capable of accumulating the celestial essence given to the ruler of the Mexicah. It progessively increased in time through the carrying of the burden of office and participation in various rituals. The tiredness and overheating it caused could be cooled down by smelling fragrant flowers, believed to be capable of attracting spiritual essences (López Austin 1996 [1980]). Smelling flowers as well as odoriferous incense was considered a privilege of nobles and they are often pictured holding flower bouquets. The fragrances were also given in offering to the gods and to the dead.
Interestingly, a recurring term designating the right to highly valued status items is the obligatorily possessed word –*tonal*. It refers to solar heat but also the spiritual essence and destiny of an individual. Indeed, the insignia decorated with turquoise mosaic and originating with the Toltecs are said to

Fig. 4
Feathered snake representing the god Quetzalcoatl

Museum der Kulturen Basel
(cat. 102)

be –*tonal* of rulers (Sahagún (1950-1982, vol. 10). The same word is used in the list of valuable things, including precious stones and feathers, food and clothes belonging to a ruler and expressing his status, power, and legitimacy. Using of the term –*tonal* implies that clothes and attributes formed individuality of rulers, adding to their status and destiny. They not only created an external appearance of nobility, but were also conceived as repositories of spiritual essence and vehicles of transformation.

The Aztec dress code also embraced sophisticated battle outfits and insignia (*tlahuiztli*), that, like royal insignia, conveyed a variety of messages. Particular insignia carried specific symbolic associations, alluding for example to the transformations of dead warriors or to their divine patrons, but the general meaning of the *tlahuiztli* related to the shining and glowing qualities of military apparel. Native accounts emphasise the shimmering, gleaming appearance of battle outfits that were conceived as particularly powerful: the terrifying figures of the coyotes, jaguars

or stellar demons spread terror among the enemy. Thus, their exuberance and brilliant colours were not only aimed to impress, but also "to sow fear and fright among the enemy" (Tezozomoc 2001, 158). On special battle occasions the rulers of Tenochtitlan wore a frightening costume of the flayed god Xipe Totec, consisting of a human skin and other attributes of this deity closely linked to bloody sacrifice and the renewal of vegetation.

The symbolism and different roles of dress code and royal insignia throw interesting light on the ideological and socio-political construction of the empire of the Triple Alliance. The imperial nobility living in the broad area controlled by the Aztec state was linked by marriage alliances, exchange of luxury goods, art styles, material culture and status items, ideology and elite-restricted knowledge. They shared activities such as religious rituals or elaborate ceremonies of the legitimisation of royal power. These and other common interests crossed political boundaries and ensured cooperation over local divisions and identities. The rulers of Tenochtitlan were able to benefit from these mechanisms, enhancing the integration of the noble class across the empire through the distribution of lavish gifts, including precious accoutrements, clothes and regalia. While in other Meso-American cultures these items were frequently acquired by means of long-distance trade, the Mexicah and other dominant groups in the Triple Alliance gained a great part of these status markers by means of tribute obligations. The intense demand for luxuries seems to have been an important factor in conquests and tribute assessments of the subjugated regions. Particularly attractive for the imperial and provincial elites was the profound symbolism of rulership as well as the powerful status of lords grounded in the heritage of the Meso-American past. Rich evidence of this can be found in preserved examples of elite images – especially in pictorial manuscript commonly called codices – coming from a number of conquered provinces in the modern Mexican states of Guerrero, Hidalgo, Morelos, Puebla, Oaxaca and Veracruz. Many of these status markers were remembered, produced and transformed by Nahuatl-speaking elites in the colonial period; echoes can be still found in the local versions of traditional costume in Nahua communities today. ⌐⌐

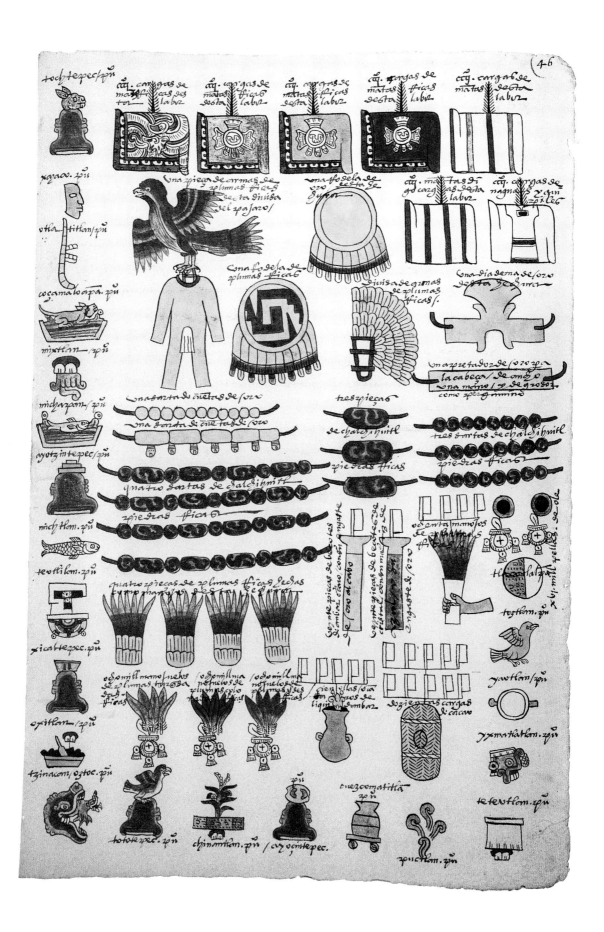

Ludo Snijders

Toltecayotl, the Aztec Artisans

Fig. 1 ◄
Coyote or young wolf

Museo Nacional de
Antropología, Mexico
City D.R. Secretaría de
Cultura – INAH (cat. 59)

The Nahuatl word *Toltecayotl* is a term which refers to what we would call craftsmen or artisans. Literally, this term means "those that are like the Toltecs", for the Aztecs believed that all their arts were passed down to them from the Toltecs. Goldsmiths, feather workers, lapidaries and scribes were all *toltecayotl*. The Spanish colonial written sources, such as the Codex Mendoza and the Florentine Codex, refer to these artisans as men. This may reflect reality to some extent, but may also be a problem of translation, as Nahuatl does not distinguish between genders. There is a depiction of a female scribe in the Codex Telleriano-Remensis, so we know that at least some *toltecayotl* were women. Artisans worked all over the Aztec empire. We know this from the Aztec tribute lists in the Codex Mendoza and the *Matricula de Tributos*. These record that subjugated provinces paid their tribute in the form of raw materials – gold powder, feathers, shells, turquoise and jade mosaic pieces – and in finished products. There is virtually no archaeological evidence for professional workshops. It seems that most artisans worked, probably on a part-time basis in addition to their agricultural activities, in their own homes. This also helps explain why the colonial sources stress that children would learn their parents' craft and inherit their tools of the trade. One notable exception to this may be the imperial workshops in Tenochtitlan where the most exclusive, sacred, and we assume most elaborate, objects were fashioned. Unfortunately, these workshops have not been found yet as they are located somewhere deep beneath the streets of Mexico City. From the analysis of artefacts and the study of the colonial descriptions of these crafts we do have a good idea how these artisans worked. Most Aztec objects made of gold were produced by hammering out a very thin sheet of the metal. This was then cut and bent into shape. In some cases, highly detailed figurative scenes were embossed in the sheets. This technique was used to decorate some of the most spectacular ceremonial shields and spear throwers. Another technique used by Aztec goldsmiths was to cast an object using the lost wax technique. First a figure was moulded out of wax. This was covered in a clay mixture and baked. Then the wax was drained through a small hole and the mould was filled with liquid gold. After cooling the mould had to be broken to release the gold figure, meaning that each figure would be unique.

The making of mosaic-covered objects was a highly developed art in the Aztec empire. Mosaics could be made with both stones and feathers and it seems that the basic process was similar. First, the feathers or mosaic tiles had to be acquired and prepared. Feathers were selected based on their colour and shape and in some cases dyed and cut to shape. When making a mosaic object such as the Quetzalcoatl mask, a wide range of materials was needed to obtain the right shades. Jade and turquoise gave green and blue colours, corals and shells were used for red and pink, mica and mother-of-pearl for grey or white, and obsidian for black. Whether stone or feather, all the mosaic pieces needed

Fig. 2 ◀
Codex Mendoza

Bodleian Library,
Oxford

Fig. 3
Sacrificial altar

Museo Nacional de
Antropología, Mexico
City D.R. Secretaría
de Cultura – INAH
(cat. 121)

Fig. 4
Mosaic mask in the
form of a bird's head

Stiftung Schloss
Friedenstein Gotha (cat. 83)

to be fixed to a base that was made of wood, or sometimes cloth in the case of feather mosaics. Pine resin and a binder made of orchid bulbs were used to glue feathers and stones to the surface. The design for the mosaic was probably first drawn out on a different material and we know from Spanish descriptions that the feather workers used a type of thin cotton tracing paper to transfer designs. Scribes also used a wide range of materials when they needed to make a book. Leather or paper was used as a support, which needed to be covered with a white gesso to create a writing surface. Then a range of organic and inorganic materials was used to paint the figures. The books also needed a cover. On the few remaining Meso-American books that still have their original cover it was made of wood with turquoise mosaic (Codex Vaticanus B), feather mosaic (the Mixtec Codex Nuttall), or jaguar skin (Codex Laud). All of this shows that Aztec artisans did not work in isolation, but that they must have worked together frequently. Feather headdresses contained gold work, books had elaborate covers, and the mosaic masks are likely to have been part of the much more elaborate regalia of a priest of Quetzalcoatl, for example. Depictions of this wind god show that the mask is part of a complex outfit that included a jaguar and feather headdress and a necklace made of shells. Depictions of the wind god show that this mask was part of a complex outfit that included a jaguar and feather headdress and a necklace made of shells. Most of the materials used in this costume are thus organic and highly perishable. Since very little has survived, it is likely that the materials worked by the *Toltecayotl* were even more diverse than we now realise. ⌐

Disssimo segundo mes

Fig. 5
Representation of Quetzalcoatl-Ehecatl, the god of
the winds, *Codex Borbonicus*,
p. 22

Library of the French
National Assembly, Paris

Gerard van Bussel

Three Works of Ancient Mexican Feather Art in Vienna

Three works of ancient Mexican feather art preserved in the Weltmuseum Wien in Vienna –, insignia or fan, headdress, and shield, were recorded as "Windmaker", "Moorish hat" and "Rondure of red feathers" with the representation of a blue dragon, in the inventory of the Cabinets of Art and Curiosities in the Ambras Castle in Tyrol in the year 1596. This collection of the Archduke Ferdinand II (1526–1595) was one of the most important of the time. They were not the only feather works in Ambras; in the same inventory eleven other feather objects as well as three birds of paradise are mentioned, which were all kept together in the so-called "feather case" of Ambras. 75 years after the fall of the Aztec capital Tenochtitlan this inventory of 1596 is the oldest documented reference of the feathered headdress. In addition to feathers and gold ornaments, this inventory points to a golden beak on the front of the headdress. In the eighteenth century, this beak or head of a bird was removed and disappeared. Since 1788 it has no longer been mentioned in the inventories. However, despite its current absence, it still has relevance.

In the sixteenth century, the Spanish sent many examples of Mexican crafts to Europe: gold objects, feather art works, wood carvings, mosaics, etc. They registered the objects, mainly, processed gold in the lists of official shipments. It is not known when the headdress arrived in Europe. None of the head-dresses mentioned in the shipping lists can be clearly identified as the Vienna artefact, especially since none of these existing written references cites the golden beak that, as indicated above, was once part of the Vienna headdress. In 1806, the quetzal feathered headdress was moved from Ambras to Vienna; the shield and, insignia or fan, were moved later, in 1891. Of the many feather artworks shipped to Europe only a few survived the passage of time and European storage practices. In addition to the three objects in Vienna and the two feathered shields in Stuttgart, there is still an Aztec shield in the Castillo de Chapultepec in Mexico City that Maximilian of Habsburg-Lorraine brought as a gift from Vienna to Mexico in 1865.

Fig. 1 ◄
Quetzal feather
headdress

KHM-Museumsverband,
Weltmuseum Wien
(cat. 98)

After the first mention as "Moorish hat", later inventories followed this interpretation as a headdress. After the golden peak had been removed, the upper and lower edges were surely difficult to recognise, so the way it was once worn was no longer clear. For this reason it was designated as an "Indian apron"in 1788. Although in 1855 it was once again interpreted as a headdress, it was later also described as a mantle, a coat and a banner, as Aztec army commanders carried on their backs. During the restoration in the year 1878, this last assumption led to its flat presentation according to the appearance of such a banner, instead of that of a headdress. Unfortunately its fragility does not allow a correction to turn it into a three-dimensional headdress, as was decided jointly during the binational research project of Austria and Mexico for the research and conservation of the ancient Mexican feather headdress (2010–2012). In the year 1878, during the aforementioned restoration, the light blue feathers and skins, the small green quetzal feathers and 24% of the metal ornaments in the lower part were added. For three decades, the function of this ancient Mexican plumed artwork was discussed until, at the International Congress of Americanists in Vienna in 1908, a commission decided on the interpretation as a headdress. In a UNAM TV documentary (2014), a name already proposed in the nineteenth century was used for this feather art work: *Quetzalapanecayotl*: "quetzal feather headdress".

From the nineteenth century, the feather headdress is repeatedly attributed to Moctezuma II. Originally interpreted as an object from the time of Moctezuma II, it was soon treated as a personal headdress of this ruler, later as his crown and in the course of the twentieth century, even as his sacred crown. Historical sources gave no reason for these revaluations and new interpretations. It has also been linked to priests or important male deities, such as Quetzalcoatl, Tezcatlipoca or Huitzilopochtli. The missing golden beak was with certainty of importance, and should be taken into account in the determination. According to a representation in the Codex Telleriano-Remensis, the headdress of the goddess Xochiquetzal offers a possible interpretation. However, not only she, but gods like Huitzilopochtli and incidentally Tezcatlipoca and Xochipilli, were also represented with beaks or heads of birds. Therefore, any allocation remains a hypothesis.

The feathered shield was registered in Ambras initially as "rondure" and in later inventories as a shield, except in the year 1788, when it was considered to be a Chinese sun shade. There is no information about its provenance until

1818, when it was designated an "Indian" shield, and in 1882, as "old Mexican". Repeatedly objects have been attributed to historical figures. In the case of the quetzal feather headdress, to Moctezuma II. The shield was also attributed to the same ruler, but more frequently to his predecessor Ahuitzotl. Serving as a basis and confirmation of this hypothesis, the blue animal represented on the shield was interpreted as the mythical *Ahuitzotl*. Since the Aztecs represented this mythical animal with a smooth and moist skin, different from the appearance of the creature on the shield, it is not an *Ahuitzotl* that is represented, but probably a dog-like animal; the usual current interpretation is that it is a coyote, possibly a *Xiuhcoyotl*, that is, a blue (turquoise) coyote. In front of the muzzle of the animal, the symbols of water and fire (*atl tlachinolli*) indicate war and its destructive effect. It is believed that the shield had been sent by Hernán Cortés in 1522 and reached Ambras, through the Bishop of Palencia and one of his successors, as well as King Ferdinand I.

With regard to the insignia or fan, after its first mention in the inventory of Ambras as a "Windmaker", in 1788 it was listed as "sun shade" and from 1818, once more as a "fan". That year it was designated as "Indian" and in 1882 as "Mexican." In Mexican codices, these objects are reproduced as banners or insignia of rank and symbols of gods, messengers, ambassadors and travellers. This work of feather art shows a flower on one side, and on the other, a butterfly. Together, they symbolically recall the flower wars between the Aztecs and the neighbouring Nahuas. This interpretation seems to find support in multicoloured chevron bands that, are known as a metaphor for the "path of war" in the codices. Accordingly, this object was interpreted as a possible standard of flower wars, although care must be taken when combining symbols from different cultural areas and interpreting them together. Like the quetzal feathered headdress, it is the only example of its kind among the works of Mexican feather art that have survived to the present day. ⌐

Inés de Castro

Xolotl or Quetzalcoatl?

This figure of a god made of greenstone inlaid with spondylus or coral in the mouth, nose, and cheeks, can be truly considered as unique. It probably embodies a nocturnal aspect of the god Quetzalcoatl.

The figure is worked as a standing skeleton with its arms by its sides, jaguar fangs, large earrings, loincloth, and sandals. Star symbols and calendar icons appear on the diadem. On the right side are the calendar icons *10 Calli* and *1 Ehecatl* with *1 Ozomatli* and *1 Calli* below, and on the left side the icons *9 Ozomatli* and *1 Cipactli* with *1 Mazatl* and *1 Quiahuitl* below. In the abdominal region, the figure presents two cavities that represent the heart and navel of the figure, which probably have inlaid pieces of jade. On the back, the figure carries a solar disc with the representation of the sun god Tonatiuh. The representation of a feathered serpent with long feathers, probably those of the green quetzal bird, can be seen above. In the lower part the god Tlaltecuhtli with eagle or feline claws is represented as well as with five skulls pointing towards the Aztec cosmogram.

The Aztec pantheon included a large number of gods in illustrated manuscripts or as marked geographical points, who, like cult images made of stone, wood or ceramics, occupied a fixed place in people's lives . In a complex ritual structure, the gods were presented with offerings such as food, animals, or human sacrifices according to strict rules, in order to venerate them and gain their benevolence. In this, the Tonalpohualli, the ritual 260-day calendar, and the Tonalamatl almanac that was based on it, had an essential role, since they recorded the positive and negative influences of certain days or periods of 13 days, the so-called *trecena*. These periods were under the protection of specific gods. Horoscopes and predictions about the future could be made through certain *trecenas* and their protective gods. Calendar data were therefore placed on important objects of all kinds. Thus the greenstone figure presents numerous calendar data that indicate certain holidays: the symbol of *4 Ehecatl* in the left hand indicates the fourth day of the seventh period of Tonalamatl that begins with *1 Quiahuitl* and the festival of the god of rain and lightning Tlaloc; the symbol *9 Ehecatl* in the right hand indicates the ninth day of the second Tonalamatl period that begins with *1 Ocelotl* and the feast day of the wind god Quetzalcoatl (Seler 1908). However, the interpretation

Fig. 1 ◄
Figure of a god,
aspect of Quetzal-
coatl, front view

Landesmuseum
Württemberg
Stuttgart (cat. 139)

155

of other days, such as the prominent date *1 Cuauhtli* on the loincloth, is still unknown.

The Aztec gods could exhibit protective or harmful characteristics and thus exert a direct influence on life. There was a god for all aspects of human life. The rituals ranged from simple field rituals or domestic altars to politically staged rituals of the state ruler, carried out with the help of religious specialists. Within the markedly hierarchical society, the noble was legitimised as a mediator with the gods. The extraordinary thing in this figure above all is an internal channel that connects the upper cavity in the abdomen with the mouth. The internal channel system leads us to suppose that it was used in such rituals. Possibly the openings are related to incense ceremonies or libation actions. To date, we do not know of internal channels in figures of similar gods, which underscores the uniqueness of this piece.

For a long time this figure was interpreted as the god Xolotl, as the renowned American scholar Eduard Seler (1849–1922) named the figure in an essay for the 14th International Congress of Americanists in Stuttgart in 1904. Seler (1908) recognised the direct link of the figure with the planet Venus in its evening star shape. On the one hand, the upper row of calendar symbols in the diadem, with a period of 293 days that reproduced half the synodic orbital period of the planet Venus (Seler 402–404), supported this hypothesis. On the other hand, however, the attributes of the god Quetzalcoatl that are present point towards that interpretation: the shell-shaped ornaments in the ears, the plumed serpent at the back, the bent bars in the hands that Seler interprets as lightning, and the star symbols in the diadem (Seler 1908).

Even if the link with Venus and its divine counterpart Quetzalcoatl, which represents the planet Venus as the morning star, seems conclusive, the classification as the god Xolotl is problematic since this deity is represented in other cases with a dog's head. Dogs were associated with the underworld, accompanying the dead on their journey to the Mictlan underworld, and serving as protectors and guides.

In contrast, in an article from 2007, Jeremy Coltman describes the figure as a reproduction of the god Tlahuizcalpantecuhtli, an aspect of the god Quetzal-coatl, who frequently appears as a skeleton with iconography of feathered stars and serpents. He indicated that, iconographically speaking, he is known in two ways: with a human face or as a skull, and that he is related to Venus as the morning star. The relationship between Venus as the morning star and the sun, which appears on the back of the figure, is the belief that the morning star in the east guides the sun when it comes out on its way from the under-world. Coltman also sees a relationship with the Aztec warriors who returned in the house of the sun after their death in the east Tlahuizcalpantecuhtli would be its deification (Coltman 2007).

The Aztec gods often combine several aspects or manifestations. In general, the gods have a human and an animal form. In addition to the gods them-selves, priests were also represented who personified the god. The large number of divine manifestations with different regional aspects often makes clear classification difficult. In addition, in this largely oral culture, our insufficient knowledge about religion is based on accounts by Spanish chroni-clers, on the iconographic analysis of Aztec legacies as well as on analogies with current indigenous followers. Therefore, the identification of this figure in green stone is not an easy task. The figure seems to be unique in its mani-festations. No parallel piece that facilitates a classification is known so far.

Fig. 3 ▶
Underside of the figure
of a god

Landesmuseum Württem-
berg Stuttgart (cat. 139)

The close relationship of the figure represented to the god Quetzalcoatl and the cycle of Venus is irrefutable. However, an exact classification as a specific manifestation of this god, is difficult.

The god Quetzalcoatl has different manifestations and appears under different aspects. He is a legendary ancestral figure among the Aztecs, by whom he is seen as a dispenser of divine gifts and the Almighty Creator. As Tlahuizcalpantecuhtli he is the incarnation of the twilight, like Ehecatl, the wind. The latter also appears as a feathered serpent, which the stone figure carries on its back. As a bringer of culture, Quetzalcoatl is usually associated with positive characteristics, whereas here the "nocturnal" and dark attributes predominate.

Due to the negative connotation of the figure, Esther Pasztory (1984) supposed it was made especially for the ruler Motecuhzoma Xocoyotzín (also called Moctezuma II, 1466–1520) and, therefore, dated from the period between 1519 and 1520. During that period the Spaniard conquest was known as well as the danger for the "strangers" of the east. For this reason, she assumes a link with rites related to destruction and death.

Almost nothing is known about the exact origin of the greenstone figure. We do not know what region of Mexico it comes from or how it finally arrived in Europe.

The first mention of the figure in the context of the Württemberg Art Room occurred in the year 1616. In a description of the collection of Duke Ludwig Frederick (acting 1617–1631), the younger brother of the regent, Philipp Hainhofer (1578 –1647) writes: "and his Highness allows me to see an idol of Pietra Isada" (Von Oechelhäuser 1891).

Around 1700, the figure was in the possession of the Mömpelgard Line of the Ducal House. After the death of Duke Leopoldo Eberhard (reigned 1699–1723) in 1723, his collections passed to the line of Stuttgart.

In the Stuttgart Art Room stocks there are records referring to the figure in the inventories. They mostly speak of a *monstrous figure of green stone (jasper) or soapstone that can represent an idol* (HStAS A 20 a Bü 85, HSTAS A 20 to Bü 130; HStAS A 20 to Bü 151).

The figure, like the two Aztec feathered shields, arrived at the "Museum für vaterländische Alterthümer", and was then transferred to the collection of the Commercial Geography Association of Württemberg, the precursor of the Linden Museum, at the beginning of the twentieth century. Together with the feathered shields, they subsequently became the property of the Württemberg State Museum, probably in the 1950s or 60s. ◢

Inés de Castro

Two Aztec Feathered Shields from the Württemberg Art Room

Fig. 1 ◂

O f the total of four pre-Hispanic feathered shields that are preserved at present, two splendid specimens can be found in the State Museum of Württemberg. Together with the so-called Feathered Shield of Ambras in the Weltmuseum Wien in Vienna and the feathered shield which Emperor Maximilian I of Mexico (ruled 1864–1867) returned to Mexico from near Vienna, and which is currently in the National Museum of History in Mexico City, the two shields of the Württemberg State Museum are witnesses of the ancient Aztec culture.

Feather shield "Meander and Sun"

Landesmuseum Württemberg Stuttgart (cat. 97a)

A large network of merchants known as *Pochtecas* was responsible for providing feathers from tropical countries such as Guatemala and Honduras. The *Amantecas* of San Miguel Amatlán in the vicinity of the capital special-ised in the production of feather art.
For this, the *Amantecas* used two different techniques: knotting the feathers, as in the famous feather plume in the Weltmuseum Wien, or sticking them onto a support material with vegetable glues, as is the case with the feathered shields.

Both shields present an enclosure made of rawhide, which was placed and stitched in a wet state around the edge of the shield. Segments of feathers, of either one colour or alternating reds and yellows, were knotted in groups onto this enclosure. When making the motifs, four to six layers of feathers were glued onto a backing of vegetable fibres. The lower layers of feathers were glued completely onto the support, while the upper layers were only glued on the underside of the feathers and partly overlapped. To create the motifs, feathers were placed on strips or circles of the felt, then cut in a straight line and attached to the support material. Agave juice or orchid bulbs were used as a base for the glue. The back of the shields is formed by a cane weave to which an enarme is attached.

The feathers used for this come from various endemic species, which were probably kept in captivity. I thank Prof. Norbert Lenz, Director of the State Museum of Natural Sciences, Karlsruhe, for the following determination of the feathers.

In the shield "Greca and Sun" the cinnamon brown feathers of the Cuckoo Squirrel (*Piaya cayana*) were used. For the yellowish feathers, the species-rich family of the turpiales (*Icterus spp.*), in particular the turpial campero (*Icterus gularis*, also known as the *bolsero de Altamira* or *trupial campero*), with its orange-red to yellow-orange plumage, is considered. The greenish feathers, which were also used in the shield "Greca" in combination with the yellow feathers of the species of the turpiales, are typical of the specimens of the trogonid family (*Trogonidae*) due to their metallic iridescence. The best-known example of this family is the resplendent quetzal (*Pharomachrus mocinno*), whose feathers, however, are lighter and have a much more intense iridescence. Other species of trogonids, such as the black-headed trogon (*Trogon melanocephalus*), also come into consideration.

Both the purple feathers and the blue ones come most likely from the "lovely cotinga" (*Cotinga amabilis*). The plumage of the blue feathered "lovely cotinga" is mainly sky blue, the throat and belly are purple, the wings and tail are darker, almost black. The carmine red feathers—and probably also the black feathers—recall the carmine red to blood red feathers of the tuft and throat of the tropical red-and-black tanager (*Ramphocelus sanguinolentus*).

The use of feather costumes was reserved for people of noble birth. In addition to the shields, the costumes of priests and rulers, ornaments for the head and body, fans and banners were also adorned with valuable feathers. Presumably the feathered shields were presented as special gifts or as a sign of distinction by the ruler and served as valuable offerings and tributes. Reproductions of feathered shields are found in some colonial sources, such as the *Matrícula de Tributos* and in the *Historia General de las Cosas de Nueva España* by Bernardino de Sahagún (1499–1590). This last chronicler also describes with the help of his indigenous informants the creation of the mosaics of the feathered shields with superposed layers of cotton, *amate* (paper made of bast from bark) and simple and valuable feathers (Sahagún 1989).

Fig. 2 ▶
Feather shield "Meander"

Landesmuseum Württemberg Stuttgart (cat. 97b)

The famous American scholar Eduard Seler (1849–1922) calls the shields adorned with feathers *mauizco chimalli*, an insigne and glorious shield (1904). However, up to now it has not been possible to make a clear assignment of a person's social rank by means of shield patterns.

The date of the shields of feathers can probably be limited to the time shortly before the Spanish conquest of Tenochtitlan in the year 1521. The boom in feather art began as early as the sixteenth century with the regency of Motecuhzoma Xocoyotzín (also called Moctezuma II, 1466–1520), who according

Fig. 3
Design for the procession of
Duke Friedrich I of Württemberg (reigned 1593–1608)
at the ring tournament of
1599, sheet 6: Friedrich I in
the costume of "Queen
America"

Stiftung Weimar, Museen,
KK 207
Photo: Hannes Bertram

to the sources maintained different species of birds at his court. However, it should not be ruled out that the feathered shields were made shortly after the Spanish conquest. Unfortunately, a more accurate determination of leather enclosures was not possible without broader studies of the materials. The use of goats, introduced by Europeans, could not be ruled out completely.

The feather objects were sent in large quantities to Europe after the Spanish conquest and enjoyed great popularity. In the European imagination, the objects made with tropical feathers of wonderful colours were equated with indigenous America. The growing interest of Europeans led to the continuation of feather art even after the Spanish conquest, albeit with a different iconography. However, in the sixteenth century a totally different feather art from Mexico achieved great fame: the feather art works of the *Purépechas* of Michoacan, with Christian content, especially devotional images and parts of ecclesiastical ornaments, where hummingbird feathers were used.

It is difficult to determine from a study of the existing sources by which route and when exactly the two feathered shields arrived in Europe. It is known that the shields were used in 1599 during a medieval tournament in a carnival parade of Duke Frederick I of Württemberg (ruled 1593–1608). Jakob Frischlin (1556/1557– after 1621) bequeathed us a detailed description of the scene in the year 1602 as well as drawings in which the parade of the "Queen of America" can be seen along with with her retinue wearing clothing and ornaments from different parts of America (Klassik Stiftung Weimar KK; Bujok 2003). Both the feather shields can be clearly recognised in these drawings. The "Greca" shield is possibly being held upside down. Presumably, at the time of the parade, the shields were in the collection of the director of the palace at Tübingen, Niclas Ochssenbach (1562–1626) (Bujok 2003). However, reliable proof of this hypothesis is made difficult by the often vague or false inventory information, which does not allow a clear allocation. The art dealer Philipp Hainhofer (1578–1647) saw the art room in Stuttgart in 1616 and noted "indigenous articles" among numerous ethnographic objects. These could have been the feathered shields described here (Carola Fey: personal notice 2018).

If the shields were in the possession of Ochssenbach, they could have been brought by their son to the Benedictine monastery of Weingarten and remained as the property of Württemberg after secularisation. In the inventory of the Art Room of Stuttgart of 1642 *an indigenous round shield of [...] derwerkh* is mentioned (HStAS A 20 a Bü 5).

Around 1870, the feathered shields were in the Numismatic Collection at Neckarstrasse 10 in Stuttgart. This is proven by the drawings of Augustus W. Franks (1826–1897), probably made in 1872 and currently in the British Museum (Martin Schultz, personal notice 2017).

At the beginning of the twentieth century, the shields became part of the collection of the Commercial Geography Association of Württemberg, the forerunner of the Linden Museum, together with the greenstone figure that is also described here. The shields were important central objects for the foundation of the Linden Ethnographic Museum of Stuttgart in 1911 and served as the foundation for the construction of a new museum. In the 1950s or 60s, they then passed into the hands of the Württemberg State Museum. However, we can only speculate on the reasons for this decision and the precise developments over time. ⌐

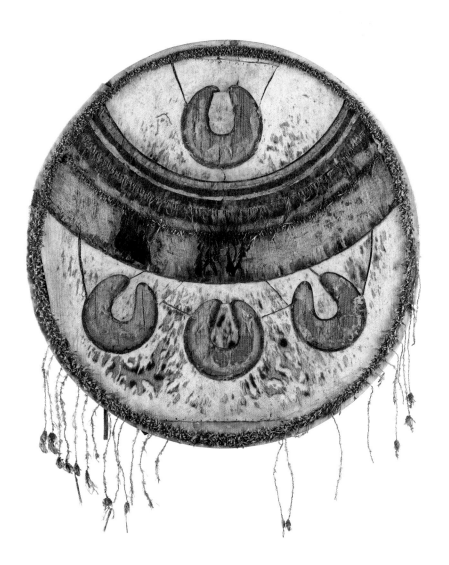

Fig. 4
Feather shield, preserved in the Museo Nacional de Historia, Chapultepec Castle, Mexico City

Museo Nacional de Historia, Mexico City D.R. Secretaría de Cultura – INAH (cat. 142)

⊡ The Sacred Precinct

Leonardo López Luján

The Sacred Precinct of Tenochtitlan

The Heart of the Island

The Sacred Precinct of Tenochtitlan was the ultimate centre of divine propitiation and one of the most important ritual grounds in Meso-American history. Clearly separated from the secular space of the city, it was framed on its four sides by a wide rectangular platform with alternate vertical walls, inclined planes and staircases on its internal and external faces. This platform, which would have measured 340 metres from north to south and 360 metres from east to west, was interrupted at three or four intervals to form the main entrance gates. The interior space, measuring more than 12 hectares, was occupied by different types of buildings: *teocalli* (pyramids of all sizes, which were always crowned by chapels), *momoztli* (small ritual platforms without roofed spaces), priestly houses and oratories (enclosures for the fasting and penitence of dignitaries), *calmecac* (temple schools for nobles), *tlachtli* (ball game courts), *tzompantli* (palisades where the skulls of the sacrificed were displayed), *tlacochcalco* (armories where weapons acquired sacred power), *yopilcalco* (temples where the foreign sovereigns who came to witness the great ceremonies stayed), ritual monoliths such as *temalacatl, techcatl,* and *cuauhxicalli* (for the sacrifice of animals and human beings, and the subsequent offering of their blood and hearts), springs and other replicas of the sacred geography (such as a small arid environment), all of which were separated from by wide squares or smaller courtyards (Marquina 1960; Lupo et.al., 2006; Nichols and Rodríguez Alegría 2019).

Historical data concerning the number of buildings within the Sacred Precinct vary greatly from one source to another. Captain general Hernán Cortés told of "forty very tall and well-wrought towers", whilst Franciscan friar Toribio de Benavente recalls 12 or 15 *teocalli* and chronicler Gonzalo Fernández de Oviedo recalls more than 60 *cus* (various types of religious buildings). Dominican friar Diego Durán signals that there were eight or nine groups of temple buildings, each with its own courtyard and staircase, distinguished by roof ornaments and fitted out with lodgings for ministers. In contrast, Franciscan friar Bernardino de Sahagún's indigenous informants describe 78 buildings of a variety of sizes and functions.

Fig. 1 ◀
The ruins of the Templo Mayor in the heart of Mexico City

Photo: Inés de Castro

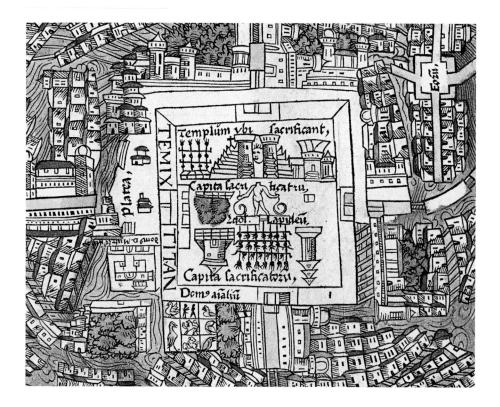

The main temples

In the eastern sector of the Sacred Precinct, with its main façade facing west, was the Huei Teocalli or "Templo Mayor". This was a vast pyramid that, at the time of the arrival of the Spaniards, had 113 or 114 steps. At its summit were two chapels: one dedicated to the god of sun and war, Huitzilopochtli, in the southern half, and one dedicated to the worship of the god of rain and earthly fertility, Tlaloc, in the northern half (Matos Moctezuma 1988; López Austin und López Luján 2009). The famous Coacalco ("Place of the Meeting House") was located in the temple of Huitzilopochtli. According to Sahagún's indigenous informants, this was "a room with grilles like a prison. Here [dwelt] the gods of cities which, in all places which the Mexicans overran, were held captive." This building existed as a consequence of the Mexica practice of stripping the defeated of their divine strength: after setting fire to their temples as a sign of victory, the victorious armies returned jubilantly to Tenochtitlan, carrying the captured cult effigies on their backs.

Close to the Templo Mayor, temples to other important divinities were constructed, which radiated the supernatural powers that gave the Mexica people the strength and protection necessary to wage war against far-flung settlements. The most notable of these temples are, according to Jesuit priest

Joseph de Acosta, an 80-step pyramid in honour of the lord of destiny, Tezcatlipoca, a "very tall and very beautifully built" building, and a 60-step temple consecrated to the wind god, Ehecatl-Quetzalcoatl, in the form of a truncated cone "because of the way the wind swirls around the sky, they made this a round temple", the entrance of which was "through a door built like the mouth of a snake and painted devilishly". The foundations of these two constructions have been uncovered recently, the first under the Palace of the Archbishopric and the second under the modern Hotel Catedral.

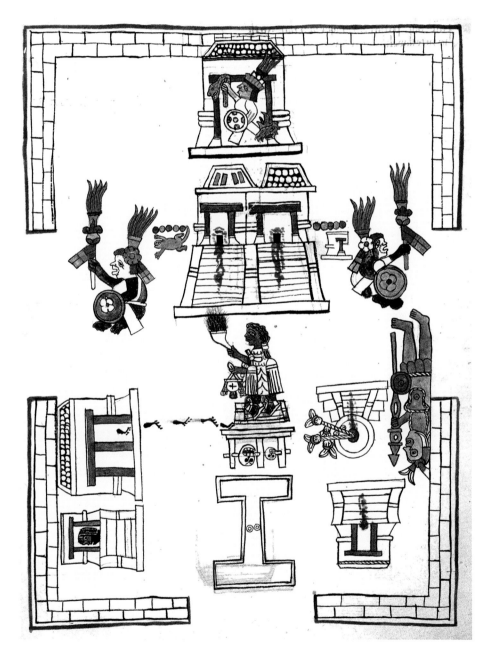

Fig. 3
The Sacred Precinct of Tenochtitlan, *Primeros Memoriales,* Sahagun 1999

175

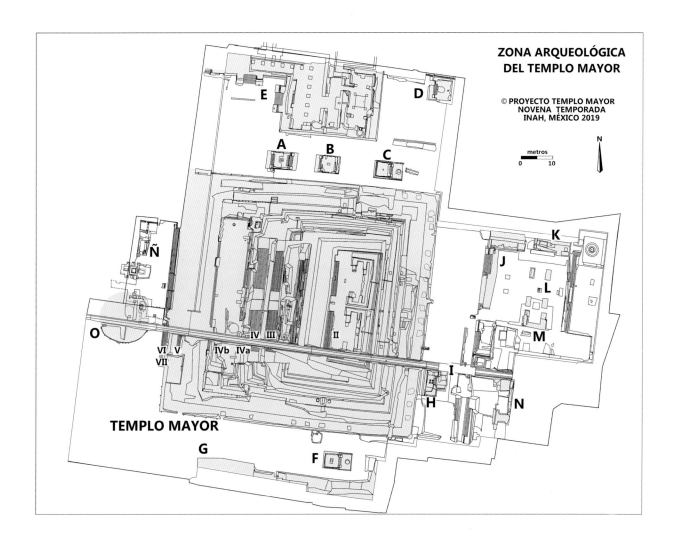

ZONA ARQUEOLÓGICA
DEL TEMPLO MAYOR

© PROYECTO TEMPLO MAYOR
NOVENA TEMPORADA
INAH, MÉXICO 2019

TEMPLO MAYOR

Fig. 4
This map shows the Templo
Mayor Archaeological Zone,
excavated by the Proyecto
Templo Mayor between 1978
and 2019 and covering
1.29 hectares.

With the kind permission of
the Proyecto Templo Mayor
Preparation and drawing:
Michelle De Anda, Saburo
Sugiyama and Leonardo
López Luján

Thanks to the work of archaeologists, we now know that there were several
buildings of a markedly archaist style, whose design and decoration evoked
the style of two renowned civilisations that had already disappeared: Teotihuacan (100–600 AD) and Tula (950–1150 AD) (López Luján 2013). First of
all, four neo-Teotihuacan shrines have been exhumed, three of which are now
known as the "Red Temples", dedicated to Xochipilli-Macuilxochitl, god of
the sun, music and dance. The mural paintings, religious iconography and
symbols of the Sun found within these temples, as well as their orientation
towards dawn and the offerings of musical instruments found within them,
clearly allude to the beginning of a new era in the mythical Teotihuacan, that
is, the creation of the Fifth Sun. Secondly, two neo-Toltec porticoed enclosures
have also been discovered. One of these is the *Huei Calmecac* associated with
the temple of Ehecatl-Quetzalcoatl, which was a school for nobles whose
patron god was Quetzalcoatl, the legendary ruler of Tula. The other building

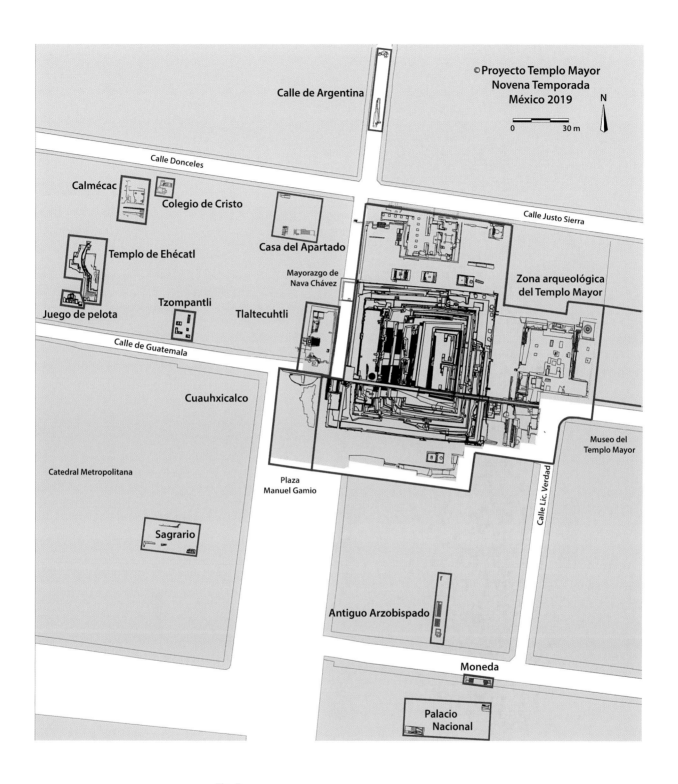

Calle de Argentina

©Proyecto Templo Mayor
Novena Temporada
México 2019

N

0   30 m

Calle Donceles

Calmécac

Colegio de Cristo

Casa del Apartado

Calle Justo Sierra

Templo de Ehécatl

Mayorazgo de
Nava Chávez

Zona arqueológica
del Templo Mayor

Juego de pelota

Tzompantli

Tlaltecuhtli

Calle de Guatemala

Cuauhxicalco

Museo del
Templo Mayor

Catedral Metropolitana

Plaza
Manuel Gamio

Calle Lic. Verdad

Sagrario

Antiguo Arzobispado

Moneda

Palacio
Nacional

Fig. 5
This map shows the heart of Mexico City's historical district with the Mexica buildings
excavated by the Proyecto Templo Mayor, by the Programa de Arqueología Urbana, and by
other older archaeological projects.

With the kind permission of the Proyecto Templo Mayor
Preparation and drawing: Michelle De Anda, Saburo Sugiyama and Leonardo López Luján

Fig. 6
Building B, related to
Mictlan, the ninth level of
the Underworld.

With the kind permission of
the Proyecto Templo Mayor
Photo: Leonardo López Luján

was named the House of Eagles by archaeologists and was the ritual ground for the handing over of power from the deceased *tlatoani* (sovereign) to his newly elected successor.

Large Public Gatherings

According to Cortés, the Sacred Precinct could fit an entire village of 500 Spanish inhabitants inside it, while soldier Andrés de Tapia reduces this figure to 400. Historian Francisco López de Gómara, meanwhile, claimed that within this site there were about 5,000 people at all times, who performed a variety of services and whose principal mission was to preserve order and harmony within this space. In contrast, Acosta recalled that on holy days, between 8,000 and 10,000 individuals would congregate inside these grounds to rejoice in dance (López Austin and López Luján 2017).

Those attending the ceremonies ranged from large crowds of locals to small and very select groups of dignitaries from other cities. Local crowds were not only made up of the inhabitants of the island, but also those of the entire region, as was stated in descriptions of the "gladiatorial" combat between the sacrificial victim and Mexica warriors, or the distribution of food that the *tlatoani* made to the poor during eight days of the twenty-day period known as *Huei tecuhilhuitl*. As far as foreign dignitaries were concerned, it can be assumed that only those from allied political entities came to Tenochtitlan; however, historical sources make it clear that the Mexica *tlatoani* also invited their rivals; they were hidden away behind lattices so that they could witness the ritual spectacles without their presence being noticed by the people. This practice was evidently motivated the desire to deter and intimidate enemy spectators, as it was not uncommon for them to witness the sacrifice of their own warriors who had been captured in battle (López Austin and López Luján 2001; Berdan 2014).

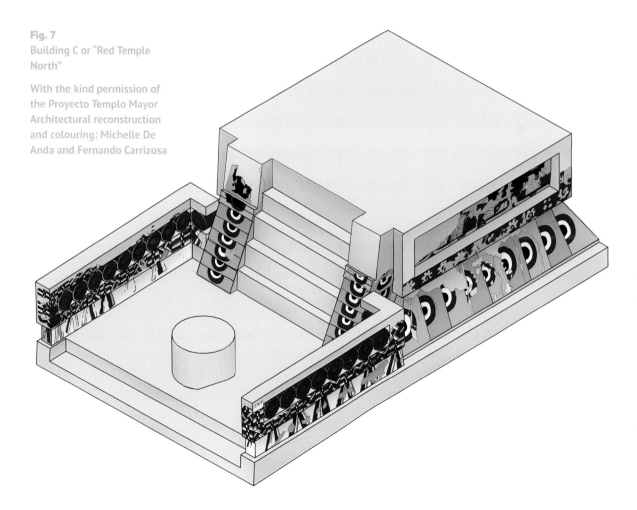

Fig. 7
Building C or "Red Temple North"

With the kind permission of the Proyecto Templo Mayor Architectural reconstruction and colouring: Michelle De Anda and Fernando Carrizosa

Fig. 8
Large stone slab in the form
of a sacrificial knife, part of
the *ofrenda* 78 found in the
Templo Rojo Sur

Museo Templo Mayor, Mexico
City, D.R. Secretaría de
Cultura – INAH (cat. 115b)

The liturgy

The state cult was endorsed by the supreme government and its purpose was to appease important gods and goddesses such as Huitzilopochtli, Tlaloc, Quetzalcoatl, Tezcatlipoca, Xipe Totec, Cihuacoatl and Chicomecoatl in order to achieve the well-being of all the inhabitants of the city and its dependent communities, as well as military and agricultural success. This cult was largely governed by the calendar, mainly the *xiuhpohualli* (solar cycle of 365 days organised into 18 twenty-day periods plus five unlucky days).

Beyond the ceremonies dictated by the calendar, the state protocol ordered lavish rituals in the sacred precinct for royal and noble funeral rites, the enthronement of rulers, the recognition of the newly elected sovereigns belonging to the Triple Alliance, the arrival of triumphant armies and the procession of captives who would become victims for the gods. In addition, both the revealing of the sacrificial monoliths and the construction and continuous expansion of the pyramid temples called for sumptuous festivals, ritual burnings and the burial of rich offerings. Lastly, ceremonies were also performed in these sacred grounds in which the people asked for an end to the great misfortunes with which the gods punished human beings, namely agricultural catastrophes, famines and epidemics (López Luján 2018). ⌐

Fig. 9
Stone of Tizoc, used as an altar stone during the festival of Tlacaxipehualiztli

With the kind permission of the Proyecto Templo Mayor
Photo: Mirsa Islas

Guilhem Olivier

The Foundational Myths of the Aztecs

When the Spaniards led by Hernán Cortés landed on the coast of Veracruz, the Mexica sovereign Motecuhzoma II sent a delegation of one hundred men bearing gifts led by a man by the name of Quintalbor, whom the soldier-chronicler Bernal Díaz del Castillo (1988) described as follows: "A great Mexican cacique, who in face, features and body was very much like Captain Cortés. The great Montezuma had deliberately sent him […] and as he looked like Cortés, we called him that in the camp, this Cortés here and that Cortés there". To unravel the meaning of this enigmatic episode of the Conquest and understand the strategy of the Mexica king in sending this individual who was Cortés' double, it is essential to turn to Mexica myths. In fact, as Michel Graulich (1994) has indicated, it is highly likely that Motecuhzoma intended to reproduce an episode in the battle between the god Tezcatlipoca, the "Lord of the Smoking Mirror" and Quetzalcoatl, the "Quetzal Serpent," in the prestigious Toltec city of Tollan). Among the stratagems used to exile Quetzalcoatl from his capital – such as getting him drunk and inciting him to commit incest with his sister – Tezcatlipoca showed Quetzalcoatl a mirror, in which the Toltec sovereign saw himself as old and ugly and was frightened (*Anales de Cuauhtitlan* 1992). In this way, Tezcatlipoca, the god of destiny, revealed to Quetzalcoatl that his position as a lunar star was about to disappear, signifying his defeat as the sun-king of the Toltec era. Clearly, Motecuhzoma II – who believed that the arrival of Cortés represented the return of Quetzalcoatl – was attempting to reproduce the mythical episode of the mirror to force the Conquistador to flee. As we know, the manoeuvre did not have the effect he had hoped for.

This anecdote demonstrates to us the importance for the Mexica – and in fact, throughout Meso-America – of the great mythic cycle of the cosmogonic Suns, revealing the indigenous conception of time and history. Linked to the creation of complex calendar systems (see the article by Martínez Gracida in this volume), Meso-Americans conceived history as a cycle comprised of different ages that preceded our era. Unfortunately the ancient myths of the Meso-Americans have come down to us in a fragmentary manner, but the surviving accounts speak of four or five eras, also known as Suns (Graulich 1997). Each era was destroyed by a cataclysm and the final era, in which we are now living, is destined to end with an earthquake. Some sources indicate

Fig. 1 ◀
Aztec Sun Stone

Photo: Jorge Perez Lara

12ª Motecuçuma. primero deste nombre. 6º Rey.

what humans were transformed into with each destruction: into fish with the flood at the end of the Sun of Water; into monkeys with the hurricane at the end of the Sun of Wind; and into butterflies, dogs and turkeys with the rain of fire at the end of the Sun of Fire. Important mythological data indicate that Tezcatlipoca and Quetzalcoatl alternated in the role of the Sun (*Historia de los mexicanos por sus pinturas* 1941). The struggle between these two deities appears clearly in the episode recounting the fall of Tollan, where Quetzalcoatl, the Sun of the fourth era, was defeated by Tezcatlipoca, as we have seen (Graulich 1997; Olivier 2003). Naturally, the fifth Sun of the Mexica, the Sun of Movement, was dominated by Huitzilopochtli, the tutelary god of this people, who was sometimes confused with Tezcatlipoca. It is not surprising that at the end of the fifth era – in other words, with the Spanish Conquest – the Mexica associated the arrival of Quetzalcoatl with the return of the "Quetzal Serpent" (Sahagún 1950–1982, vol. 12; Nicholson 2001; Olivier 2003).

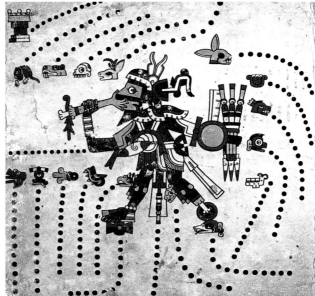

Other myths tell us of the creation of the gods by the supreme couple
Ometecuhtli and Omecihuatl. Among the gods that were begotten at that
time, Tezcatlipoca and Quetzalcoatl were given the task of creating Heaven
and Earth from a being known as Tlalteotl – "the Earth Deity" – that floated
on primeval waters. Quetzalcoatl and Tezcatlipoca entered the body of
Tlalteotl and split it in two, with which they created Heaven and Earth.
They then erected four posts to prevent Tlalteotl from reassembling itself.
Ometecuhtli and Omecihuatl were angered by the outrage committed against
Tlalteotl because, in a way, Quetzalcoatl and Tezcatlipoca had violated
Tlalteotl. In order to make amends, they had plants grow out of its body and
ensured it would be nourished with the blood of sacrificial victims (*Historia
de los mexicanos por sus pinturas* 1941; Thévet 1905).

The birth of the Sun and the Moon represents another fundamental myth in
the Mexica worldview. The gods gathered at Teotihuacan to choose two from

Fig. 5
Men are transformed
into monkeys after the
hurricane has destroyed
the Sun of Wind, *Codex
Vaticanus Latinus* 3738
1996, reverse, p. 6

Biblioteca Apostolica
Vaticana

among them to be transformed into stars. When asked to be the Sun, the rich and proud Tecuciztecatl could not bring himself to jump into the fire, while the poor but brave Nanahuatzin leapt into the flames and became the star of the daytime sky. Tecuciztecatl followed him but fell into the ashes and was transformed into the moon. Both stars remained motionless in the sky. The Sun then demanded the sacrifice of all the gods in order to be able to start moving. Quetzalcoatl was elected to sacrifice the gods and tore out their hearts. In his manifestation as Ehecatl, he was also the god of the Wind and blew on the stars to launch them on their trajectory in the sky (Sahagún 1950–1982, vol. 7; Mendieta 1980).

The practice of human sacrifice figures prominently both in the myth of the creation of Heaven and Earth, and the myth of the birth of the Sun and the Moon (López Luján and Olivier 2010). Most sacrifices were intended to nourish the Sun and the Earth. As we have seen, the Earth deity produced fruit only in exchange for the blood of sacrificial victims. Moreover, had the gods themselves not given their lives in Teotihuacan so that the stars could move? Men had the duty to reproduce these primeval sacrifices to obtain the gifts of the gods in exchange.

Moreover, the gods needed human sacrifice as nourishment. Myths explain how the Sun and the Earth were fed by means of the sacrifice of the Mimixcoa, the "Cloud Serpents," immolated by their brothers, among whom Mixcoatl, the god of the ancestors and hunting, stands out. This account constitutes the model of the practice of the Sacred War, which was waged to capture prisoners in order to feed the gods (Olivier 2015).

To understand the phenomenon of human sacrifice, it is necessary to stress the Meso-American idea that life is born from death (Matos Moctezuma 2010). The myth of the creation of man describes how Quetzalcoatl descended to the underworld, where the god of Death Mictlantecuhtli stored the bones of the giants who had inhabited the earth in an earlier era. After several tests, such as blowing into a sealed shell that had been perforated by bees, Quetzalcoatl gained access to the bones and brought them to the surface of the earth. The bones were ground like corn by the goddess Quilaztli, and Quetzalcoatl drew blood from his penis to shower these bones with his blood: the men of today were born from this mixture (*Leyenda de los Soles* 1992; see also Mendieta 1980).

Fig. 6
Underside of the stone chest of Moctezuma II with a representation of the earth goddess Tlaltecuhtli

Museum am Rothenbaum Hamburg (cat. 72c)

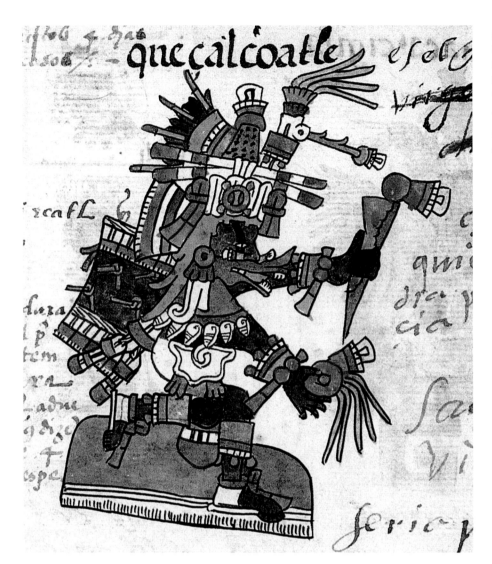

Fig. 7
Quetzalcoatl with his mouth mask, which distinguishes him as Ehecatl, the god of the wind, *Codex Telleriano-Remensis*, p. 8r

Bibliothèque nationale de France

The myths described hitherto are probably extremely ancient; archaeological testimonies attest to their deeply rooted past. The Mexica, recently-arrived newcomers to the Basin of Mexico, would turn to these old tales to create their own myths which were intended to justify their new power. One of these is the myth of the birth of Huitzilopochtli, the Mexica tutelar deity. It recounts how Huitzilopochtli was born on the hill of Coatepec, the "Serpent Mountain," where his mother Coatlicue had been impregnated with a feather – the soul of a dead warrior – as she was sweeping. Angered by this, her first children, the Centzon Huitznahua and her daughter Coyolxauhqui, decided to kill their mother, and so they set off for Coatepec. But at the moment his sister arrived, Huitzilopochtli was born fully armed and he decapitated her

Fig. 9
A sacrificed Mimixcoa, the prototype of the warriors who were sacrificed as food for the Sun and the Earth, *Codex Borgia*, p. 19

Biblioteca Apostolica Vaticana

with his weapon, the fire serpent (*xiuhcoatl*). He then chased after his brothers and killed several of them, taking possession of their weapons (Sahagún 1950–1982, vol. 3). On an astral level, the fact that the earth goddess Coatlicue gave birth to Huitzilopochtli could be considered the rising of the Sun, which defeats the Moon (Coyolxauhqui) and the stars (Centzon Huitznahua) (Seler 1902–1923). This episode may also be interpreted as an attempt by the Mexica to recover the prestigious figure of Quetzalcoatl and replace him with their tutelary god Huitzilopochtli (Graulich 1997). In fact, the myth of Coatepec includes many elements of

Fig. 10
Mictlantecuhtli, the god of the dead and lord of the underworld, *Codex Borgia*, p. 13

Biblioteca Apostolica Vaticana

Fig. 11
Huitzilopochtli fights against
his brother, the Centzon
Huitznahua, on Mount
Coatepec, *Codex Florentinus*,
vol. 1, Book 3, reverse, p. 3

Biblioteca Medicea
Laurenziana, Florence

incidents involving Quetzalcoatl, specifically the episode in which the
"Quetzal Serpent" defeats his uncles or brothers who wanted to kill him
on a hill, the Mixcoatepetl. In this way, the Mexica identified Huitzilopochtli
as the Sun of the Fifth Era and assumed the role of feeding the sun and the
Earth by means of human sacrifices, thereby justifying their conquests. The
Great Temple of Tenochtitlan, a replica of Coatepec, constituted the centre
of the Mexica religious universe, from which the chosen people of Huitzilopochtli, with the cooperation of Tlaloc, the god of the autochthonous population, would dominate other peoples and control the fragile equilibrium of the
universe (López Austin and López Luján 2009).

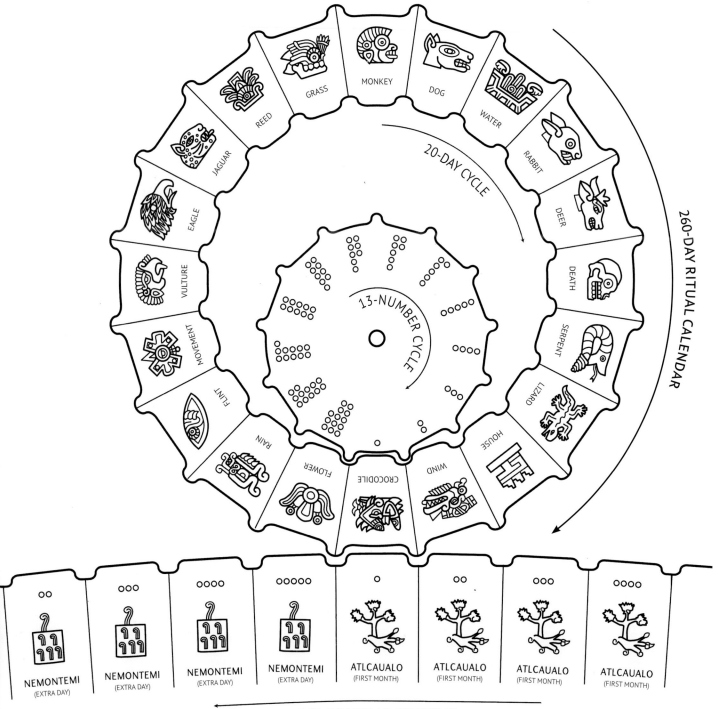

20-DAY CYCLE

13-NUMBER CYCLE

260-DAY RITUAL CALENDAR

GRASS

MONKEY

DOG

WATER

REED

RABBIT

JAGUAR

DEER

EAGLE

DEATH

VULTURE

SERPENT

MOVEMENT

LIZARD

FLINT

HOUSE

RAIN

WIND

FLOWER

CROCODILE

NEMONTEMI
(EXTRA DAY)

NEMONTEMI
(EXTRA DAY)

NEMONTEMI
(EXTRA DAY)

NEMONTEMI
(EXTRA DAY)

ATLCAUALO
(FIRST MONTH)

ATLCAUALO
(FIRST MONTH)

ATLCAUALO
(FIRST MONTH)

ATLCAUALO
(FIRST MONTH)

365-DAY SOLAR CALENDAR
(consisting of 18 months at 20 days each, plus 5 additional days at the end of the cycle)

Araceli Rojas Martínez Gracida

The 260-day Calendar

Time for the Meso-American peoples was a fundamental aspect of daily, ritual, scientific and philosophical life (as previously established by Caso in 1967, López Austin in 1990, León Portilla in 1956; Boone in 2007, and others). Different permutations of time – cycles or calendars – denoted festivities, public ceremonies, rites and appeals to the gods and ancestors, designated days for going to market and making exchanges, guided farming activities, established tax obligations, dictated a person's name, signalled the best time for travel, new enterprises and wars and provided the basis for astronomical observations. Time was closely linked to the order of space; an understanding of time afforded an understanding of how the world (including the Other World) worked. This time management was so fundamental to life that, despite the European invasion and the devastation and genocide attendant upon it, it still survives, in some cases only as an echo of the past, among some indigenous populations, such as the Ayöök (Mixes), K'ichés, Binizaa' (Zapotecs), Ha Shuta Enima (Mazatecs), Tsa Juj Mí (Chinantecs), Totonacs, Ixiles, Sots'il and Batz'il Winik (Tzeltales) and, of course, the Nahuas. What follows is a description of the fundamental aspects of the 260-day calendar structure, which formed the basis for all other calendars. This information has been taken from the archaeological archive, historical sources that deal principally with the cultures that inhabited the ancient Anahuac (the basin of Mexico or region of the lakes of Texcoco) and a recently documentation of the current use of one of these calendars among the Ayöök of Oaxaca.

The basic cycle

The natural marker par excellence for measuring time is the day: the period of time that elapses following the movement of the sun, from a certain point on the horizon until it reappears at the same point. In Meso-America, given its geographical location between latitudes of approximately 25° and 10° north, it is also possible to observe the passage of the sun through the zenith. However, natural time is not homogeneous, and consequently nor are the instruments and systems created to measure and organise time. In fact, they

Fig. 1 ◄
Diagram showing
the Aztec calendar

Diagram: OPERA
Amsterdam

are imperfect: for example, we have to make adjustments by means of leap years. Natural-astronomical time dictates the rythm of cultural time, which is also full of symbolisms and meanings.

Among Meso-Americans, the most basic ordering for counting days consisted of combining twenty symbols and thirteen numbers (Ayala Falcón 1995; Urcid 2001). This combination results in a cycle of 260 days, that is, 260 different combinations of signs and numbers. We cannot be certain of where this method came from. To date, the first archaeological record of a combination of numbers and signs is a ceramic seal dated ca. 650 B.C.. It bears the image of a bird from whose beak emerge the glyphs "U" and "3 Ajaw" and was found at the Olmec site of San Andrés, Tabasco (Pohl et al. 2002).

Figs. 4 a, b, c

a) Calendar Temple and stone slabs; b) Wall painting in the Calendar Temple (drawing after Guilliem Arroyo 1998); c) Fragment of page 21 of the *Codex Cihuacoatl*, formerly also *Codex Borbonicus*

Library of the French National Assembly, Paris

This cycle gives nomenclature to days. For Meso-Americans, each cycle began and ended at noon, in a constant death and rebirth of the sun and cycles of appearance-disappearance-appearance on the horizon. These days could be ordered into larger time cycles, such as the thirteen groups of twenty days and five additional days -making a total of 365 days-, the Long Count calendar used by the Maya, or the periods of sixty-five days or *cocijos* among the Binizaa'. These calendars were drawn up through precise astronomical observations, the formalisation of mathematical concepts and a system of conventional symbols that in the past were recorded in special writing system (Broda 1996, Mikulska 2014).

There are numerous Aztec ruins that evidence the use of this counting system. A prime example is at Tlatelolco, in the so called Templo Calendárico, with date of dedication on 1468, where the first three thirteen-day periods (39 days) of the 260-day sequence are engraved in stone slabs (Guilliem Arroyo 1998) (fig. 1a). Here, inside a circular structure in front of the staircases, a mural was also found showing Cipactonal and Oxomoco, the first human couple to whom the creation of this calendar is attributed (fig. 1b). It is interesting to note that these gods hold instruments of sacrifice and

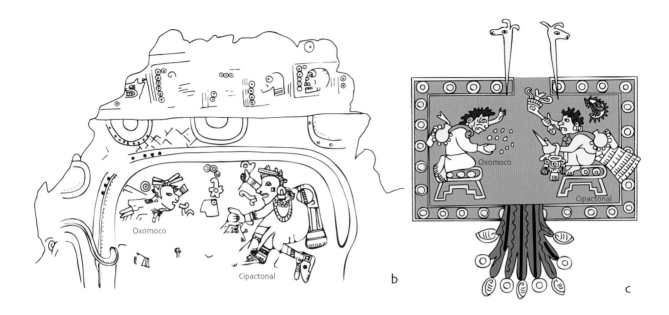

self-sacrifice. Likewise, in page 21 of the Cihuacoatl Codex (Borbonicus, XVI century), these gods are surrounded by 26 years of a cycle of 52 "years"; Oxomoco can be seen throwing maize, demonstrating the close link between the calendar, medicine and divination (fig. 1c). Arguably the most colourful example, also laden with symbolism, may be found in the Teoamoxtli (Borgia Group) codices, in which the basic 260-day cycle usually starts and continues as shown in Table 1.

As mentioned above, this cycle was used simultaneously together with other time cycles. Colonial missionaries, such as Toribio de Benavente, Bernardino de Sahagún and Diego Durán, told of this and other calendar systems, as well as the organisation of the 260-day into 13-day periods and the festivities that took place within each 20-day period. In the Nahuatl language, the 260-day cycle was called *tonalpohualli,* the 18 twenty-day periods were called *xihuitl,* the five additional days were *nemontemi,* and the cycle of 52 "years" was called *xiuhmolpilli.* Unfortunately, these sources are veiled through an obscurantism that makes them hard to access, thereby preventing a true understanding of the systems. Accordingly, these sources must be handled with scepticism and criticism.

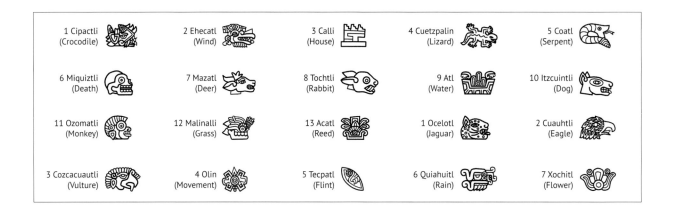

1 Cipactli (Crocodile)	2 Ehecatl (Wind)	3 Calli (House)	4 Cuetzpalin (Lizard)	5 Coatl (Serpent)
6 Miquiztli (Death)	7 Mazatl (Deer)	8 Tochtli (Rabbit)	9 Atl (Water)	10 Itzcuintli (Dog)
11 Ozomatli (Monkey)	12 Malinalli (Grass)	13 Acatl (Reed)	1 Ocelotl (Jaguar)	2 Cuauhtli (Eagle)
3 Cozcacuautli (Vulture)	4 Olin (Movement)	5 Tecpatl (Flint)	6 Quiahuitl (Rain)	7 Xochitl (Flower)

Prognosis and prescriptions in the 260-day cycle

The friars also related the significance of certain days, categorically labelling them as "good" or "bad". Sahagún (2006) noted that, when faced with the misfortune of a bad omen, the *tonalpouhque* (experts in the art of the *tonalpohualli*) advised and instructed offerings, as well as the place and the day on which to make them. Along with Duran (1967, vol. 1), he reported that diviners recommended going out and fighting wars on certain days as well as sowing seeds and harvesting on "good" days. The *tonalpouhque* were consulted to determine the cause of diseases, to find lost things, to foretell the fate of marriages, the fortune of newborns, or the auspices of a trip or new enterprise (Durán 1967, vol. 1; Benavente 1971; Ruíz de Alarcón 1953; Serna 1953).

Today, the Ayöök consult the calendar for similar reasons. This community turns to the 260-day calendar to find out whether they will receive money or a job, if a marriage will work out, if something that was lost will be found, if an illness will have a cure, to ask for good fortune and make promises, or to interpret a dream or pressage. However, the portent of days is neither absolute nor fatalistic. There is no intrinsic evil in time. Some events in life are important when they happen at significant times and only then can events, rather than days, be categorised as "good" or "not so good" (the *ethos* of a community). Furthermore, even if something happens on a day with negative connotations, there will always be something that can be done to remedy or mitigate unfavourable conditions. Hence, good and evil, as well as black and white, or light and darkness, are not absolute opposing forces into which the universe can be divided, but inherent aspects of every facet of the gods or life (Anders et al. 1994).

Furthermore, each day has a different level of significance, which overlaps without being hierarchical; they are polysemic. The sign associated with each day serves to denote 1) "good" or "not so good" symbols that serve to interpret dreams or omens; 2) prescriptions consisting of acts of respect (rituals); 3) character traits according to a person's day of birth. A fourth level of meaning could be added, signalled by the number, which refers to the intensity of the previous categories; the higher the number, the stronger the influence of the symbol. Depending on the situation, one level will come to the fore; that is, a day may have a "not so good" or a neutral connotation according to its more general prognosis, but at the same time it may be "good" or even ideal for making certain "ritual" requests, or fortunate for newborns, or vice versa. For example, the *Tëjk* day is a fairly neutral day in terms of the significance of pressages or dreams, but it is a good and very effective time to ask for the protection of the family home. *Mëy* is a day that can herald bad things, but it is a good day for visiting the graveyard and the church to pray for the welfare of the family. *Kaa* is a day without any particular significance, but it is appropriate for remembering the dead, and auspicious for a person's strong and brave character. Time has an influence on personality or brings to the fore certain human characteristics in the same way horoscopes (from the

Fig. 5
Pendant with calendar sign

KHM-Museumsverband,
Weltmuseum Wien (cat. 13)

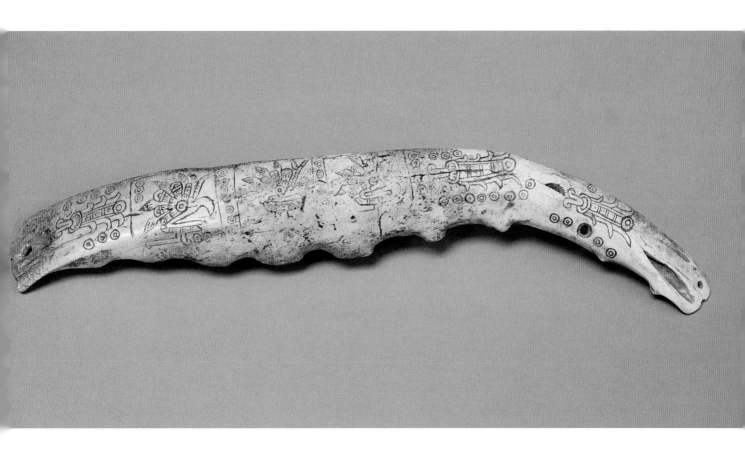

Greek "hõra", hour, and "skopos", observe) do in Western culture. Inspired by the Ayöök worldview, it can be said that there are twenty signs that correspond to the twenty personality archetypes: stubborn, friendly, aggressive, disobedient, relaxed, artistic, etc., the dominant characteristic of which depends on a person's day of birth or certain moments in life. Furthermore, acts of respect by parents and family members will reinforce good predictions and mitigate not-so-good ones.

In short, there are 260 different combinations of days that cannot be categorised according to absolutes. These days are not just ambivalent, they are multivalent. Among the Ayöök, the timekeepers and fortune tellers are called *xëë maypë machopë,* "the ones who divine and count the days ". They are often elderly and are treated with great respect and considered wise by their communities. They are consulted in concerning and distressing circumstances. During the consultation, inquiries are made as to the symptoms and questions are posed regarding when the ailments or illness began, dreams or premonitions occurred, the thing was lost, whether an argument took place, when the trip is planned to take place, for what reason, and so on. This is the *prognosis* step. In order to reach a diagnosis, maize is read, using a divination technique with its own reading system (see Rojas 2014). Once this information has been obtained, a medicinal treatment is prescribed, which consists of performing *customs* or, in the Ayöök language, *winstë'ëkë*, which literally means "to show respect". These acts are directed by the *xëë maypë machopë* towards the ancestors and deities, the most important of which is It Naaxwin, the Earth, and are performed in sacred places depending on the situation that needs resolving. Thus, the acts of respect in which one asks for work, money, fortune, health and protection, or a happy marriage, are performed on good days and in accordance with religious norms. These acts last one, two, seven, nine, thirteen or twenty days depending on each case. These steps of prognosis and prescription can be clearly seen in the Teoamoxtli (Borgia) codices.

Without a doubt, the art of calendars was, and still is, a complex and noble knowledge. Hence books and manuals such as the codices of the Teoamoxtli Group (Borgia) have been a very useful memory aid for diviners and calendar experts, or *tonalpouhque,* as they were known among the Aztecs. Given the unique character of each of these books, it is thought that the *tonalpouhque* themselves were the authors of the paintings and writing of the *tonalamatl* or the "books of the days". In the past, although the Spanish condemned the practice, colonial sources recognised the *tonalpouhque* as figures of authority and even prophets (Torquemada 1986:196). They should be recognised as true doctors and therapists, who used time to find out the symptoms of ailments in order to cure illnesses and bad pressages, consulting their books to identify warning signs in dreams and premonitions and ways to counteract possible misfortunes (Nowotny 2005). The same must be said of the *xëë maype machopë* in the Ayöök community today, and in other towns where these calendars have been conserved. Finally, the fact that the men and women who possess this wisdom do not need to refer to written or painted books or notebooks, but rely on their memory alone, should be acclaimed. This fact represents a form of dignified resistance to centuries of colonial oppression and more recently, the subjugating force of "the coloniality of power". ⌐

Leonardo López Luján

The Templo Mayor

History and archaeology

Prior to 1978 there was relatively little structured archaeological information about Tenochtitlan. Compared to Mayan, Zapotec and Teotihuacan archaeology, there were few material vestiges of Mexica culture and only sparse information regarding the subsoil layers in which they had been uncovered. Of course, the main obstacle that has limited – and continues to limit – archaeological knowledge of the illustrious pre-Hispanic capital lies in the buildings from the colonial and independent periods that rest atop its ancient ruins (López Luján 2015, 2018). Only in exceptional circumstances and in very small areas of modern Mexico City has it been possible to shed light on small portions of ancient Tenochtitlan (see the article on the archaeology of Tenochtitlan in this catalogue). This problem is compounded by the fact that a large part of the explorations prior to 1978 took place as a result of unexpected discoveries during urban works. Such explorations were often limited to the hasty recovery of some of the most exceptional Mexica works of art, usually in the form of large-scale sculptures, and this prevented detailed archaeological recording.

There was, however, a well-rounded picture of Mexica society and of the general physiognomy of Tenochtitlan, thanks to the innumerable historical sources from the sixteenth, seventeenth and eighteenth centuries, in obvious contrast to the meagre pictographic and written information available on the Maya, the Zapotec and, above all, the Teotihuacan people. For example, extensive information abounds in the codices of local artists regarding the main pyramid of the Mexica capital, known as Huei Teocalli or the "Templo Mayor": in the stories of the indigenous sages written in Latin, Nahuatl and even in Spanish in the chronicles of the Spanish conquistadors, who bore eyewitness to the pyramid when it was in use; in the accounts of Franciscan, Dominican and Jesuit friars, often based on the indigenous tradition; and even in the fantastic publications – with outlandish illustrations – which were written in Europe by people who had never set foot on the American continent.

Fig. 1 ◀
The construction phases
of the Templo Mayor
Phase I, 1325–1375
Phase II, 1375–1427
Phase III, 1427–1440
Phase IVa, 1440–1469
Phase IVb, 1469–1481
Phase V, 1481–1486
Phase VI, 1486–1502
Phase VII, 1502–1520

Diagram: www.latin-
americanstudies.org

Fig. 2
Drawing showing a reconstruction of the Templo Mayor
in the heart of Mexico City

With the kind permission of Proyecto Templo Mayor
Drawing of the reconstruction: Michelle De Anda

ano se qua tro cat

Figs. 3, 4, 5
Extension of the Templo
Mayor, begun by Tizoc and
finished and inaugurated by
Ahuitzotl with the blood of
war captives.

Bibliothèque nationale
de France
Codex Telleriano-Remensis.

In this sense, it can be said that no other monument in ancient Mexico attracted as much attention among both the Mexica and foreigners as the Templo Mayor. As a consequence, we now have a unique documentary archive of practically its entire history, from the very moment of its foundation, through its continuous extensions and architectural modifications, to its destruction and complete dismantling. These written accounts also provide insight into the construction of the pyramid and the physiognomy of the two chapels that crowned it; the number of steps from the base and the top; its structural and decorative elements; its religious imagery and ritual furniture; and the wide variety of ceremonies – religious and political, scheduled or otherwise, public or private – that it housed.

While it is true that the archaeological discovery of the Templo Mayor dates back to 1914 and is attributable to the Mexican anthropologist Manuel Gamio, it was not until the period between 1978 and 1982 that another famed Mexican, Eduardo Matos Moctezuma, and his team completely liberated the pyramid from the rubble that had covered it for centuries (Broda et al. 1987; Matos Moctezuma 1988). Since then and by means of the valuable combination of historical and archaeological testimonies we know that, at the time of the arrival of the Europeans, this monument measured exactly 78 metres at its base from north to south and 83.6 metres from east to west, while it had around 45 metres in height, like the Pyramid of the Moon in Teotihuacan and the Column of Independence (nicknamed "The Angel") in the modern Paseo de la Reforma in Mexico City. It was also discovered that this architectural complex consisted of a quadrangular platform, on which stood a pyramid with four superimposed bodies, which served as a base for two chapels: the southern one dedicated to Huitzilopochtli, god of the sun and war, and the northern one dedicated to the worship of Tlaloc, god of the rain and earth (López Austin and López Luján 2009). From ground level, these chapels were reached by a double staircase on the western façade, flanked by large snake heads carved in basalt.

The Templo Mayor of Tenochtitlan, like many of the Meso-American pyramids, is a solid mass of stone, earth, limestone, sand and wood. It was principally built from extrusive igneous rocks as the result of a deliberate decision on the part of its architects, but also due to two factors worthy of consideration (López Austin and López Luján 2009). Firstly, the Basin of Mexico had been the site of significant volcanic activity in its recent past and as a consequence there were no outcrops of sedimentary or metamorphic rocks. And secondly, pre-Hispanic civilisations lacked draught animals, and never implemented the mechanised use of the wheel. It is logical to suppose that the combination of these factors inhibited the transfer of allochthonous rocks – especially large blocks – from regions that were not only distant, but also located on the other side of the high mountains that surround the Basin.

To date five types of rocks have been found during excavations. The first of these is dense grey and black basalts (*metlatetl*), ideal for building foundations, load-bearing walls, staircases and floors for exteriors. Next is light but highly resistant volcanic slag (*tezontli*), which is reddish, violet or blackish in colour and forms part of the building's fillings and façades; it is also found in the staircases, stucco floors, paving stones and walls. Thirdly, there is the pale pinkish lamprobolite andesites (*tenayocatetl*), whose pseudostratification makes it easy to obtain flat faces which can be used to make magnificent floor slabs, corner stones, covering ashlars and drains. Pyroxene andesites (*iztapaltetl*) are grey or off-white, dense stones with flat and smooth faces used for floors, foundation templates, façade ties and drains. And finally there is limestone (*tetizatl*), a sedimentary rock of whitish, grey, rose and ochre tones. To date, these stones have only been detected on the platform of stage IVa of the Templo Mayor, where they were used in the luxurious tile floors of two small rooms that flank the steps leading to the upper chapels. Unlike the other rocks, these were brought from far-off sources located in what is now the state of Puebla.

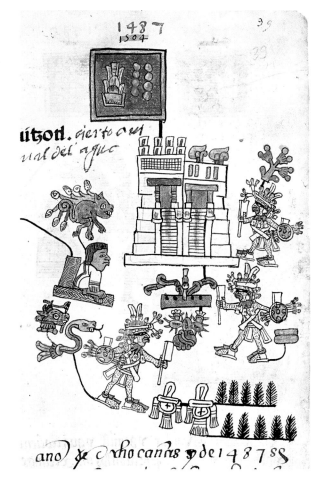

207

grasas,

patio

Soil formed the basic component of the construction fillings. It is characterised by a clay-like texture and dark brown colour resulting from of its high content of organic matter. Evidence indicates that the soil was obtained from the shallow beds of the lake or in the swampy zones along its shores. In fact, when examining the botanical content of the various fillings we can observe a clear predominance of seeds belonging to species found in lake and marsh habitats. It was also possible to identify significant concentrations of fish scales and freshwater snails.

Sand and lime were also essential to construction. They were used to make plaster and stucco coverings for floors, walls and staircases of all stages of the building, and they also served as ingredients for the preparation of concrete and mortar (Miriello et al. 2011). The sand used, given its volcanic origin, was probably obtained from any of the numerous deposits in the Basin of Mexico. In contrast, limestone had to be imported from more remote locations. Historical sources and chemical analyses point to the region of Tula, in what is now the state of Hidalgo. Lastly, wood was used to make stakes for the foundations, door posts and lintels, as well as beams, planks and roof rafters. We know from botanical analyses that the Mexica also made use of pine, cedar and willow trees from the cold and temperate forests, located between 2,350 and 4,000 metres above sea level within the Basin.

Fig. 6
The Templo Mayor with the chapels for Tlaloc and Huitzilopochtli, *Codex Durán*

Biblioteca Nacional de Madrid

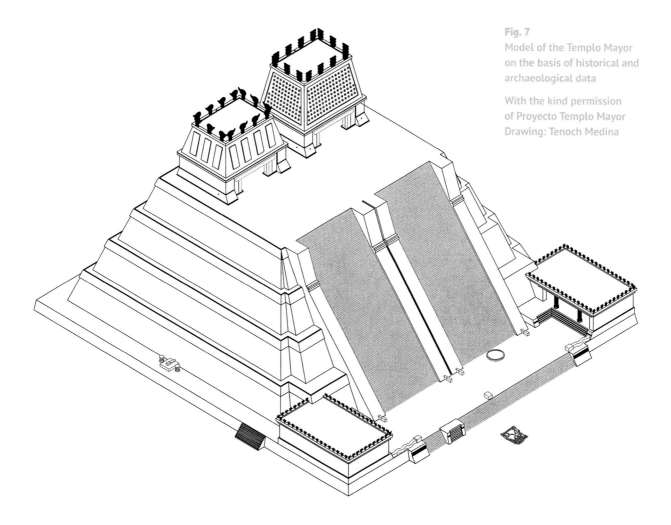

Fig. 7
Model of the Templo Mayor
on the basis of historical and
archaeological data

With the kind permission
of Proyecto Templo Mayor
Drawing: Tenoch Medina

A tireless activity

The geological formations and forests where these building materials could
be found extended almost to the shores of the lake system surrounding the
island of Tenochtitlan, which made it relatively easy to exploit them. Despite
this, the Mexica forced all the riverside towns to participate in obtaining and
transporting supplies for the expansion of their pyramidal temples. Among
them were the Chalca, who had to travel the longest distance, as their territory was located around 38 kilometres from the Mexica capital. This distance
does not seem excessive if we consider that for most of their journey the

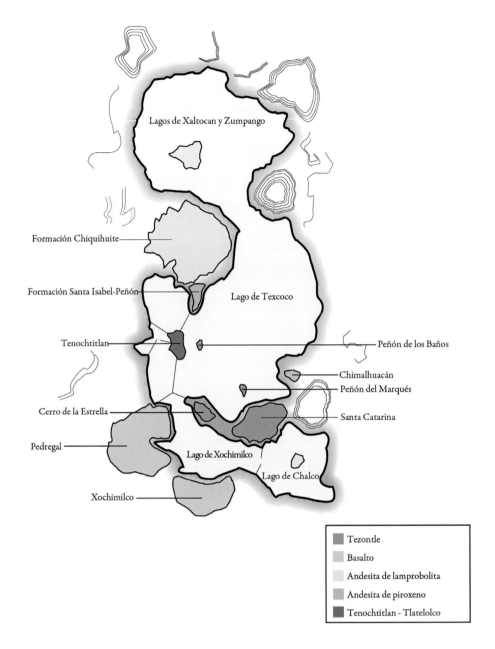

Fig. 8
Map of the Basin of Mexico
with the sites of the building
materials which were used
for the Templo Mayor and
other temples in Tenoch-
titlan

With the kind permission
of Proyecto Templo Mayor
Drawing: Jaime Torres

Lagos de Xaltocan y Zumpango

Formación Chiquihuite

Formación Santa Isabel-Peñón

Lago de Texcoco

Tenochtitlan

Peñón de los Baños

Chimalhuacán

Peñón del Marqués

Cerro de la Estrella

Santa Catarina

Pedregal

Lago de Xochimilco

Lago de Chalco

Xochimilco

Tezontle
Basalto
Andesita de lamprobolita
Andesita de piroxeno
Tenochtitlan - Tlatelolco

people of Chalco were not carrying heavy loads on their shoulders, as almost
all transportation was done by canoe. This mode of transport was between
forty and fifty times more efficient than *tlamamaque* or human carriers.
According to fairly reliable calculations based on historical, ethnographic and
experimental data, a man capable of carrying a maximum load of 23 kilograms over the course of a day on his back was able to transport up to 1,200
kilograms in a canoe. In addition, it must be considered that people advanced

at the same speed both on foot and by canoe, covering between 2.6 and 3.5 kilometres per hour. Accordingly, the transportation of more than a tonne of materials from Chalco to Tenochtitlan by boat would take just ten hours (López Luján et al. 2003).

In light of the vestiges excavated by the Templo Mayor Project, it is evident that the main pyramid of Tenochtitlan was subject to constant renovation from its erection in the fourteenth century to its destruction in the sixteenth century. This is demonstrated by the discovery of at least seven complete extensions, corresponding to its four façades (stages I–VII); six partial extensions of only of the main façade or the northern façade (stages IIa, IIb, IIc, IIIa, IVa and IVb); a complete renovation of the platform staircase (stage VIa); multiple re-levellings of the upper façades of some pyramidal structures; and numerous minor refurbishments of the lateral façades (López Austin and López Luján 2009). We also know that when each of these stages was underway, on more than one occasion the level of the platform and also the floor height of the surrounding square were raised.

Etapa	Matos Moctezuma	Umberger
II-IIc	1375-1427 Acamapichtli Huitzilíhuitl Chimalpopoca	
III	1427-1440 Itzcóatl	
IV	1440-1469	1440-1469 Motecuhzoma I
IVa	Motecuhzoma I	
IVb	1469-1481 Axayácatl	
V	1481-1486 Tízoc	1469-1481 Axayácatl
VI	1486-1502 Ahuítzotl	1481-1502 Tízoc Ahuítzotl
VII	1502-1520 Motecuhzoma II	

Fig. 9
Chronology of the construction phases of the Templo Mayor

With the kind permission of Proyecto Templo Mayor
Plate: Alfredo Lopez Austin and Leonardo López Luján

Fig. 10 ▶

The binary division of the sculptures at the Templo Mayor: in the middle of the south side, which is dedicated to Huitzilopochtli, the serpents are ochre-coloured and some are feathered, a symbol of the sky. In the middle of the north side, which is dedicated to Tlaloc, the serpents are blue and some show symbols of jade beads, symbols of water droplets. In fact, ocher alludes to the Dry season of the year and blue-green to the Rainy season.

With the kind permission of Proyecto Templo Mayor
Drawing: Michelle De Anda

Undoubtedly, there were many different reasons for this exaggerated constructive fervour recorded in the relatively short period of 150 years. One such reason was the natural phenomena such as earthquakes, floods and land subsidence that the pyramid was subject to as a result of its location on a lake bed containing compressible clays. Some researchers have also suggested that the Templo Mayor was renovated every 52 years; however, there are few facts to support this theory. Other more plausible theories set forth that with each enlargement, successive Mexica sovereigns sought to leave their personal mark on history.

However, most of the expansions recorded in historical sources seem to be the direct result of an expansionist policy that began when Motecuhzoma Ilhuicamina took power in 1440 and ended with the Spanish conquest (López Luján et al. 2003). A careful reading of the work of the indigenous chronicler Hernando Alvarado Tezozómoc reveals an important factor relating to these expansions: each enlargement was inaugurated with the blood of warriors from a kingdom conquered solely for the celebration. Thus, the new building symbolised, celebrated and sanctified the inclusion of new tributaries within the sphere of the Mexica Empire. In exceptional circumstances in which the troops of the Triple Alliance (made up of Tenochtitlan, Texcoco and Tlacopan) failed to conquer an independent settlement – as was the case in the unsuccessful expedition of King Axayacatl to Tarascan lands – the celebration was postponed until a successful conquest had taken place. In other words, the Templo Mayor grew at the same rate as the empire expanded. This helps explain why it grew 13 times in such a short time.

Stage of mythical re-enactment

Like many other pyramids in pre-Hispanic Mexico, the Templo Mayor emulates a sacred mountain. In this specific case it evokes Mount Coatepetl, a mythical place where the dramatic birth of the god Huitzilopochtli took place. Fortunately, several versions of this fantastical event have survived to the present day, the most complete and well-known of which is included in the *Florentine Codex* of friar Bernardino de Sahagún and his indigenous informants (Matos Moctezuma 1988; López Austin and López Luján 2009). The basic story goes like this:
It all began with a woman called Coatlicue performing her daily penance at the top of Mount Coatepetl, the "Hill of the Serpents". One day, when she was sweeping, she noticed a feather fall right in front of her eyes. Without hesitating, she grasped hold of it and used it to touch her stomach, an act that

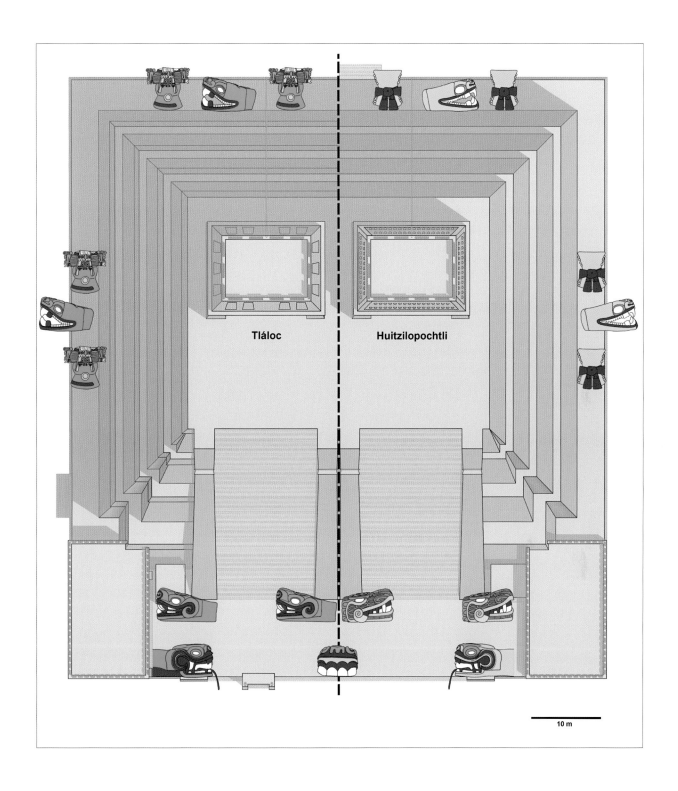

Tláloc   Huitzilopochtli

10 m

resulted in a miraculous pregnancy. Shortly afterwards, Coyolxauhqui and the Centzonhuitznahuah, the sons of Coatlicue, learned of this inexplicable transgression and, feeling that their honour had been besmirched, decided to go and kill their mother.

They set out for Coatepetl, passing through the sites of Tzompantitlan, Coaxalpan, Apetlac, and then reaching the slope of the hill and finally its summit. When they reached their mother, they witnessed the birth of their brother Huitzilopochtli, who emerged from his mother's womb as a fully armed young man ready to fight them. He immediately gouged a magic *xiuhcoatl* or fire serpent into the torso of his sister, Coyolxauhqui, and then decapitated her with it and threw her to the foot of the hill, where she fell inert and her body shattered into pieces. Huitzilopochtli's exploits came to an end when he attacked his brothers and chased them away towards the sky.

More than a century ago, the different versions of this story were analysed by the German sage Eduard Seler, who astutely identified Huitzilopochtli as the young rising Sun, Coyolxauhqui as the Moon and the Centzonhuitznahuah as the stars, explaining the myth as the astral struggle between the forces of day and night. Inspired by these ideas, Matos Moctezuma (1988) affirmed that the Templo Mayor of Tenochtitlan is the material manifestation of the myth of Huitzilopochtli. The most convincing proof of this theory is the spectacular monolith of the moon goddess Coyolxauhqui at stage IVb, found in 1978, in which the goddess was depicted decapitated and dismembered. Matos Moctezuma notes that this monolith symbolising the defeat of the night was placed precisely at the foot of the steps leading to the top of the pyramid, where the image of the sun god Huitzilopochtli was placed triumphant at the zenith. Matos Moctezuma also points out that certain architectural features of the Templo Mayor recall the name Coatepetl, such as the four large serpent heads at the foot of the staircases' balustrades and the coarse stones embedded in the successive bodies of the pyramid. According to this logic, the serpents would have the phonetic value of *coa[tl]*, while the stones would respond to the wild character of the word *tepetl*.

On this firm basis, the Mexican archaeologist then constructed a series of hypotheses that attempt to give coherence to other elements of the iconographic programme of the Templo Mayor. It is suggested, for example, that the great anthropomorphic sculptures discovered on the southern staircase of stage III were the effigies of the Centzonhuitznahuah referred to by Alvarado Tezozómoc when he stated that the warrior brothers of Coyolxauhqui were depicted with shields around the pyramid.

Fig. 11
The Earth goddess Coatlicue
gives birth to the sun god
Huitzilopochtli. As an adult
the latter, armed with a fire
serpent, vanquishes his
brothers, the moon and the
stars, *Codex Florentinus*.

Biblioteca Medicea
Laurenziana, Florence

To the monuments listed by Matos Moctezuma we could add, on the one hand, the mural paintings he discovered in 1979 inside the chapel of Huitzilopochtli corresponding to stage II and, on the other, the three sculptures that were exhumed completely in 1987 in stage IVa. The pictorial ensemble in question, although almost completely destroyed, represents a jumbled heap of weapons and luxurious military effects, among them shields, darts and banners, all linked to the god of the sun and war. On the other hand, the sculptural ensemble consists of a rudimentary effigy of Coyolxauhqui, a mat of snakes and a slab with a shield, a flag and four darts in relief. The headless, dismembered goddess is depicted here as the archetypal victim lying at the base of the pyramid hill. The weapons, on the other hand, commemorate the confrontation between the Sun and the Moon, while at the same time sanctifying war as a means of satisfying the gods. Finally, the mat alludes to the omen that those who sat on this web of snakes would soon meet their death, as happened to Coyolxauhqui, or discover power, as happened to Huitzilopochtli.

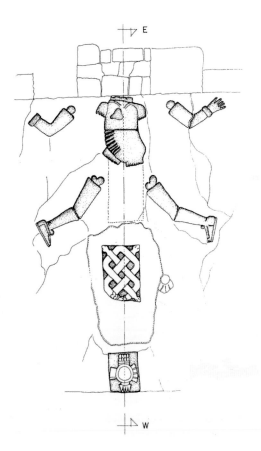

Fig. 12
Drawing of Coyolxauhqui, beheaded and hacked to death, on the platform of building stage IVa of the Templo Mayor

With the kind permission of Proyecto Templo Mayor
Drawing: Leonardo López Luján

According to Seler, the fact that the Templo Mayor is referred to as Coatepetl in historical documents clearly identifies it as an arena for ritual reenactment. On this stage a procession of faithful carrying the image of Huitzilopochtli dramatised the mythical offensive against the Centzonhuitznahuah during the *Panquetzaliztli* festival. The German researcher pointed out that this connection was made even more evident by the names Tzompantlitlan, Coaxalpan and Apetlac, received by both the places visited by Coyolxauhqui and the Centzonhuitznahuah in the myth as well as three existing constructions in the sacred site: the line of trophy-skulls opposite the Great Temple (the *tzompantli*), the base of the pyramid (called *coaxalpan*) and its platform (named *apetlac*).

Fig. 14
Excavation of the monolithic
stone sculpture of the
goddess Tlaltecuhtli at the
foot of the Templo Mayor

With the kind permission of
Proyecto Templo Mayor
Photo: Leonardo López Luján

The dual pattern of the pyramid

According to some foundational myths, the original *tlalmomoztli* – the
humble earth chapel, which with the passage of time became the majestic
Templo Mayor of Tenochtitlan – was built on the exact spot where the
miraculous sign that marked the end of the Mexica migration took place: the
stone and the cactus (*nopal*) where the eagle landed and spread its wings. In
some versions of this story it is said that under the stone and the *nopal* there
were two caves or two large rocks from which two streams flowed, foreshad-
owing the double features of the pyramid of Huitzilopochtli and Tlaloc. For
Matos Moctezuma (1988) (Broda et al. 1987), the unique design of the
monument and its devotion to two divinities is the clear ideological reflec-
tion of an economy based both on the tribute of the towns conquered by the
Mexica empire and on obtaining the fruits of the earth through agriculture.

Fig. 15
Monolithic stone sculpture
of the goddess Tlaltecuhtli
in situ

With the kind permission
of Proyecto Templo Mayor
3D-scan: Guido Galvani and
Martia Sanchez

Another group of theories suggests that the dual composition of the Templo Mayor is fully in line with the Meso-American cosmovision, which was mainly binary (López Austin and López Luján 2009). Indeed, the division into opposing pairs has its roots in the oldest cultural manifestations of ancient Mexico and became a true obsession. According to the defenders of this hypothesis, the Templo Mayor was the consolidation of the universe's opposing and complementary forces: dry season/rainy season, riped/tender, winter solstice/summer solstice, life/death, sky/earth, day/night, stars/vegetation, fire/water, heat/cold, ochre/blue, and so on.

This recurring pattern is clearly expressed in the binary distribution of the architectural, sculptural, pictorial and oblatory elements that have been archaeologically excavated to date, which are listed in the following table:

Vertical section	Middle North Section	Middle South Section
Merlons	Clouds, pots, barrel cactus, *cuechtli*, *tecciztli*	Flames, fire, feathered snake, *tecciztli*
Summit	Plinth for the image of Tlaloc	Plinth for the image of Huitzilopochtli
	Paintings of the maize god and water imagery	Paintings of weapons
	Water and fertility offerings	Burials of cremated dignitaries
	Sacrificial *Chacmool*-Tlaloc	Sacrificial polyhedron
		Head of a *Huitznahua* decapitated
Tlatlacapan (Pyramid)	Moulding decoration	Without moulding decoration
	Four superimposed bodies: rough flanks	Four superimposed bodies: rough flanks
	Reliefs of *chalchihuitl* and spiral	Reliefs of *chalchihuitl*, spiral and astral
	Offerings of overturned blue pots	
	Chalchihuitl snakes entwined	*Centzonhuitznahuah*
	Snake heads with jade beads	Snake heads with feathers
	Scaled snake heads with jade beads	Scaled snake heads without jade beads
	Tlaloc braziers	Braziers with red ribbon
Apetlac (West platform)	Chamber 2: blue and aquatic/terrestrial cave	Chamber 1: ochre and astral cave
	Water and fertility offerings	Burials of cremated dignitaries
	Tepetlacalli of water and fertility	*Tepetlacalli* of water and fertility
		Coyolxauhqui, weapons, *petlacoatl*
	Consecration offerings with Rain and Fire gods effigies	
Coaxalpan (West platform and square)	Great undulating blue snake	Great undulating ochre snake
	Central axis: Large blue/ochre snake head	
	Altar of the Frogs	Altar of the Celestial Serpents
	Tlaloc, spring, cloud and corn slabs	Astral, fire, captive, snake, weapon and eagle slabs
	Central axis: Anthropomorphic Tlaltecuhtli monolith	
	Central axis: Zoomorphic Tlaltecuhtli slabs	

Fig. 16
Monolithic stone sculpture
of the goddess Tlaltecuhtli

With the kind permission
of Proyecto Templo Mayor
Colour reconstruction:
Michelle De Anda and
Kenneth Garrett

Fig. 17
Dedicatory offering
box found under the
Tlaltecuhtli monolith

With the kind
permission of
Proyecto Templo
Mayor
Photo: Jesus López

222

Fig. 19
Skeleton of a she-Mexican
wolf dressed as a warrior.
Offering box 120.
The Mexica buried several
kinds of dressed animals, all
of them related to war
orders: Jaguars, pumas,
wolves, eagles.

223

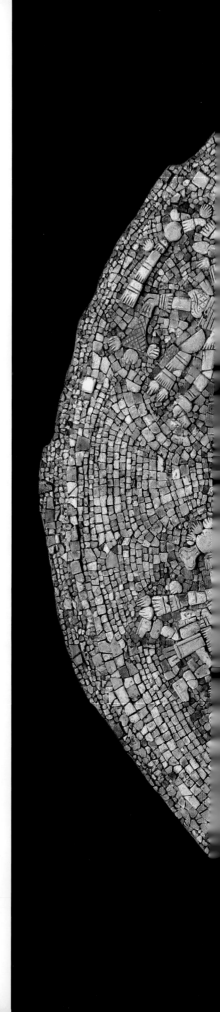

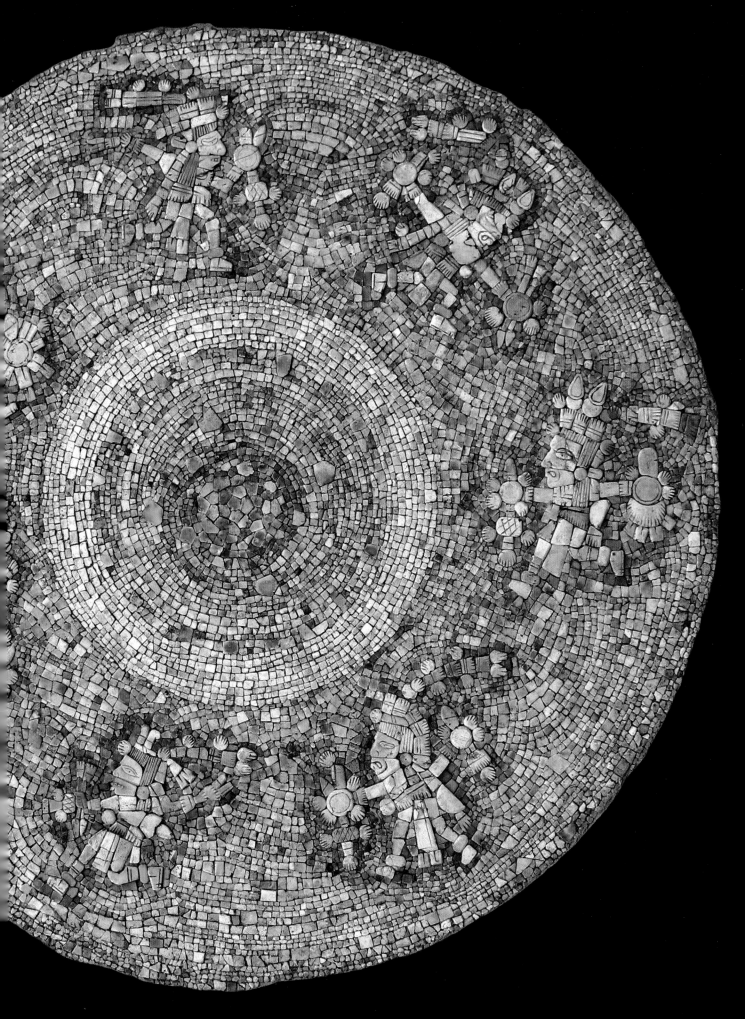

Leonardo López Luján

The House of Eagles

To the north of the Templo Mayor

The Casa de las Águilas (House of Eagles) is one of the most impressive religious buildings discovered in the ruins of Tenochtitlan to date. It was built and enlarged three times between 1430 and 1502 AD, and stands out not only due to its proximity to the Templo Mayor, its large dimensions and staircases decorated with eagle heads, but also for its rich neo-Toltec ornamentation, inspired by a style that was fashionable four centuries before in the city of Tula (950-1150 AD) (López Luján 2013).

Unfortunately, of the last two construction phases of the House of Eagles (stages 3–4) only the platform survives, as the upper half of the building was razed between 1521 and 1523 AD following the Spanish conquest. The platform has an L-shaped floor plan and is comprised of two connected areas: the east wing and the north wing, with two access staircases in the southwest corner. Although it has not been possible to excavate it completely, it is estimated to measure 32 metres in a north-south direction and 52 metres in an east-west direction.

When excavating the interior of stages 3 and 4, an older stage (stage 2) was located. This had been built between 1469 and 1481 AD, during the reign of Axayacatl (López Luján 2006, 2017). This stage also consists of a solid, small, L-shaped platform which serves as the base for a portico, several rooms and a small interior courtyard. In pre-Hispanic times the east wing of the building was accessed via a staircase that rose from the public plaza to the portico, supported by a regularly distributed series of pilasters (fig. 3). In order to reach the main room, it was necessary to pass through a door guarded by two ceramic, full-body, life-size sculptures of individuals dressed in eagle costumes. From the main room, occupied by a large altar, the next rooms were reached through a narrow corridor. This led to a rectangular courtyard flanked by two rooms, one to the north and one to the south. Each of these had a small altar and a pair of ceramic incense burners decorated with Tlaloc's face shedding tears of rain.

Fig. 1 ◄
Ceramic in the form of the god Mictlantecuhtli, the lord of the kingdom of the dead

With the kind permission of Proyecto Templo Mayor
Photo: Michel Zabé

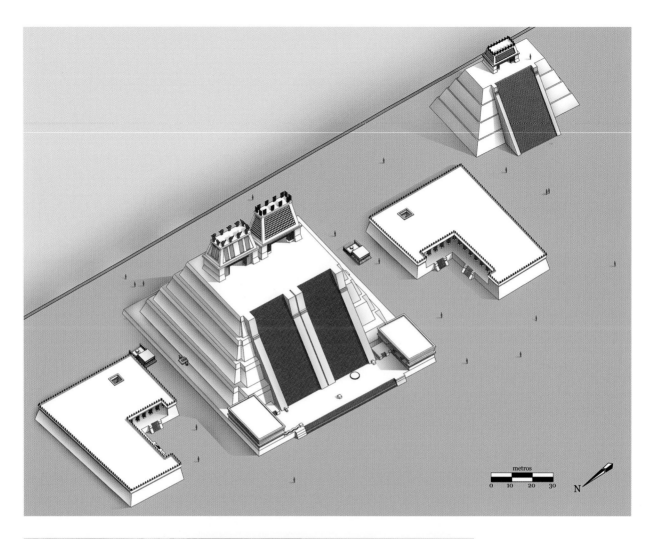

Fig. 2 ▲
The House of Eagles lies to
the north of the Templo
Mayor

With the kind permission
of Proyecto Templo Mayor
Reconstruction drawing:
Michelle De Anda

Fig. 3 ◀
The House of Eagles in the
northern inner plaza

With the kind permission of
Proyecto Templo Mayor
Photo: Leonardo López Luján

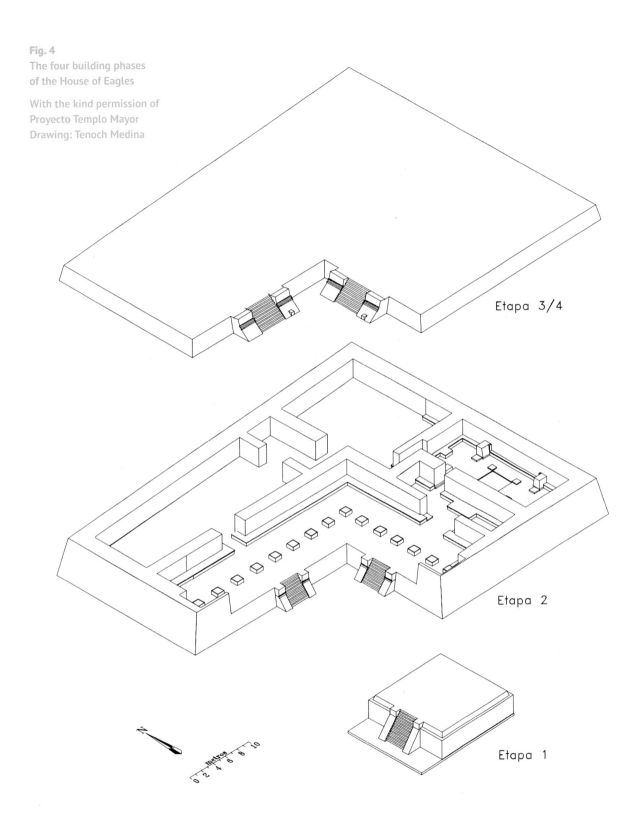

Fig. 4
The four building phases
of the House of Eagles

With the kind permission of
Proyecto Templo Mayor
Drawing: Tenoch Medina

Etapa 3/4

Etapa 2

Etapa 1

N

metros

0 2 4 6 8 10

Fig. 5 ◀
Incense burner

Museo del Templo Mayor,
Mexico City, D.R. Secretaría
de Cultura – INAH (cat. 111)

Fig. 6 ▶
Tlaloc braziers and carved
benches in neo-Toltec style

With the kind permission of
Proyecto Templo Mayor
Photo: Salvador Guilliem

The interior spaces of the House of Eagles have stucco floors and masonry walls decorated with bench-like structures of basalt running around the perimeter and paintings on flat, smooth earth plastering. So far, 86 metres of benches have been excavated, all decorated with rich polychrome reliefs, in addition to 90.5 square metres of paintings that are unfortunately in a very poor state of conservation.

The tunnel excavation

Since the northern half of the House of Eagles is buried under the street Justo Sierra and the colonial building of Librería Porrúa, in 1994 two long tunnels were dug under the tourist walkway of the archaeological zone. In the first tunnel, a room of large proportions was uncovered. It was decorated with mural paintings and more than 13 metres of polychrome benches, which were mostly intact.

Even more impressive was the discovery in the second tunnel, where the access to the north wing of the building was found, guarded by two impressive ceramic figures representing Mictlantecuhtli, the Lord of the World of

the Dead. Both were broken into smithereens due to the high level of humidity in the subsoil and the great amount of pressure exerted by the weight of the colonial and modern buildings. After five months of work inside the tunnel and eight more months in the conservation laboratory, these real-life puzzles measuring 1.74 metres tall and 128 kilograms in weight were finally put together.

Fig. 7 ▲
Comparison of a Neo-Toltec
Rain God ceramic braziers
from the House of Eagles
(top) with a Toltec incense
burner found in Tula (below)

With the kind permission of
Proyecto Templo Mayor
Drawing: Fernando Carrizosa

The areas of ritual activity

The House of Eagles was an important stage in the religious life of Tenochtitlan. Architecturally, the interior spaces of the building provided ideal conditions for performing private rites in which only a few individuals participated. Its isolation from the outside, restricted lighting conditions and reduced dimensions create a secluded atmosphere ideal for activities such as prayer, meditation and penance. In addition, the rich interior decoration would suggest that blood offering was one of the main ceremonies to take place there. The vertical faces of the benches depict religious processions of armed warriors that converge in a *zacatapayolli*, a ball of hay, into which worshippers stuck bloody bone knives during the ritual of self-sacrifice.

Architecture and benches are not the only sources of information available
for reconstructing the ceremonies that took place in this monument. Stucco
floors also offer valuable data. For this reason, they were studied under the
assumption that they were chemically "clean" when they were first used and
that, with the passage of time, the solutions spilled during the performance
of specific rites accumulated in their porous structure. According to this logic,
floor samples were taken every metre and were subjected to ten different
analyses. The results make it clear that the spatial distribution of chemical

40 cm

values cannot be attributed to chance: the highest indices were always recorded in front of the altars with incense burners, revealing that these were the places where most ritual activity took place. There, residues from the ritual use of copal and other aromatic resins, animal fats, human blood and fermented beverages such as *pulque* can be found.

An archaic style

In stage 2 of the House of Eagles, allusions to Toltec civilisation abound to convey to the faithful the idea of a glorious past, such as ceramic braziers bearing the face of the God of Rain. While it is true that these Mexica imitations are fairly similar to Toltec originals of the Abra Café Burdo ceramic type, their raw materials, smaller dimensions and certain stylistic details point towards a different origin.

The murals of the House of Eagles also bear the unmistakable Toltec stamp. Mexica artists made use of technical and stylistic solutions that were already in vogue in Tula. The exterior masonry wall of the building was coated on

Figs. 9 and 10
Comparison of a Neo-Toltec "bench seat" from the House of Eagles (top) with a Toltec bench seat found in Tula (below)

With the kind permission of Proyecto Templo Mayor
Drawing: Fernando Carrizosa

both sides with a thin layer of beaten earth. The lower part of the walls, about one third in each case, was covered with a thin layer of stucco, a mixture of lime and sand. The upper part of the walls was treated with a clay plaster (dark, very malleable clay with a low lime content). The painting layer was applied to these plaster layers. Toltec ornamental motifs such as the multicoloured borders were also copied. These are made up of four horizontal bands that are always repeated in the same colour sequence: black, blue, red and ochre succeed each other from bottom to top.

The neo-Toltec programme of the House of Eagles is finished off with an impressive sequence of benches. Each one is composed of two panels carved in bas-relief. The top panel is a frieze containing images of snakes with undulating bodies. As previously mentioned, the lower panel, shows a procession of warriors making a blood offering.

A rigorous study of historical sources has allowed us to conclude that this neo-Toltec building served as a stage for the rites of dynastic transition. It was here that the vigil for the corpse of the king was held and it was here, too, that the successor to the throne performed the death and rebirth rituals prior to coronation a few days later. In this regard, it should be considered that, for the Mexica, the legitimacy of power was based on two beliefs: that their ruling lineage was descended from the god Quetzalcoatl and that it was linked to the ancient Tula through the blood ties of Acamapichtli, the founding king of the dynasty of Tenochtitlan.

The closing rites

Between 1486 and 1502 AD, the Mexica decided to enlarge the House of Eagles once more, perhaps because its dimensions and the quality of its finishes no longer reflected the splendour that Tenochtitlan had achieved. As was the custom, a group of priests ritually closed the sacred space just before the new building work began. In

234

the first rite identified by archaeologists, the images of Mictlantecuhtli and the figures dressed in eagle costumes flanking the main entrances to the building were literally soaked in human blood and biochemists. Then one of these entrances was blocked with a sculpture depicting a threatening rattlesnake. Then the stucco floors, the Tlaloc braziers, the rattlesnake, the polychrome benches, the ceramic sculptures and the mural paintings were covered with a thin layer of lacustrine clay. Lastly, several human jaws were placed in front of the torso of each of the large images, possibly to emphasise their ritual death and definitive burial.

Once the ritual was over, the whole complex was meticulously protected with walls made of large stones. Finally, the rooms were filled with earth, and the flat roofs were taken down to create a solid platform that would serve as a base for the new building. ⅃

Fig. 11 ◂
Wall paintings in the north wing of the House of Eagles with symbols of death and brightly coloured Neo-Toltec bands

With the kind permission of Proyecto Templo Mayor

Fig. 12 ▾
Blood sacrifice for the god Mictlantecuhtli, *Codex Magliabechiano*

Biblioteca Nazionale Centrale

Raúl Barrera Rodríguez

The *Huei Tzompantli*, the Ball Court and the Temple of Ehecatl Quetzalcoatl

A Trilogy of Recent Discoveries

In recent years, the Urban Archaeology Program (known as PAU after its Spanish acronym) of the National Institute of Anthropology and History (INAH) has carried out important archaeological work in the area comprising the sacred precinct of Tenochtitlan, located in the heart of Mexico City. This text discusses the discovery of three significant Mexica buildings located in the square in front of the Templo Mayor; namely the *Huei Tzompantli* "wall of skulls," the Temple of Ehecatl Quetzalcoatl, the "god of wind", and the Ball Court or *Teotlachco,* "the game of the gods". These efforts continue today thanks to a whole team of specialists, who also go to great lengths to preserve these areas and make them available as museum spaces.

Fig. 1 ◀
View of the excavations of the Temple of Ehecatl-Quetzalcoatl

Photo: Raúl Barrera Rodríguez

The *Huei Tzompantli*

The restoration of a building located at 24 calle Guatemala, in the Historic Centre of Mexico City in 2015, gave PAU the opportunity to carry out an archaeological intervention. Just before the end of this research phase, a surprising discovery was made. The appearance of dozens of fragments of human skulls and a circular wall also made of skulls associated with the remains of a Mexica platform located at the southern end of the historic building, confirmed to archaeologists that they had unearthed the *Huei Tzompantli* ("Wall, Row or Banner of Heads" in Nahuatl,) that some historical accounts claim was dedicated to Huitzlilopochtli, the divine protector and Mexica god of the sun and war (Matos Moctezuma et al. 2017).

As a result of this important discovery for Mexican archaeology a second season of excavations was proposed. On this occasion, excavations focused on exploring the circular wall of skulls and defining the architectural characteristics of the platform on which, according to historical sources, the skulls of those sacrificed in the Templo Mayor and those decapitated during the Ball Game were exhibited. This new season took place between 2016 and 2017 (Barrera 2018a).

From the progress of the investigations so far, we know that this platform was low, north-south facing and perhaps consisted of two stacked architectural bodies. The walls that give it its shape were made with ashlars of volcanic rock and have a stucco coating on their façades. The remains of the first architectural body are 70 cm high. As of the present, three construction stages have been identified, which were possibly concurrent with stages IVb (1469–1481), V (1481–1486) and VI (1486–1502) of the Templo Mayor at Tenochtitlan. In the last two construction stages, there is evidence of a total of four levels of stucco floors made of lime and tezontle (ground volcanic rock), which leads us to believe that each of the floors was remodelled at least once during each construction stage. The floor of the penultimate stage has a series of circular holes which are 25 cm in diameter and are positioned at 80 cm linear intervals, where wooden posts or beams supported sticks from which skulls pierced through the temporal and parietal lobes were suspended. The overall dimensions of the platform are still unknown; however we can assume that it must be between 36 or 40 metres long by about 14 or 16 metres wide. (Barrera 2018b).

As for the circular wall or tower of skulls glued together with lime and clay that was located at the northern end of the platform, it would appear they were arranged row upon row in a sequence of concentric circles; in some rows the skulls have been positioned facing toward the centre of the circle while others are facing toward the outside. Although excavations have focused on the third part of the skull tower, archaeologists have discovered that it is 4.70 metres in diameter.

This architectural feature should originally have been taller, protruding well above the surface of the platform of the building, perhaps reaching a height of 4 or 5 metres. The destruction of this skull tower by the Spaniards during the conquest of Tenochtitlan and in the first years of the viceroyalty means that only part of this circular skull tower, which measures between 1.25 metres and 1.80 metres in height and has an approximate thickness of 1.60 metres, was preserved until today.

As evidenced in physical anthropology studies, 10,577 skull fragments unearthed in the first season of archaeological excavations have been counted and analysed. They were associated with the filling during the last stage of construction of the platform and with the basalt floors that surround it, as well as with the filling during the early viceroyalty. The number of fragments has made it possible to determine that they correspond to a minimum number of 221 individuals.

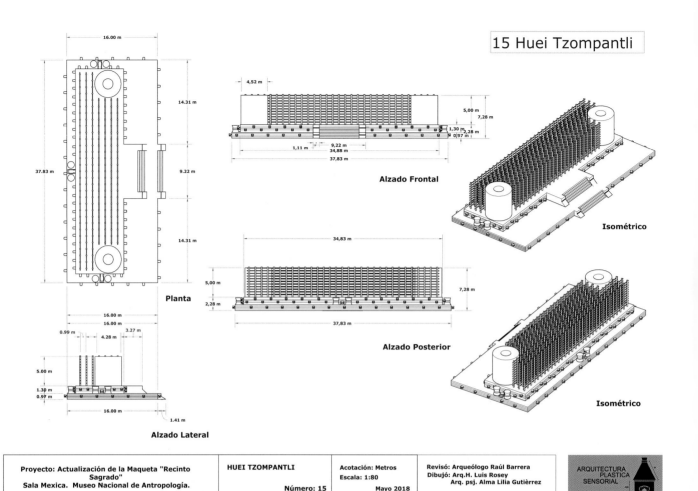

15 Huei Tzompantli

16.00 m

14.31 m

37.83 m

9.22 m

14.31 m

Planta

4,52 m

5,00 m
7,28 m
1,30 m
2,28 m
0,97 m

1,11 m
9,22 m
34,88 m
37,83 m

Alzado Frontal

34,83 m

5,00 m

2,28 m

7,28 m

37,83 m

Alzado Posterior

Isométrico

Isométrico

16.00 m
16.00 m
0.99 m
4.28 m
3.27 m

5.00 m

1.30 m
0.97 m

16.00 m

1.41 m

Alzado Lateral

Proyecto: Actualización de la Maqueta "Recinto Sagrado" Sala Mexica. Museo Nacional de Antropología.	HUEI TZOMPANTLI	Acotación: Metros Escala: 1:80	Revisó: Arqueólogo Raúl Barrera Dibujó: Arq.H. Luis Rosey Arq. psj. Alma Lilia Gutièrrez
	Número: 15	Mayo 2018	

ARQUITECTURA PLASTICA SENSORIAL

Fig. 4 ⌃
Plan of the *Huei Tzompantli*

Drawing: Raúl Barrera Rodríguez

Fig. 5 ◂
The Tower of Skulls

Photo: Oliver Santana

Fig. 7 ▲
Three skulls embedded in
the Tower of Skulls

Photo: Oliver Santana

These fragments showed signs of intentional deformation of the crania (tabular erect, tabular oblique and superior flattening) and at least 845 fragments of parietal, frontal, occipital and maxillary bones show signs of differential weathering. In 188 of these cases it has been possible to spot the typical bilateral perforation of the skulls so they could be placed in the *Tzompantli*. Cutting marks were also detected, consisting of skinning in order to remove the skin and then remove the muscle masses. Only in 15 cases was the possibility of heat treatment observed.

Regarding the circular wall of skulls, 179 such walls have been found and extracted. They were intact but very fragmented due to the destruction of the *Huei Tzompantli* during the Spanish conquest. Although we do not know the exact number of skulls that would have comprised this tower in an archaeological context, it is estimated that in the excavated section (the third part), there must be approximately one thousand skulls, most of which, it has been observed, correspond to young male adults and a handful of female adults, as well as some infants.

Fig. 8 ▶
The PAU team at work under
the direction of Raúl Barrera
Rodríguez

Photo: Ignacio Urquiza

Andrés de Tapia, who was one of the Spanish soldiers who accompanied Hernán Cortés during the conquest of Mexico-Tenochtitlan, left behind a detailed description of the *Huei Tzompantli* at Tenochtitlan:

"Opposite this tower there were sixty or seventy very high timbers, stuck in the ground, as far from the tower as a crossbow shot, atop a great theatre, made of lime and stone, which on its steps had many heads of the dead stuck together with lime, with their teeth sticking outward. On either side of these timbers, there were two towers made of lime and the heads of the dead with their teeth sticking outward and no other stone, as far as one could see; the timbers were separated from one another by little less than a measuring rod, and from top to the bottom as many sticks as would fit were placed between them, on each stick there were five heads of the dead strung by the temples: he who writes this and Gonzalo of Umbría counted the sticks, and multiplying each of the sticks between each timber by five heads, found there to be one hundred and thirty-six thousand heads, without counting those of the towers" (Tapia 2008).

Figs. 9
View of the excavations of the ball court

Photo: Raúl Barrera Rodríguez

We continue to believe the number of skulls that Andrés de Tapia and Gonzalo de Umbría claim were on display in the *Huei Tzompantli* to be exaggerated. What we do know from historical sources and now through archaeological findings is that the skulls that were exhibited on the palisade were taken down after some time and affixed to either of the two skull towers described by Andrés de Tapia.

The ball court or *Teotlachco*

In works carried out in the year 2014 at 16 calle Guatemala, the remains of the north side of the ball court or *Teotlachco* "the game of the gods", described by Fray Bernardino de Sahagún (1999), were discovered in the same lot where in 2010 the back of the Temple of Ehecatl Quetzalcoatl was discovered (Barrera 2018a).

With regard to the context, it is worth mentioning that since the beginning of the twentieth century some evidence of the ball court had already been found. During waterworks under calle Guatemala, a deep ditch was opened that allowed the archaeologist Leopoldo Batres to carry out an archaeological rescue, in which an altar consisting of five stone balls 15 cm in diameter, one of which was painted blue and another painted red, were discovered behind the Metropolitan Cathedral. (Batres 1990). In 1967, when line 2 of the Metro was being built, the then Archeological Salvage Department intervened by locating an altar containing nine stone models depicting two ball games and two balls (one white and the other black obsidian), as well as various musical instruments very close to the area explored by Batres. Meanwhile, between 1991 and 1997, PAU reported the discovery of the end of the ball court and rubber offerings as well as other objects by the Capilla de Ánimas.

The 2014 excavations, which continued in 2016 and 2017, revealed an east-west facing platform, with three monuments whose construction stages may coincide with stages V (1481–1486), VI (1486–1502) and VII (1502–1521) of the Templo Mayor. The penultimate stage, which is the best preserved, is approximately 9 metres wide and is located 6.45 metres south of Ehecatl's temple. The excavation work also uncovered two overlapping

Fig. 10
One of the embankments within the ball court

Photo: Raúl Barrera Rodríguez

Fig. 11 ▲
Front view of the temple of
Ehecatl-Quetzalcoatl

Photo: Raúl Barrera
Rodríguez

Fig. 13 ▶
Miniature model of a Temple
of Ehecatl-Quetzalcoatl

Nationaal Museum van
Wereldculturen (cat. 49)

staircases, with their respective benches on the north side. These staircases are built into platforms measuring under one metre in height respectively (Barrera 2018b).

At the foot of one of these staircases an altar containing human neck vertebrae that still retained their anatomical position were found. These corresponded to 32 individuals (children and young people). The other end of the platform (south side) is formed by the superposition of three sloping stucco walls, the wall of the penultimate stage of construction measures 1.95 metres in height. In its upper part there are the remains of benches, and a stucco floor with holes for wooden posts. In later excavations, the remains of a staircase that we believe to be associated with the western end of the ball court, through which the players entered the court, was found at the north side of the ball court. This staircase was generally east-west facing, and thus in line with the Huitzilopochtli shrine in the Templo Mayor.

We know that during the feast of *Panquetzaliztli* dedicated to Huitzilopochtli, god of war, sacrifices of captives were made during the *Teotlachco*:

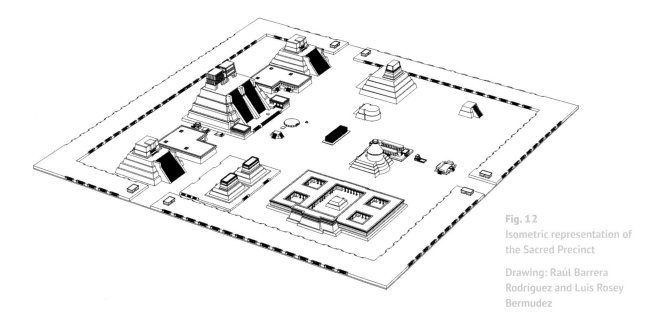

Fig. 12
Isometric representation of
the Sacred Precinct

Drawing: Raúl Barrera
Rodríguez and Luis Rosey
Bermudez

"And at dawn, before the sun had even completely risen, they summoned the god Páinal from the top of the hill of Huitzilopochtli, and then went straight to the ball court that was in the middle of the courtyard, which they called *Teotlachco*; ...– there they killed four captives, two in honour of the god Amapan and two in honour of the god Oappatzan, whose statues were next to the tlachco; once the captives were dead they were dragged along the tlachco – bloodying the ground as they were dragged along-...". (Sahagún 1999).

The temple of Ehecatl-Quetzalcoatl

In the lot located at 16 calle República de Guatemala, between 2009 and 2010, the PAU discovered a section of the temple of Ehecatl-Quetzalcoatl (God of the Wind). The building has many levels and consists of a rectangular platform containing two structures measuring approximately 34 metres from north to south, with an 18-metre diameter circular platform at the rear. It has not yet been possible to determine its east-west extension, since part of its main façade that faces east remains hidden beneath the surrounding buildings.

These initial works confirmed that the Temple of Ehecatl is in front of and aligned with the chapel of Tlaloc in the Templo Mayor (Matos Moctezuma and Barrera 2011). Although it must have different construction stages, so far, three have been identified that were simultaneous with stages V

Fig. 14
The PAU team at work on the
excavation of the Temple of
Ehecatl-Quetzalcoatl

Photo: Raúl Barrera
Rodríguez

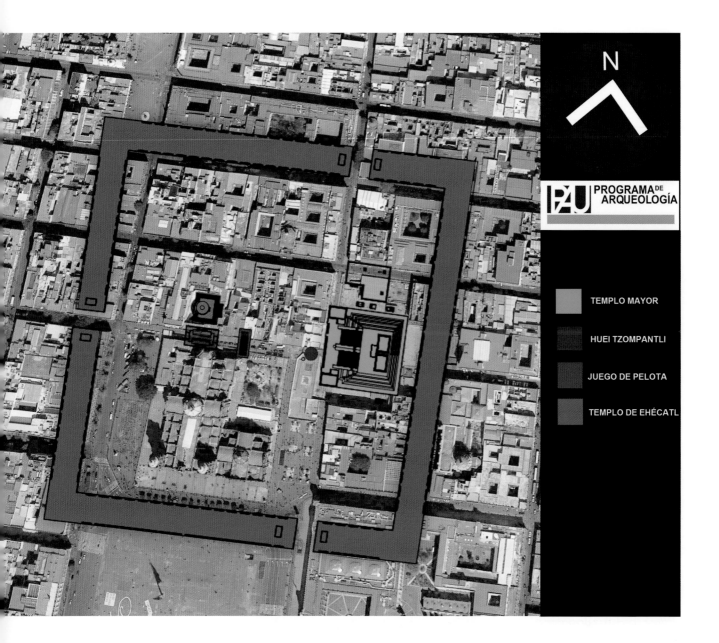

N

PROGRAMA DE
ARQUEOLOGÍA

TEMPLO MAYOR

HUEI TZOMPANTLI

JUEGO DE PELOTA

TEMPLO DE EHÉCATL

Fig. 15
Plan of the Sacred Precinct

Drawing: Raúl Barrera
Rodríguez and Luis Rosey
Bermudez

(1481–1486 AD), VI (1486–1502 AD) and VII (1502–1521 AD) of the Templo Mayor (Barrera 2014).

In a third season of excavation activities carried out between 2016 and 2017, the liberation and restoration of almost all of the two semi-circular architectural structures attached to the back of the platform continued. Both architectural structures, which measure almost 3 metres in height, have an imposing air as they loom from their base consisting of a floor of basalt slabs in a large courtyard surrounding the base platform of the Temple of Ehecatl (Barrera 2018a).

Some sixteenth-century sources refer to temples dedicated to the god of wind and his powers. Diego Durán (1995) and Fray Juan de Torquemada (1986) describe it as a high basement that served as a base for a round building with a conical thatched roof whose entrance resembled the jaws of a snake. The reason why it faces east is surely due to its relationship with the story of the birth of the Fifth Sun in Teotihuacan, when the gods asked where the star would go. Xipe and Ehecatl were the ones who said it would be in the east: "But some stared over there toward the course of the red colour, the east. They said, 'Truly from there, from there the sun will rise.' It was true what those who looked there said, who pointed in that direction with their fingers. As it is said, the ones who were looking over there were Quetzalcoatl, the second was Ehecatl and Tótec, that is, the Lord of Anáhuatl and Red Tezcatlipoca". (*Códice Matritense del Real Palacio* 1983).

Comments

The discovery of the *Huei Tzompantli,* the Temple of Ehecatl-Quetzalcoatl and the Ball Court represent a great opportunity, although the existence of the latter had already been verified since the previous century. Although it has not been possible to uncover these Mexica buildings entirely, as they lie buried under the buildings of the Historic Centre of Mexico City, we believe their relationship to the sacred grounds of the Templo Mayor of Tenochtitlan and the fact that they were located within these grounds, to be extremely important. The *Huei Tzompantli* and the ball court are believed to be on an east-west axis that coincides with the shrine to Huitzilopochtli, god of war, in the Templo Mayor. The Temple of Ehecatl-Quetzalcoatl, meanwhile, is also located on an east-west axis that coincides with the shrine to Tlaloc, god of rain and fertility of the earth, which was in the upper part of the Templo Mayor. The link between these buildings and the main temple of the Mexica denotes a complex ritual landscape that will allow us in-depth insight into aspects such as the religion, myths and cosmovision of the Mexica. ⌐

Fig. 16
Stone sculpture of the god Ehecatl-Quetzalcoatl

Rautenstrauch-Joest-Museum, Cologne, donation of Peter and Irene Ludwig (cat. 140)

Maarten E.R.G.N. Jansen and Gabina Aurora Pérez Jiménez

Sacrifice in Ancient Mexico

According to Meso-American religion the universe is a complex, living landscape in which multiple animated entities and divine beings dwell, interact and manifest themselves. Humans are dependent upon these superior creative forces of nature for their health, well-being and survival. The powers of the sun and other astral bodies, the rain, mountains, stone formations, water, wind, fire, plants and other life-giving elements are divine and addressed with respect, as well as the deceased ancestors and the principles that orient and animate human society. Animals but also artefacts are part of this animated universe. Through metaphorical speech and ritual acts the humans invoke these beings, all with their specific names, and cultivate a spiritual relation with this 'Other World', a covenant of cooperation, reciprocity and mutual care. As the divine powers nurture the humans, especially through agriculture, so the humans have to express their gratefulness through worship with pious service and offerings.

Offerings could include the first fruits of the harvest or hunt, as well as specially prepared meals and drinks, but also precious artefacts, all accompanied, of course, by prayers and diverse forms of veneration, which would normally include processions, pilgrimages, chants, music and dance. Slashing the throat of quails, lighting fire, scattering ground tobacco (*piciete*) in the air and burning incense (*copal*) were often the central acts. Today such ingredients continue to be part of traditional ritual in the form of chickens, candles, cigars and of course incense (Jansen and Pérez 2017).

Most valuable, however, was the gift of some of the personal life force through bloodletting, as a true bodily expression of devotion and conscious connection to the sacred powers that surround us (Baudez 2012; Graulich 2005b). This was a form of self-sacrifice, performed by the perforation of body parts such as tongue, ear or intimate parts with a pointed bone or maguey spine. The blood would be captured on leaves or feathers, or flow into the maw of the earth. The libation of drops of blood as well as spilling a little of an alcoholic beverage (*pulque*) seem to have been a frequent and common act of daily religiosity. A more intense and mystic aspect, however, was the combination of this act with prolonged fasting and vigil as well as with the consumption of hallucinogenic seeds, snuff or mushrooms. This was bound to provoke visionary experiences and so a direct mental contact

Fig. 1 ◄
Personified "sacrificial knife"

Museo del Templo Mayor, Mexico City, D.R. Secretaría de Cultura – INAH. (cat. 124c)

with the 'Other World', a touch of the sacred which would have a profound impact on the individual. Ancient Meso-American art offers many examples of rulers and priests performing this ritual at important occasions such as the inauguration of a temple or an enthronement ceremony, often in front of Sacred Bundles, which contained the relics of ancestors. The visionary experience is then represented as a large serpent rising from darkness and encircling the penitent, possibly speaking to him or her in an oracle.

Many elements of ancient Meso-American ritual art are to be understood
in the context of such a religious trance as symbolic representations of
devotional experiences and related concepts. The serpent, for example, is a
symbol of the mysterious (sometimes also dangerous) part of earth (nature):
in pictography the open jaws of a serpent represent a cave, an entrance to
darkness and the 'Other World'. Darkness itself, in combination with wind,
represents the mysterious essence of the gods.

A famous Aztec sculpture is the statue of the goddess Coatlicue, "She with the Skirt of Serpents" (Pasztory 1983; Matos Moctezuma and López Luján 2012). Her name and her representation as being surrounded by many serpents evoke in Meso-American terms a metaphoric image of Mother Earth. She wears a necklace consisting of hearts and hands, which, as we know from a colonial source, are to be read as "a sign that meant that with their hands and heart they asked for a good harvest, because it was already the time…" (Durán 1967, Ritos: ch. 16). In other words: the goddess's necklace of hands and hearts is not to be taken literally but symbolises a Meso-American prayer.

Similarly we find that artistic representations of skulls and bones do not stand for killings or macabre acts, but are pictorial references to the (deceased) ancestors, very much as they are still today in the images of the Mexican Days of the Dead. In line with such imagery, we may venture to interpret the scene of a god ripping out an eye of a human not in a literal sense but rather symbolically as the impact of the mystic encounter: the deity overpowers the individual and takes away his or her cognitive capacity.

Eyes and faces qualify natural elements, mountains, and plants but also artefacts as being alive and animated. Blood and heart are a logical metaphor for life, sustenance and off-spring. Thus we find, for example, corncobs represented as human heads, the harvest of new corncobs being a form of decapitation, while the old corncobs of the past year are painted as skulls. Similarly, the cutting down of a tree to make firewood is like killing it, taking its heart (life) out. It is important to be aware of this layer of metaphors and figures of speech in pictorial writing, which had a particular need to represent abstract notions through concrete iconic images. When the Spanish colonisers looked at Aztec art, however, they were horrified: to their mind the many serpents were references to the devil; things with eyes and faces, as well as other unfamiliar combinations, evoked images of demons, while skulls and bones made them think of hell. The sculptures of deities, of course, were to them already clear proof of idolatry. Severed heads and hands, ripped out eyes, blood etc. were indications of massacres, torture and cruelty. Such early intercultural misunderstandings have haunted the interpretation of pre-colonial art until today.

This brings us to the famous but complex topic of human sacrifice, which is generally presented as emblematic of Aztec culture and Meso-American civilisation in general (Graulich 2005a; López Luján and Olivier 2009). The custom was reported in abundant detail by Spanish authors and explicitly identified as "sacrifice" already in their earliest references. The first reports are those of the conquistador Hernán Cortés himself, elucidated further by the work of Bernal Díaz del Castillo, who participated in the conquest but wrote his work much later from memory.
The idea that human sacrifice was practised in Meso-America actually already emerged before the campaign of Cortés, namely during the earlier incursion led by Grijalva (1518), as reported by Bernal Díaz:

"We found two houses, which were strongly built of stone and lime; both were ascended by a flight of steps, and surmounted by a species of altar, on which stood several abominable idols, to whom, the previous evening, five Indians had been sacrificed. Their dead bodies still lay there, ripped open, with the arms and legs chopped off, while everything near was besmeared with blood. We contemplated this sight in utter astonishment, and gave this island the name of Isla de Sacrificios" (Díaz del Castillo 1844, *Memoirs*, ch. 13).

Bernal Díaz states that he himself saw the dismembered bodies, but he did not see the act itself. At a later similar occasion an interrogation through signs (without interpreters) made the Spaniards think that the killing was a sacrifice that had happened on the orders of the Aztecs who would become the main adversary once the expedition of Cortés was under way. Thus we find here the beginning of an argument that the human sacrifices were an imposition of the Aztec empire (and therefore not something the local population really wanted to do). Later on, Bernal Díaz and other authors would stress that the practice of human sacrifice was widespread, continuous and directly related to anthropophagy, confirming that this practice took place first and foremost in the Aztec capital (Tenochtitlan) and that the Aztec ruler Motecuhzoma (also written as Moctezuma or Montezuma) had himself a daily routine of sacrificing people and consuming human flesh.
There are several reasons to doubt the veracity of the Spanish accounts in this respect. Due to fanciful medieval literature about "strange peoples" in distant lands, the conquistadors and missionaries were expecting to encounter

Fig. 3 ◄
Personified "sacrificial knives": stone knives with eyes, teeth and painted facial features which allow them to appear like living beings, manifestations of certain gods. Hitherto they have usually been described as "sacrificial knives" that were used to kill people, but there is no evidence of this. These objects may have been used as revered items and/or as offerings in order to invoke the divine power of the stone knives during certain rituals.

Museo del Templo Mayor, Mexico City, D.R. Secretaría de Cultura – INAH (cat. 124a–c)

Fig. 4 ▶

Codex Yoalli Ehecatl (Borgia), p. 33: Ritual ceremonies in and around the great Temple of Heaven, which is filled with divine powers. The gable of the temple roof is connected with the sun (borne by a stag) and the moon (carried by a rabbit).

At the front (top left), a priest is dancing on a round stone (altar) and frees the flaming spirits who run off towards the four points of the compass.

Thereafter, represented under the altar scene, two priests who serve the god Quetzalcoatl and the god of love Tlahuizcalpantecuhtli, are sacrificing the heart of a tree spirit on an altar. That means, they kill (fell) a tree (original colour green), in order to have fuel for the ceremonial centre. Above them on the right stands a person with raised hands who was originally also green and who probably symbolises a prayer for the tree god.

At the entrance to the temple stands a round altar, on which the god Xipe Totec (Lord of the Skin, protector of slash-and-burn agriculture) is covered with woven fabric (which means he will be made into a Sacred Bundle). In the interior of the temple we can see the priest of Quetzalcoatl once more: aided by the priest of Tlahuizcalpantecuhtli, he performs an act of self-sacrifice by piercing his tongue with an agave thorn. These ritual ceremonies took place in the Aztec month of Tozoztontli ("bloodletting").

abhorrent customs. At the same time they were in the grip of late medieval demonology (witchcraze) and saw themselves in a "crusade" against the devil. These preconceived notions clouded their observations and interpretations, the more so as their descriptions of human sacrifice are not eyewitness accounts but texts produced later during the colonial period, based on hearsay and imagination, often with a Eurocentric bias. Allegations of irrational killing and cannibalism served to stigmatise the native peoples as barbarians, who had to be subjugated in order to be civilised, Christianised and saved. This was the ultimate justification of conquest and colonisation (Arens 1979; Isaac 2002; Sued Badillo 1978).

Visual representations leave no doubt that the killing of individuals did occur in Meso-America, as in many other societies. Actually, there existed several forms of such acts, stabbing in the chest being one. In those cases the image may show the extraction of the heart, but it is difficult to tell whether this really refers to the removal of the heart (which is not a very easy operation) or was just a pictorial way to express the taking of a life. People could also be killed in "gladiatorial combat" (fighting superior armed warriors), by being shot with javelins, by decapitation or lapidation. The contexts of such scenes may be religiously charged by the location in front of a temple with a divine

image or Sacred Bundle, the use of an altar, and/or the adornment with
special attributes of consecration (e.g. down balls). But this religious dimen-
sion seems more the consequence of the idea that a life that was taken had
to return to the creator deities that had given it (Olivier 2015). The context
indicates that these acts were not motivated by a wish to make sacrifices per
se, but were mainly the consequence of military activities (the executions of
prisoners of war), of the implementation of justice (capital punishment for
criminals) or even of political murder (for critical views of Western interpretations concerning Aztec human sacrifice see Graham and Golson 2006;
Graham in press; Gunsenheimer 2011; Hassler 1992).

It is easy to see how such killings were convoluted in the eyes of non-
informed hostile outsiders (the Spanish conquistadors and missionaries)
with the self-sacrificial bloodletting and with the sacrifice of animals that
was customary in Meso-American civilisation: the early colonial sources do
not distinguish clearly between these practices and what they called human
sacrifice. Consequently, the frequency of the bloodletting ritual and other
offerings could be projected onto the ritualised death penalties and executions, so that a propagandistic image of continuous cruel butchering could
be constructed.

Although the killing of criminals and enemies would not have been uncommon in ancient Meso-America, it most likely occurred on a much smaller
scale than the numbers mentioned by the colonial authors suggest. Reviewing
the evidence, we conclude that instead of speaking about "human sacrifice"
it might be better to use a term like "ritualised execution", or, as Elizabeth
Graham has suggested, "socially sanctioned killing". ⌐

Fig. 6
Slit drum *teponatzli*. The carved motif on the two-tone drum is recorded in the
style of the Codices. It shows two people in bird costumes who sing and dance
as they move around a ceremonial object, depositing thorns for blood
sacrifices. On both sides we can see the sign for "Flower and Song" (*in xochitl,
in cuicatl*), the Nahuatl expression for very fine songs or ceremonial discourse.

Museum der Kulturen Basel (cat. 103)

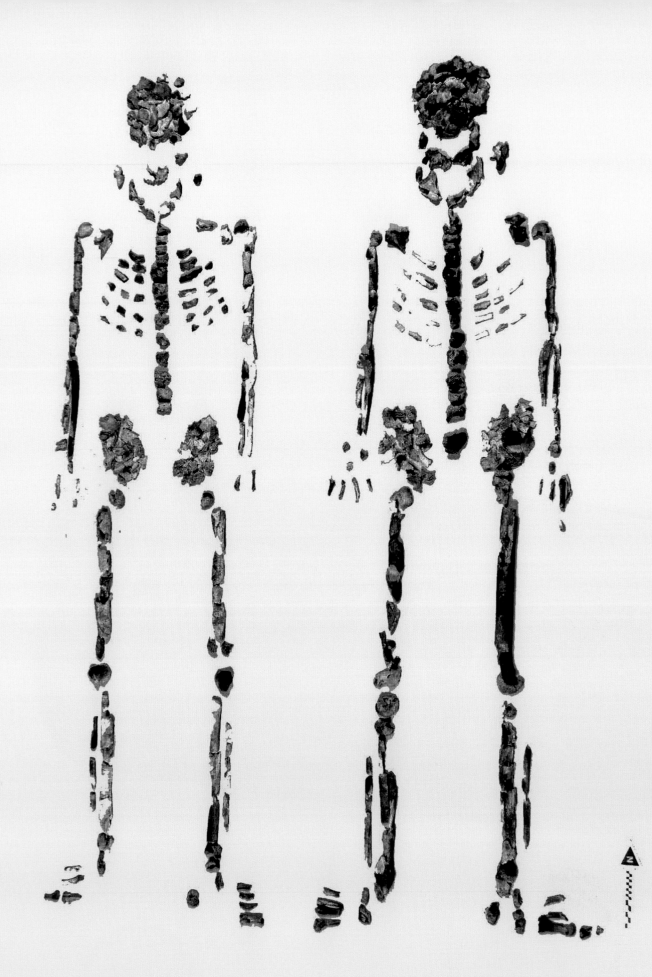

Ximena Chávez Balderas

Bioarchaeology at the Sacred Precinct of Tenochtitlan

The skeletal remains found at the Sacred Precinct of Tenochtitlan reveal the complexity of Mexica treatment of the human body. They correspond to two types of rituals: funeral rites and ritual death, although it is possible that the two overlap. Funeral rites were performed following the death of an individual and were designed to dispose of the corpse, offer a time of mourning and, on a symbolic level, help the immaterial part of the body reach the afterlife. Ritual death, for their part, involved the offering of human life: the ceremony was not performed as a consequence of death but to establish communication with the gods.

With respect to funerals, seven graves of Mexica dignitaries have been identified at the Templo Mayor, the House of Eagles and Building I (Chávez Balderas 2007, López Luján 2005, Román Berrelleza and López Luján 1994). These dignitaries were cremated and their bones were buried in containers. Not everyone received the same funeral treatment since the latter depended on their identity, occupation and cause of death. By analysing these remains I have been able to identify three different types of cremation. The first is represented by the remains of two people who were burned on individual pyres made of wooden sticks along with a very small number of funeral items; these fires did not last long or did not reach high temperatures. The cremated bones were collected by hand and even the smallest of fragments was recovered. These fragments were deposited in two orange ceramic urns bearing the reliefs of the gods Tezcatlipoca and Mixcóatl dressed as warriors and were buried in the vicinity of the defeated goddess Coyolxauhqui. These remains are of male adults who had walked great distances and worked hard with their forearms, which modified their muscle structure. It is possible that they were warriors, as suggested by Matos Moctezuma (1989) and previously by this author (Chávez Balderas 2007, 2017). The second type of cremation corresponds to two elite individuals buried at the top of the Templo Mayor. Their individual pyres reached very high temperatures and so their bones were extremely fragmented. A small part of the remains of each was divided into two containers that were buried in the most important part of Tenochtitlan: at the foot of the effigy of Huitzilopochtli, along with some funeral items that were burned and others that were intact. It is not known where the

Fig. 1 ◄

Remains of bones from two burned bodies which were removed from the interior of the *ofrendas* 10 and 14. They came from two adult males.

With the kind permission of Proyecto Templo Mayor
Photo: German Zuniga

Fig. 2
Funerary urns of the *ofrendas* 10 and 14. One is decorated with the image of the god Tezcatlipoca and the other with the image of the god Mixcoatl. They contained the remains of burned human bodies.

With the kind permission of Proyecto Templo Mayor
Photo: Mirsa Islas

remaining bones were taken. These graves could correspond to early Mexica rulers, but we do not have sufficient artefacts to confirm their identity. Finally, offerings 3 and V, as they are known, are two sides of the same coin. In each of them, a body was cremated at high temperatures along with luxury items; the remains were collected when they had been reduced to embers and were divided into several containers. The remains of one of these individuals were buried in offering V, while the residues of the fuel from the pyre, sumptuous funeral items and a few bone fragments were deposited in Offering 3.

Most evidence of ritual death is found in the West Square, the Cuauhxicalco, the Huei Tzompantli, the Calmécac and the Ball Game courts. This strip runs from the southern half of the Templo Mayor to the western limit of the site. These findings consist mainly of skulls, although some bones and thousands of bone fragments with cut marks, signs of boiling and perimortem fractures have been discovered. Historical sources suggest that most were killed by cutting out the heart, slitting the throat or starvation; throwing people from heights or shooting them with arrows were also used as means of torture or forms of killing. Although not all of these techniques leave traces on bones, evidence of removing hearts from two humans and three animals has been collected. Although there are few examples of this, it should be remembered that only the heads of decapitated victims were kept at the sacred site, while their bodies were taken to the *calpulli* or the lake. Toribio "Motolinía" Benavente (1967:62), Bartolomé de las Casas (1967, II:192) and Bernardino de Sahagún (2000, II:240) confirm this in their writings. Historical records have stated that victims were killed in ceremonies performed according to the calendar and during special rituals, such as coronations or funerals. Most were decapitated by removing the neck vertebrae with stone tools, a relatively slow procedure. Some heads were immediately buried in sacred offerings at the Templo Mayor. However, a large number had all or some flesh removed to achieve a skeletal appearance. Some may have been transformed into breast plates or effigies of the gods, but most were perforated on either side so they could be hung from the palisades of skulls (*tzompantli*). Skulls were displayed on these palisades until they were brought down to be reused in the offerings of the Templo Mayor, in other rituals, or to be stored in the towers that flanked the *Huei Tzompantli*; these were recently discovered by the Urban Archaeology Program.

So, who were these victims? They were mostly adult men, although some were women, adolescents and children. Isotope studies have revealed a very peculiar pattern: most of the individuals analysed spent the last years of their lives in Tenochtitlan, that is to say, they were not brought there after a conquest and immediately killed. With the exception of children dedicated to

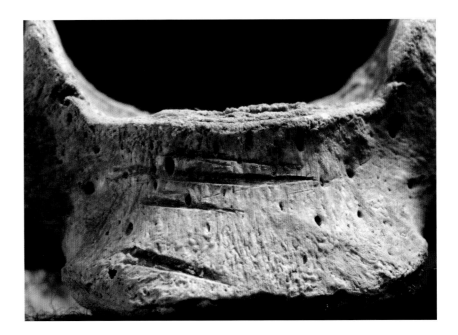

Fig. 3
Cervical vertebra with incision marks from a beheading carried out with a cutting tool

With the kind permission of Proyecto Templo Mayor
Photo: Jesús López

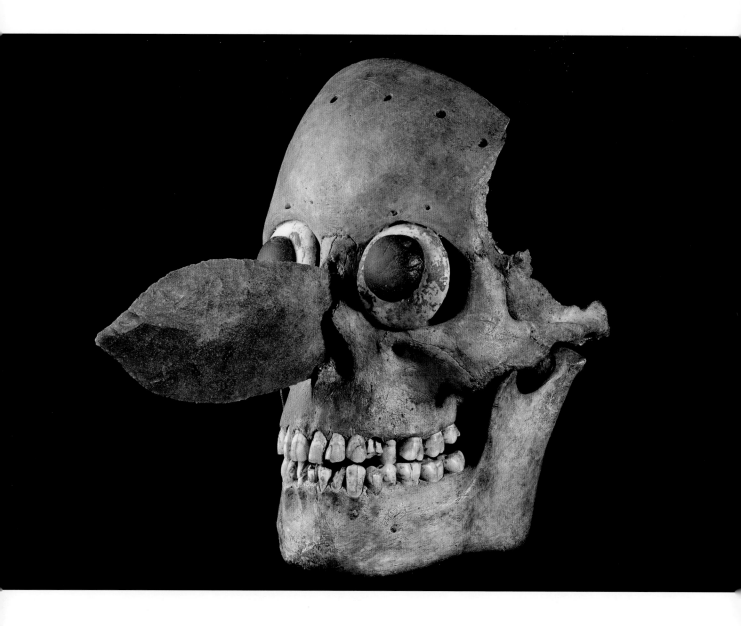

Tlaloc, their state of health is as expected for pre-Hispanic populations (Barrera 2016, Chávez Balderas 2017, Moreiras and Longstaffe 2018, Román Berrelleza 1990). The diversity of victims allows to conclude that they were mainly slaves, captive warriors, individuals offered as tribute and others as the spoils of war. The type of victim would be chosen depending on the occasion. The question arises as to how many individuals were killed, and although we have tangible evidence of this practice, it is clear that they were not as common as reported by chroniclers who did not actually witness these ceremonies. The archaeological evidence recovered by the Templo Mayor

Project and the Urban Archaeology Program has so far allowed us to identify roughly 1,000 individuals, although there are still more to be counted. The active participation of researchers from both projects and the new techniques available make the future analysis of human remains from the sacred site of Tenochtitlan both promising and fruitful. ⌐

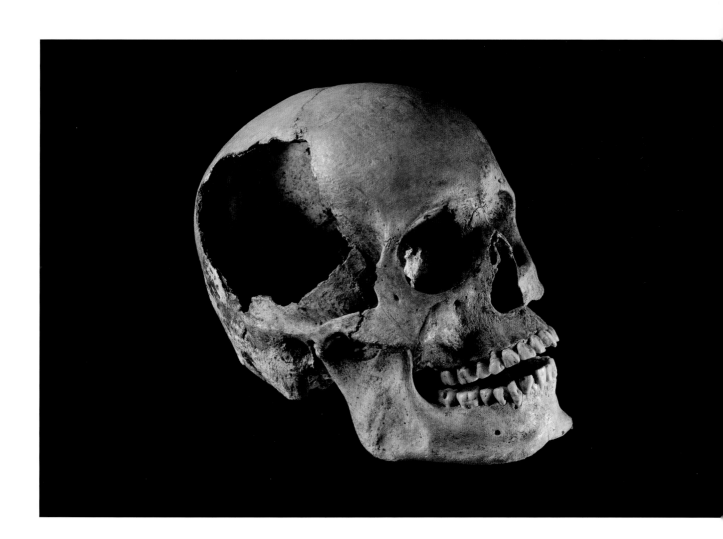

Raul Macuil Martínez

Nican tiistoque! ("Here we are!")

For centuries, indigenous peoples have suffered deep-seated discrimination and marginalisation at the hands of a monolingual Spanish-speaking
society, with our ritual life being stigmatized as the work of the devil, our
sacred sites described as places of evil, and our traditions denigrated as beliefs
and "Indian things". For centuries, those responsible for preserving ritual life
have been called witches, sorcerers, charlatans, ignorant, traditional doctors
or "witch" rather than sages, which is the name they are given in a great
number of indigenous languages.

In the Mexican or Nahuatl language, the word used to describe someone who
cares for and protects the community, both physically and psychologically, is
tlamatqui ("wise"). For hundreds of years these people have cherished the
sacred and florid words in their hearts and on their lips, the *xochitlahtolli*, and
have been marginalised and labelled as ignorant or sorcerers by a society that
refuses to see their inherent cultural richness since it is considered backward
and an obstacle to progress.

The community

Our peoples have always lived in communities. Their solidarity, friendship
and verbal commitment can be seen in community rituals, which can be
very expensive. Community leaders are responsible for managing economic
resources with government bodies, while the rest of the community is
organised into commissions to collect money from community members or
to store surplus maize, chili, squash and beans to be sold or exchanged for the
goods necessary for these rituals. This organisation serves as the foundation
of the community.

Walking with our own people and speaking to them in our own language
means we are little understood when entering the outside world, with
language being one of the main barriers to communication since the Nahua
world has been understood from a Spanish perspective. This is evidenced in
the extensive academic literature that ignores important and basic concepts:
for example, in referring to the wise members of the community as *shaman*,

Fig. 1 ◄
Doña Isabel Flores
sanctifies the first food
offering for Santa
Catarina by presenting
her with a goblet
containing burning
copal. The smoke
purifies and sanctifies
the offering (Santa
Catarina Acaxochitlan).

Photo: Raul Macuil
Martínez

Fig. 2
Women and children take
part in a procession during
the *novenario de difunto*, the
nine-day period of mourning
following the death of a
family member.

Photo: Raul Macuil Martínez

the names that the community itself has given them, such as *tlamatque* ("wise") and *tiachca* ("big brother"), are ignored. The latter word is used for the wise members of Tlaxcala who have offered their work and service to their communities. They are also known as "judges" (*fiscales*).

Nahua peoples divide time into a great cycle of rituals and community and family work. At the beginning of the new year, civil and religious community leaders are replaced. They are elected through assemblies held at sites representing the heart of the community, such as the plaza of the *xantocalli* ("house of the saint") or in the temple courtyards, depending on the customs of each community.

The authorities

These new authorities will receive "bastones" (staffs), also called "varas de mando" (staff of office), which are symbols of authority, work and service. These roles will be performed for a period of one year, the period in which they occupy the position. One of the primary community service positions in a large number of indigenous villages is that of police officers or *topiles*, used to integrate young people into community life. In this way, they serve the community, learning how it is organised and how it works, while discovering at first hand the symbolic value of the staff, which is not a symbol of power, but of service and respect.

Throughout the year, the delegates, "judges" or *tiachcauh*, will provide a reliable record of their work as leaders and in service and, when a "public" ritual is performed, the leaders carry their staffs. These figures are responsible for preserving and working for the common good, which is quite the opposite of what we see in urban life, where the interests of the individual override those of the collective.

It should also be noted that no money is received for holding these positions, and that, for a whole year, the delegates, *tiacha* or "judges", will work without remuneration to keep the community united by means of collaboration in the *tequio* or community labour, while strengthening family relations and friendship.

The eternal cycle: the ritual life of the community

Communities in the states of Hidalgo, Tlaxcala and Puebla have a calendar of rituals that must be adhered to by community members and leaders. This means that, throughout the year, these people occupy two different times: the ritual-sacred and that of their daily work. After the changing of local leaders and on February 2, the Day of the Candelaria, community members take selected seeds and grains, mainly maize, beans and squash, to mass.

Along with the blessing of the seeds and grains, the communities of Santa Catarina and Tochtla – in the state of Hidalgo – invite their friends or community members to be godparents in a ceremony referred to locally as *Sacamisa*. As part of this ceremony, young children up to the age of five are blessed as part of a Catholic Mass with the priest sprinkling holy water on their heads. The ceremony is necessary for the children of the community to grow strong and healthy, while the seeds and grains are expected to grow and yield maize, beans, and squash. In this way, both peoples secure their future.

The rituals performed by these communities are, to a great extent, intertwined with the Catholic religion, especially during the days of Holy Week or during the festival of their patron saint. Delegates, "judges" or *tiacha* offer food to the entire community, and the church façade and main altar are decorated. In these cases, it is immediately apparent how patron saints from colonial times have become the heart of these communities.

May 3 is dedicated to the Holy Cross. Indigenous people climb the hills to celebrate Catholic Mass and request that the forces that surround the communities bring the rain necessary for the fields to produce the crops they need. They also call for the intervention of Catholic saints. Here, both worlds come together and work for the good of the community. These worlds meet again during the final days of October and the first days of November, in the period

Fig. 5
Doña Paula Martínez Bartolo and Senovio Bartolo Vargas pray to the images of Santa Catarina and Christ. They are holding bowls of incense with copal in their honour (Santa Catarina Acaxochitlan).

Photo: Raul Macuil Martínez

called the *Xantolo*, *Micailhuitl* or the celebration of the Day of the Dead. This is, perhaps, one of the most important festivities for indigenous communities.

In the Huasteca region of Hidalgo, November 1 and 2 are a time of celebration, during which groups of dancers parade through the streets of local communities. In the privacy of their homes, families celebrate *Xantolo* by saving money for a long period of time so they can purchase items for their offerings. In the state of Tlaxcala and many communities of Puebla, the Day of the Dead is more solemn and not as festive as in the Huasteca. The deceased are remembered and are expected to arrive between October 27 and November 2. The *Xantolo, micailhuitl* or Day of the Dead is an encounter with ancestors and with the past. It is a time when the dead come to eat and drink with us. It is, therefore, a time when the protective forces of the communities, our ancestors and we ourselves come together in the same space and time.

The knowledge that has been transmitted from generation to generation for hundreds of years is in serious danger of disappearing as *modernity* considers community activities a product of fantasy due to their lack of scientific and academic weight. However, despite this, sages refuse to disappear, and they see the community as a unit that helps keep rituals alive.

We, the indigenous peoples, are duty bound to watch over, care for and ensure that our religious and ritual world passes on to the next generation. We must create specialized core groups within our communities that will provide us with a complementary vision of what has been written about our language, our culture and, above all, our ancestors and gods.

When society in general becomes aware of and recognises these community values and treats them as knowledge, then we will be very close to returning the due dignity that was wrested from our ancestors, from our grandmothers and grandfathers, and from our mothers and fathers.

In spite of all the difficulties we face, we say, "Nican tiistoque!" ("Here we are!") and that our culture is still alive. ⏎

Fig. 6
The images of Christ and
Santa Catarina receive the
food and drink offerings
dedicated to them (Santa
Catarina Acaxchitlan).

Photo: Raul Macuil Martínez

PRE-AZTEC
BEFORE 1000

AZTECS
CA. 1000 – 1521

CA. 2500 BC – 100 BC

Meso-America is a cultural area that includes parts of Mexico, Guatemala, Honduras, Belize and El Salvador. The first settled farmers appear around 2500 BC, the first supra-regional culture of the Olmec begin around 1500 BC, the Classic Maya around 250 BC.

800 – 1150 AD

Tula, the capital of the Toltec empire, reaches its highpoint between 900 and 1150 AD.

100 BC – 650 AD

Teotihuacan, "Seat of the Gods", is the capital of the largest early state in Meso-American history. It is considered sacred by the Aztecs. In it's heyday it has around 125,000 citizens.

1064
1 Tecpatl (Flint)*

The Aztec people leave their homeland in the North of Mexico guided by their patron god Huitzilopochtli.

1325
2 Calli (House)*

The Aztec capital of Tenochtitlan is founded on an island in Lake Texcoco. The site was chosen after the Aztecs found an eagle perched atop a cactus, as had been prophesied to them.

1487
8 Acatl (Reed)*

The fourth expansion of the Templo Mayor, the Great Temple of Tenochtitlan, is completed.

1428
1 Tecpatl (Flint)*

The Triple Alliance is formed consisting of Tenochtitlan and neighbouring city-states Texcoco and Tlacopan, giving the Aztecs two powerful allies.

1440–69
13 Tecpatl (Flint) – 3 Calli (House)*

Rule of Moctezuma I. He expands the Aztec empire as far as the Gulf Coast in the east and Oaxaca in the south.

* Aztec calendar

1096–1099

First crusade and conquering of Jerusalem

1271

Italian explorer Marco Polo departs for Asia

1347

The "Black Death" (the plaque) ravages Europe

1453

Fall of Constantinople and the end of the Byzantine Empire

1492

End of the reconquest of Spain from the Moors, referred to as "Reconquista"

Columbus arrives on the Island of Hispaniola in the Caribbean

VICEROYALTY OF NEW SPAIN
1521 – 1820

PRESENT-DAY MEXICO
FROM 1820

2019

About 25 million people in Mexico self-identify as indigenous. They speak indigenous languages, follow traditional customs and/or live in indigenous communities. Around 1.5 million people still speak Nahuatl, the language of the Aztecs. While many of them live in Mexico, an increasing number lives in the United States because of extensive migration.

1701

The Bourbons take over the reign of the Spanish monarchy from the Habsburgs.

1521
3 Calli (House)*

The Spanish conquer Tenochtitlan and thereby end the Aztec empire.

1550

Triggered by the reports of Brother Bartolomé de las Casas and others, the "Disputation of Valladolid" deals with the cruel treatment of indigenous peoples by the Spanish Empire. As a consequence, the "New Laws" are enacted, which, however, bring only limited improvements.

1836–1848

After numerous wars, Mexico loses former provinces of Texas, California, Nevada, New Mexico, Arizona and Utah to the United States.

2016

Pope Francis asks the indigenous peoples for forgiveness for the crimes committed against them 500 years ago.

1519
1 Acatl (Reed)*

Spanish conquistador Hernán Cortés arrives in Mexico.

1810

Miguel Hidalgo, a Mexican born priest with Spanish ancestors, pleads for the independence of Mexico. His rousing speech leads to the rebellion against Spain.

1820

Mexico becomes an independent federal republic after a 10 year war. It is the birth of the Mexican flag with the Aztec symbol as its center: an eagle sitting on a cactus eating a serpent.

1502
10 Tochtli (Rabbit)*

Moctezuma II. becomes ruler of the Aztec Empire. He is the ninth of the Aztec kings.

1535

Don Antonio de Mendoza becomes the first viceroy to rule New Spain. The most famous colonial codex is named after him.

1910–1920

The Mexican Revolution ends General Porfirio Diaz' dictatorship, also called Porfiriato, as portrayed in Diego Rivera's painting.

1516

Charles V becomes King of Spain and in 1519 Holy Roman Emperor

1517

Proclamation of Luther's theses, beginning of Reformation

1568–1648

Eighty Years' War or Dutch War of Independence against Spanish rule. The Netherlands win and become independent.

1789

Start of the French Revolution

Cat. no. 1
Mask

Greenstone
H: 16 cm; W: 14.5 cm
Mexico, Teotihuacan,
ca. 250 – 600 A.D.
Linden-Museum Stuttgart; Inv. no.
M 34079 L, Acquired with funding of
the Zentralfonds Baden-Württemberg
Photo: Dominik Drasdow

Teotihuacan was the centre
of one of the largest states in
Pre-Columbian Meso-America.
It was an important place for
the Aztecs, because according
to their mythology the sun and
the moon were created in this
magnificent city. Masks of this
type were produced on a large
scale in Teotihuacan. The Aztecs
carried out excavations at
Teotihuacan and placed the
objects they found in sacrificial
chests in order to offer them to
their gods. MB

Cat. no. 2
Mask

Greenstone
H: 14.5 cm; W: 12.5 cm
Mexico, Teotihuacan,
ca. 250 – 600 A.D.
Linden-Museum Stuttgart;
Inv. no. M 30268
Photo: Dominik Drasdow

Cat. no. 3
Carrier figure

Volcanic stone, pigment
H: 78.5 cm; B: 34.5 cm; D: 26 cm
Mexico, Tlaxcala, 1000–1500 AD
KHM-Museumsverband, Weltmuseum Wien, Inv. no. 59.144
Photo: KHM-Museumsverband

The Confederation of Tlaxcala made a significant contribution to the Spanish
victory over the Aztecs. Today the Mexican state of Tlaxcala continues to
emphasise its former relationship with the Spanish crown and the Habsburgs.
The monograms of the Spanish monarchs Isabel, Karl and Ferdinand and the
golden flag with the black eagle are depicted in the state coat of arms. According to the inhabitants of Tlaxcala, their ancestors defeated the Aztecs with the
assistance of Spain. Later, the Tlaxcaltecs helped Spain to (military?) success in
northern Mexico, Guatemala and the Philippines.
A plate, perhaps an altar or a bench, once lay on the raised hands of several
warrior sculptures like the one shown here. The back shield, the ribbons
around its arms and legs and the pointed "Toltec" loincloth identify the figure
as a victorious warrior, as do the arms raised to grab the hair of the beaten
opponent. Carrier figures were known from Tollan, the capital of the Toltecs
and residence of the legendary prince Quetzalcoatl. The Aztecs, Tlaxcaltecs
and their contemporaries collected items of this revered predecessor cult and
made objects in the Toltec style. Accordingly, a statue from Tollan was
worshipped in Tlaxcala. GvB

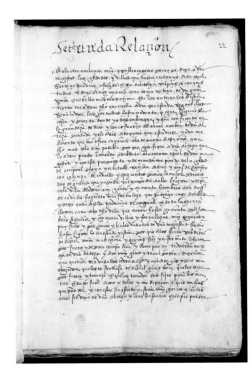

The Spanish conqueror Hernán Cortés wrote several so-called "Cartas de relación", which literally translated means "letter tales", and sent them to Emperor Charles V. These letters have been published several times and describe the conquest of the Aztec empire as well as life in Tenochtitlan.   DK

The desire for gold was the prime incentive for the invasion of the Americas by the Spanish. The individual soldiers wanted to become rich as quickly as possible, while at the same time the Spanish Crown needed resources in order to pursue their ongoing wars against the Protestant powers in Europe. Indigenous art objects were melted into bullion for transport to Europe. This particular gold ingot was probably lost by a Spanish soldier whilst fleeing from Tenochtitlan during the so-called "Noche Triste", 30 June 1520. MB

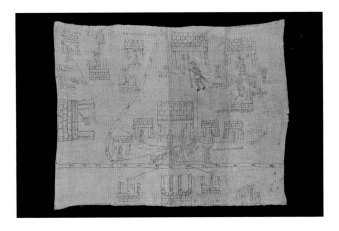

After the fall of the Aztec empire, local indigenous rulers attempted to maintain power. They created documents that showed their genealogy, establishing them as the rightful owners of their lands. The information was painted on *lienzos*, large cotton cloths. In accordance with pre-colonial traditions, they used a pictographic script combined with alphabetical glosses. This *lienzo* belonged to Don Juan Chichimecatecuhtli, a local lord from Tlaxcala. MB

Cat. no. 7
Greenstone figurine
with calendar signs

Serpentine
H: 34 cm; W: 17.5 cm; D: 7 cm
Mexico, Teotihuacan, 250 –750 A.D.,
re-worked by Aztec artists
Museum am Rothenbaum Hamburg,
Inv. no. FSB 264
Photo: Paul Schimweg

This standing figure was made at
Teotihuacan, between 250 and 750 A.D.
The dates "1 Flint" and "13 Reed"
engraved on the figure's chest are,
however, of Aztec origin. For the Aztecs,
"13 Reed" refers to the birth of the sun.
"1 Flint" was the birthday of their tutelary
deity Huitzilopochtli. These dates were
applied to a statue from Teotihuacan, the
birthplace of the Sun and the Moon. MB

Cat. no. 9
Humpbacked deity Nanahuatzin

Volcanic stone
H: 29 cm; W: 17 cm; D: 23.5 cm
Mexico, Puebla, Tianguismanalco, Nahua, around 1500 AD
KHM-Museumsverband, Weltmuseum Wien, Inv. no. 59.129
Photo: KHM-Museumsverband

Historical sources and images show that hunchbacked and small
people held a special position at the courts of the rulers of Meso-
America, for example as musicians, dancers and fools. This figure
may represent the hunchbacked god Nanahuatzin ("The Leper").
The chronicler Bernardino de Sahagún reported how the gods
gathered in the darkness of Teotihuacan after the destruction of the
"Fourth Sun" and decided to recreate a new sun and thus the world.
Tecuciztecatl, who was rich, beautiful and proud, was to take on the
role of the new sun. The second was Nanahuatl, poor, sickly and
conscientious. Four days of fasting and sacrifice followed, during
which Tecuciztecatl sacrificed treasures such as quetzal feathers,
jade and gold. Nanahuatzin offered thorns soaked in his own blood.
When the gods asked Tecuciztecatl to jump into the sacred fire to
become the sun, he hesitated; Nanahuatzin jumped into the fire.
Ashamed, Tecuciztecatl followed him. The next day both stood in
the sky, but did not move until the gods finally sacrificed themselves
for the new creation, as they could only set the two in motion in
this way. Nanahuatzin illuminates the new creation as the sun and
appears during the day, Tecuciztecatl appears during the night as the
moon. GvB

Cat. no. 10
Stone slab showing the calendar date "Flint"

Basalt
H: 30 cm; W: 32.5 cm
Mexico, Aztec, mid-14th century, before 1521
Museo Nacional de Antropología, Mexico City,
D.R. Secretaría de Cultura - INAH, Inv. no. 10-46541
Photo: D.R. Archivo Digital de las Colecciones del Museo Nacional de
Antropología, Secretaría de Cultura – INAH

Stone slabs like this were included in buildings as commemorative plaques. This one contains two dates: "3 Flint", composed of the central image of a flint blade and three dots for the number "three", and "12 Lizard". The smaller image is badly eroded but probably reads "12 Lizard". Together these form the date "3 Flint" (year), "12 Lizard" (day). MB

Cat. no. 8
Sculpture of a Deity, the Sun God Tonatiuh

Volcanic tuff, haematite
H: 31.5 cm; W: 16.2 cm; D: 24.5 cm
Central Mexico, Aztec, mid-14th century before 1521
Museum der Kulturen Basel, Coll. Lukas Vischer, Inv. no. IVb 634
Photo: Peter Horner

The sun god Tonatiuh is carrying the solar disc on his back. The disc is marked with the date "4 Movement" – *nahui ollin* in Nahuatl – the name of our present sun. Tonatiuh rose as the sun after emerging from the fire into which he had cast himself at Teotihuacan. His body was painted red to represent the heat of the sun. MB

Cat. no. 11
Relief stone showing the day "13 Jaguar"

Stone (andesite?), Haematite
H: 24.1 cm; W: 23.8 cm; D: 8.4 cm
Mexico, Aztec, between ca. 1350 and 1521 AD
Museum der Kulturen Basel, Coll. Lukas Vischer, Inv. no. IVb 645
Photo: Omar Lemke

This relief stone shows the date "13 Jaguar", one of the days in the 260-day ritual calendar *tonalpolhualli*. The stone probably originates from a building and indicates an important event. This might be directly related to the building itself, commemorating the day of its completion. MB

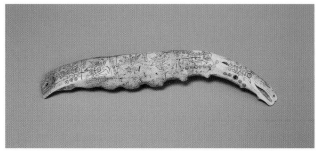

Cat. no. 12
Stone sculpture, reed bundle *xiuhmolpilli*

Basalt
H: 57 cm; W: 35 cm
Mexico, Aztec, between ca. 1350 and 1521 AD
Museo Nacional de Antropología, Mexico City, D.R. Secretaria de
Cultura - INAH, Inv. no. 10-1116
Photo: D.R. Archivo Digital de las Colecciones del Museo Nacional
de Antropología, Secretaría de Cultura - INAH

Every 52 years, the two most important Aztec calendars
would start on the same day. This momentous occasion
was marked by the New Fire Ceremony, during which
bundles of 52 reeds were burned. Stone versions of
these bundles – *xiuhmolpilli* – were created in commemoration and as offerings. This *xiuhmolpilli* was made for
a celebration on the day "1 Death". MB

Cat. no. 13
Pendant with calendar signs

Shell, pigment
L: 25.5 cm; W: 6.5 cm; D: 3.6 cm
Mexico, Nahua-Mixteca, around 1500 AD
KHM-Museumsverband, Weltmuseum Wien, Inv. no. 60.300
Photo: KHM-Museumsverband

The inner side of this lip of a sea snail (*Cassis tuberosa*)
shows six day signs: 7 Flower, 13 Eagle, 5 Eagle, 9 Eagle,
12 Flower, 5 Flower; on the outside it says "5 Monkey".
Two days are related to gods. Bernardino de Sahagún
reports that among the Aztecs a feast for Chicomexo-
chitl ("7 Flower"), an aspect of the god Xochipilli, took
place on the day "7 Flower". "5 Flower" is the calendar
name and day of Macuilxochitl, the god of games and
music, who was also connected to Xochipilli. The
engraved lines were rubbed with black pigment. Three
perforations made it possible to attach or hang the
pendant. Neither its function nor the place where it was
found are known. GvB

Cat. no. 14
Stone sculpture, turtle

Basalt
H: 15 cm; W: 28.8 cm; L: 46.3 cm
Mexico, Aztec, between ca. 1350 and
1521 AD
Museo Nacional de Antropología,
Mexico City, D.R. Secretaria de Cultura
– INAH, Inv. no. 10-1099
Photo: D.R. Archivo Digital de las
Colecciones del Museo Nacional de
Antropología, Secretaría de Cultura
– INAH

The stone sculpture could
be the representation of a sea
turtle, which would then be
associated with water. Turtle
shells were worked into musical
instruments, usually small
drums. DK

Cat. no. 15
Stone sculpture, grasshopper

Basalt
H: 16.7 cm; W: 16.8 cm; L: 26.2 cm
Mexico, Aztec, between ca. 1350 and 1521 AD
Museo Nacional de Antropología, Mexico City,
D.R. Secretaría de Cultura – INAH, Inv. no. 10-41689
Photo: D.R. Archivo Digital de las Colecciones del Museo Nacional de
Antropología, Secretaría de Cultura – INAH

The stone sculpture representing a grasshopper has been worked
in an abstract way, so the species cannot be identified. Grasshop-
pers are frequently found in the Basin of Mexico after the rainy
season. DK

Cat. no. 16
Stone sculpture, owl

Basalt
H: 21 cm; W: 11.6 cm; D: 21.5cm
Central Mexico, Aztec, between ca. 1350 and 1521 AD
Museum der Kulturen Basel, Coll. Lukas Vischer, Inv. no. IVb 632
Photo: Omar Lemke

The owl as a nocturnal creature is a frequently recurring subject
in Pre-Columbian art. It is frequently perceived as an intermedi-
ary between this world and the afterlife. DK

Cat. no. 17
Stone sculpture, barrel cactus

Basalt
H: 51 cm; D: 76 cm
Central Mexico, Aztec, between ca. 1350 and 1521 AD
found under the Librería Porrúa.
Museo del Templo Mayor, Mexico City, D.R. Secretaría de
Cultura – INAH, Inv. no. 10-650351
Photo: Gliserio Castañeda, D.R. Secretaría de Cultura - INAH

Mexico is the country with the largest number
of cactus species apart from Bolivia. Cacti are
important in the Aztec culture: in the founding
myth of Tenochtitlan, the eagle lands on a cactus.
Cactus spines were used for blood sacrifices and
some cactus species contain hallucinogenic
substances. DK

Cat. no. 18
Stone sculpture, water flea

Andesite
L: 18.3 cm; W: 14.3 cm; L: 28.2 cm
Central Mexico, Aztec, between ca. 1350 and 1521 AD
Museo Nacional de Antropología, Mexico City,
D.R. Secretaría de Cultura – INAH, Inv. no. 10-41987
Photo: D.R. Archivo Digital de las Colecciones del Museo
Nacional de Antropología, Secretaría de Cultura – INAH

Taken together, the stone sculptures representing animals that are related to water are seen as recreating the natural environment of the rain god Tlaloc. Water fleas were among the tribute payments due to Tenochtitlan. DK

Cat. no. 19
Ceramic sculpture, maize goddess Xilonen (replica)

Ceramic
H: 100 cm; W: 62 cm; D: 52 cm
Central Mexico, Aztec, between ca. 1350 and 1521 AD
Museo Nacional de Antropología, Mexico City, D.R. Secretaría de Cultura – INAH
Photo: D.R. Archivo Digital de las Colecciones del Museo Nacional de Antropología, Secretaría de Cultura - INAH

Maize formed the nutritional basis of Meso-American cultures. The calendar was developed to reflect its growth periods. Each such period had its own god or goddess: Xilonen was the goddess of the freshly germinated maize sprouts. DK

Cat. no. 20
Stone sculpture, earth and maize goddess Chicomecoatl

Stone
H: 46 cm; W: 24.5 cm; D: 9.5 cm
Central Mexico, Aztec, between ca. 1350 and 1521 AD
Collection Nationaal Museum van Wereldculturen. Coll. no. TM-3503-1
Photo: Irene de Groot

Chicomecoatl, literally translated as "Seven Snakes", was the goddess of food products, the earth and the maize. Her face and body were usually painted red and she wore a headdress made of *amatl* paper. DK

Cat. no. 21
**Relief plate,
rain god Tlaloc**

Basalt
H: 35 cm; W: 28.3 cm; D: 9.7 cm
Central Mexico, Aztec, between
ca. 1350 and 1521 AD
Museo Nacional de Antropología,
Mexico City, D.R. Secretaría de
Cultura – INAH, Inv. no.
10-222120
Photo: D.R. Archivo Digital de las
Colecciones del Museo Nacional
de Antropología, Secretaría de
Cultura - INAH

The rain god Tlaloc was one
of the most important, if
not the most important god
in the high Basin of Mexico.
He caused rain, but – like all
gods – he had two sides. He
was responsible for fertility
and the preservation of life,
but he could also destroy it.
Floods or droughts were
interpreted as the will of
the gods. He is always
recognisable by his "goggle
eyes", which stand for
water, and his jaguar-like
fangs. DK

Cat. no. 22
**Brazier, water and fertility
goddess Chalchiuhtlicue**

Ceramic, pigment
H: 55.2 cm; W: 64.3 cm;
D: 49.4 cm
Central Mexico, Aztec, late
period, early 16th century;
discovered near the sacred
district of Tlatelolco
Museo Nacional de Antropología,
Mexico City, D.R. Secretaría de
Cultura – INAH, Inv. no. 10-1125
Photo: D.R. Archivo Digital de las
Colecciones del Museo Nacional
de Antropología, Secretaría de
Cultura - INAH

Chalchiuhtlicue, "the one
who wears a jade skirt", is
the goddess of rivers,
springs, lakes and all fresh
water. She was thought to be
the wife, and in some myths
also the sister of Tlaloc. DK

Cat. no. 23
Stone stele with the goddess Chalchiuhtlicue

Basalte, pigment
H: 108 cm; W: 41.5 cm; D: 9.5 cm
Central Mexico, Aztec, between ca. 1350 and 1521 AD
Museo Nacional de Antropología, Mexico City,
D.R. Secretaría de Cultura – INAH, Inv. no. 10-613348
Photo: D.R. Archivo Digital de las Colecciones del Museo Nacional de
Antropología, Secretaría de Cultura - INAH

Chalchiuhtlicue is the goddess of water flowing from
underground springs. Depicted on her back are *tlaloque*,
helpers of the rain god Tlaloc, who break water jugs to make
it rain. On the front, Chalchiuhtlicue rises from the throat of
an earth monster. She stands for the growth of maize during
the rainy season. DK

Cat. no. 24
Mould for small figurines, with plaster figure

Ceramic, plaster
Model: H: 12 cm; W: 8.5 cm; D: 3 cm;
plaster figure: H 13 cm; W: 8.5 cm; D: 4 cm
Central Mexico, Aztec, between ca. 1350 and
1521 AD
Royal Museum of Art and History Brussels,
Inv. no. AAM 3347

Small figures like models of temples and especially anthropomorphic figures were mass-produced. They were made in moulds like the one exhibited here and served as pendants or decorated house altars. DK

Cat. no. 25
Figure of a goddess

Ceramic
H: 12.5 cm; W: 7.5 cm
Mexico, Aztec, around 1500
KHM-Museumsverband, Weltmuseum Wien, Inv. no. 6.133
Photo: KHM-Museumsverband

This massive, kneeling female figure with a high feather headdress is interpreted as the mother goddess or the goddess Xochiquetzal ("flower-quetzalfeather"), the sister or partner of the gods Xochipilli and Tlaloc. Her responsibilities included sexuality, fertility, birth and growth as well as female crafts such as spinning and weaving. The two holes refer to the figure's function as a pendant, although it is also possible that the goddess was placed on a (house) altar. Such figures were mass-produced. GvB

Cat. no. 29
Painted bowl

Ceramic, pigment
H: 6 cm; D: 17.5 cm
Mexico, Aztec, between ca. 1350 and 1521 AD
Collection Nationaal Museum van Wereldculturen. Coll. no. RV-2849-3
Photo: Irene de Groot

This coloured ceramic (black-orange ware) was an everyday commodity. It was produced in the households in the countryside and reached the cities via the markets. DK

Cat. no. 26
Figure of a goddess

Ceramic
H: 20.9 cm; W: 11 cm
Mexico, Aztec, around 1500
KHM-Museumsverband, Weltmuseum
Wien, Inv. no. 59.570
Photo: KHM-Museumsverband

The massive standing female figure produced with the help of a mould is wearing a feather headdress ending in two strands, hanging earrings, a necklace, a blouse called *huipil* and a wrap skirt. Both hands are raised. The figure is a well-known type that can represent different fertility and mother goddesses; it is usually interpreted as Xochiquetzal ("flower-quetzal feather"). Although the figure may have been placed on a (house) altar, two holes also indicate its function as a pendant. GvB

Cat. no. 27
Female figure holding an infant

Ceramic
H: 11.1 cm; W: 5.4 cm; D: 3.3 cm
Mexico, Aztec, between ca. 1350 and
1521 AD
Collection Nationaal Museum van
Wereldculturen. Coll. no. TM-3523-10
Photo: Irene de Groot

The significance of these female figures has not been clarified. Since they all hold infants, we could assume the context of a fertility cult. Perhaps it was also a ritual in which the children were presented to the gods or the representation of fertility goddesses. DK

Cat. no. 28
Female figure

Ceramic
H: 12.5 cm; W: 5.2 cm; D: 4.1 cm
Mexico, Aztec, between ca. 1350 and
1521 AD
Collection Nationaal Museum van
Wereldculturen. Coll. no. RV-2971-13
Photo: Irene de Groot

The female figures are particularly interesting with regard to their traditional costumes. The women wear different hairstyles and clothes and reflect the ethnic diversity of the Aztec empire. DK

Cat. no. 30
Stamp, monkey

Ceramic
H: 5.3 cm; W: 4.5 cm; D: 3.5 cm
Mexico, Aztec, between ca. 1350 and 1521 AD
Collection Nationaal Museum van Wereldculturen.
Coll. no. RV-2971-57
Photo: Irene de Groot

Stamp for decoration on body or clothes. DK

Cat. no. 31
Stamp

Ceramic
H: 6.6 cm; W: 8.7 cm
Mexico, early 16th century
KHM-Museumsverband, Weltmuseum Wien,
Inv. no. 57.065
Photo: KHM-Museumsverband

Many museums and private collections keep clay stamps, some of them still with remnants of red paint. They were made with the help of moulds and have a handle on the back. Many stamps show stylised depictions of interwoven flowers surrounded by butterflies, birds and monkeys as well as abstract motifs. It is believed that these stamps were used to decorate bodies or clothing, clay or baked goods, and perhaps even paper or walls. GvB

Cat. no. 32
Spindle whorl

Ceramic
H: 2 cm; D: 5.9 cm
Mexico, early 16th century
Collection Nationaal Museum van Wereldculturen. Coll. no. RV-5409-37
Photo: Irene de Groot

Spinning and weaving were among the most important activities of women. They obtained the raw cotton at the markets and processed it at home. Girls also learned this craft from an early age. The more cotton cloths a woman made, the wealthier the family was. DK

Cat. no.33
Spindle whorl

Ceramic
H: 1.1 cm; D: 3 cm
Mexico, early 16th century
Collection Nationaal Museum van Wereldculturen. Coll. no. TM-3842-1035
Photo: Irene de Groot

Cotton cloths were an important tribute item. After the conquest of a province, the Aztec Empire increased the number of cotton cloths to be delivered, in order to supply the aristocracy in Tenochtitlan. DK

Cat. no. 34
Stamp, abstract motif

Ceramic
H: 2.7 cm; W: 4.5 cm; D: 2.3 cm
Mexico, early 16th century
Collection Nationaal Museum van Wereldculturen.
Coll. no. TM-3842-1041
Photo: Irene de Groot

Stamp for decoration on body or clothes DK

Cat. no. 35
**Female figure
in typical costume**

Ceramic
H: 11.5 cm; W: 4.5 cm;
D: 2.5 cm
Mexico, Aztec, between
ca. 1350 and 1521 AD
Royal Museum of Art and
History, Brussels, AAM 2948

What is particularly interesting about this female figure is her traditional costume. She wears a wrap skirt with a diamond pattern. Textiles of this kind were found during the excavations in the Templo Mayor. DK

Cat. no. 36
Mould for skeletal skull

Ceramic
H: 14.5 cm; W: 12 cm; D: 8.5 cm
Mexico, Aztec, between ca. 1350 and 1521 AD
Royal Museum of Art and History, Brussels,
Inv. no. AAM 3334

Mould for series production of ceramics. DK

Cat. no. 37
Small ceramic skull, made in mould

Ceramic
H: 13 cm; W: 11 cm; D: 11 cm
Mexico, Aztec, between ca. 1350 and 1521 AD
Royal Museum of Art and History, Brussels, Inv. no. AAM 1847

Cat. no. 38
Vessel, skull motif

Ceramic
H: 16 cm; W: 14 cm; D: 14 cm
Mexico, Aztec, between ca. 1350 and 1521 AD
Royal Museum of Art and History, Brussels, Inv. no. AAM 3060

The vessel was used to serve pulque and therefore belonged in a ritual context. ᴰᴷ

Cat. no. 39
Female figure holding an infant

Ceramic
H: 16 cm; W: 6.5 cm; D: 5 cm
Mexico, Aztec, between ca. 1350 and 1521 AD
Royal Museum of Art and History, Brussels, Inv. no.
AAM 2949

This figure probably depicts a fertility ritual. The woman may be thanking the gods for the child by presenting it to them as part of a ritual. Her elaborate earrings identify her as a noble woman. ᴰᴷ

Cat. no. 40
Female figure holding an infant

Ceramic
H: 14 cm; W: 5.5 cm; D: 4 cm
Mexico, Aztec, between ca. 1350 and 1521 AD
Royal Museum of Art and History, Brussels,
Inv. no. AAM 2932

Cat. no. 41
Female figure holding an infant

Ceramic
H: 16 cm; W: 7 cm; D: 4.5 cm
Mexico, Aztec, between ca. 1350 and 1521 AD
Royal Museum of Art and History, Brussels,
Inv. no. AAM 2954

Cat. no. 42
Painted plate

Ceramic
H: 9 cm D: 19 cm
Mexico, Aztec, between ca. 1350
and 1521 AD
Linden-Museum Stuttgart,
Inv. no. 025133
Photo: Dominik Drasdow

Plates of this kind were
everyday items and are
found throughout the Basin
of Mexico. The carved inner
surface indicates that they
were used as graters. DK

Cat. no. 43
Painted bowl

Ceramic
H: 9 cm; D: 20.4 cm
Mexico, Aztec, between ca. 1350 and 1521 AD
Linden-Museum Stuttgart, Inv. no. 034731
Photo: Dominik Drasdow

Cat. no. 44
Stone tool for papermaking

Stone
L: 7.5 cm; W: 6 cm; H: 3.3 cm
Mexico, Aztec, between ca. 1350 and 1521 AD
Collection Nationaal Museum van Wereldculturen.
Coll. no. RV-2142-32
Photo: Irene de Groot

Pre-Columbian paper, *amatl*, was made from the bark of the fig tree. It is comparable to textiles made from bark cloth, which we find in many cultures. Coated with a layer of plaster, it served as the basis for pictorial manuscripts. *Amatl* is still produced today. DK

Cat. no. 46
Xipe Totec

Ceramic
H: 13 cm; W: 5 cm
Mexico, early 16th century
KHM-Museumsverband, Weltmuseum Wien, Inv. no. 6.143
Photo: KHM-Museumsverband

Xipe Totec ("the skinned, our Lord"), the god of war and vegetation is shown here on a pyramid. Xipe Totec is wearing his typical *yopitzontli* headdress. The skin of a sacrificed person in which he is dressed is characteristic of representations of this deity and is recognisable by the mouth opening and the hands hanging down at the arm joint. Although possibly made for a (house) altar, the two holes also indicate a pendant function. GvB

Cat. no. 45
Model of a temple pyramid
Clay
H: 11.8 cm; W: 6.8 cm; D: 7.9 cm
Mexico, Aztec, around 1500
KHM-Museumsverband, Weltmuseum Wien, Inv. no. 6.144
Photo: KHM-Museumsverband

Temple models were produced in series with the help of moulds. They convey the symbolic meaning of the pyramids as centres of society in general, as places of worship of the gods, or sometimes of an ancestor, and as burial places. Pyramids symbolised holy mountains, while temples (*teocalli*, "House of the God") symbolised the dark grottos which served as gateways permitting entry into supernatural worlds and through which the ancestors entered the earth. Rain clouds also gather around mountain tops, making the mountains the source of life. The gods influenced earthly life directly on every social level. They were worshipped by the entire society. The models may have been used for private purposes. They demonstrate the canon of religious architecture: a stepped pyramid with stairs at the front, flanked by balustrades at the top. A sacrificial stone (*techcatl*) is located in front of the temple entrance; it resembles the sacrificial stones in front of the temples of Huitzilopochtli depicted in the Codex Durán and the Codex Tudela. The numbers realised in this 4-stage pyramid and 13-stage staircase were symbolic for the Aztecs: the four cardinal directions, the four preceding creations ("suns") and the four year bearers. 13 was the number of completion and refers to the 13 levels of the upper world. In addition, their multiplication alludes to the 52 years of a calendar cycle. The structure of the temple roof, decorated with circles ("starry sky"), is reminiscent of the temples of Huitzilopochtli.
Pyramids were the stages on which priests performed their rituals. As focal points of the Meso-American religions, the Spaniards were anything but neutral towards the temple pyramids. Many of these religious places were razed to the ground, and it was not unusual for the Spaniards to build their own places of worship on the site. GvB

Cat. no. 47
Miniature of the god Ehecatl
Ceramic
H: 10.5 cm; W: 4 cm; D: 3 cm
Mexico, Aztec, between ca. 1350 and 1521 AD
Museum am Rothenbaum Hamburg, Inv. no. B 408
Photo: Paul Schimweg

Ehecatl was the god of the wind. He can be recognised by his mouth mask. DK

Cat. no. 48
Model of a temple
Ceramic
H: 18.2 cm; W: 12.2 cm; D: 5.6 cm
Mexico, Aztec, between ca. 1350 and
1521 AD
Collection Nationaal Museum van
Wereldculturen. Coll. no. RV-2971-4
Photo: Irene de Groot

Cat. no. 49
**Model of a temple of the god
Ehecatl-Quetzalcoatl**
Ceramic
H: 13 cm; W: 6 cm; D: 4cm
Mexico, Aztec, between ca. 1350 and 1521 AD
Collection Nationaal Museum van Wereldculturen.
Coll. no. RV-2971-4
Photo: Irene de Groot

The temples of Ehecatl-Quetzalcoatl were
usually round, so that the wind could
blow around them unhindered. The large
temples to the deity discovered in Mexico
City also have a circular floor plan. One of
these temples was located in the sacred
district in the centre of Tenochtitlan;
numerous others were scattered throughout the city. DK

Cat. no. 50
Small pottery item with the god Ehecatl-Quetzalcoatl on a temple
Ceramic
H: 18.2 cm; W: 12.2 cm; D: 5.6 cm
Mexico, Aztec, between ca. 1350 and 1521 AD
Collection Nationaal Museum van Wereldculturen. Coll. no. RV-2971-4
Photo: Irene de Groot

Cat. no. 51
Stone sculpture of the god Huehueteotl-Xiuhtecuhtli

Basaltic lava with whitish eye filling
H: 31 cm; W: 21.5 cm; D: 18 cm
Mexico, Aztec, between ca. 1350 and 1521 AD
Museum der Kulturen Basel, Collection Lukas Vischer, Inv. no. IVb 627
Photo: Peter Horner

The remains of the painting and the pierced earlobes indicate that the figure of the god, like many other Aztec sculptures, was realistically decorated. The "Old Fire God" is a Meso-American deity who was worshipped in many cultures. He is always depicted as an old man and often carries a smoking bowl on his head, symbolising a volcano (see also Bankmann and Baer 1990) DK

Cat. no. 52
Maize carrier

Volcanic stone, pigment
H: 42.3 cm; W: 18 cm; D: 26 cm
Mexico, Post-classical Era
KHM-Museumsverband, Weltmuseum Wien, Inv. no. 6.052
Photo: KHM-Museumsverband

Maize carrier

Volcanic stone
H: 26.5 cm; W: 12.2 cm; D: 19 cm
Mexico, Puebla, Post-classical Era
KHM-Museumsverband, Weltmuseum Wien, Inv. no. 59.138
Photo: KHM-Museumsverband

Two men bending slightly forward are carrying baskets filled with maize on their backs. Maize was one of the staple foods of Meso-America, along with beans and pumpkins. The men's arms are raised so that they can hold the straps on their foreheads with both hands. There were no pack animals in Meso-America; goods were therefore transported with the help of carriers, often slaves, and also by canoe. GvB

Cat. no. 53
Stone sculpture depicting a dog

Volcanic lava stone
H: 28 cm; W: 13.5 cm; D: 19 cm
Central Mexico, probably Aztec, Post-classical Era, between ca. 1350 and 1521 AD
Museum am Rothenbaum Hamburg, Inv. no. B3640
Photo: Paul Schimweg

Dogs were regarded by the Aztecs as companions of the soul of their deceased master on its journey into the afterlife. The sculpture can be placed in this context. In addition, like turkeys they were also bred as food. DK

Cat. no. 54
Axe money

Copper
H: 12-14 cm; W: 4.5-5 cm
Central Mexico, Post-classical Era, between 10th
century and 1521 AD
Royal Museum of Art and History Brussels, Inv. no.
AAM 48.26.1 and following

At the markets within the Basin of
Mexico, there were three forms of
payment available in addition to exchange: cotton cloths, cocoa beans and
small, non-functional copper axe blades.
It is not yet known why these axe blades
were used as a means of payment. DK

Cat. no. 55
Pendant

Seashells
L: 4.5-6.7 cm; D: 2-3.5 cm
Mexico, unknown date and provenance
KHM-Museumsverband, Weltmuseum Wien, Inv. no. 60.302
Photo: KHM-Museumsverband

The tip (apex) of the snail shells has been trimmed and carved for
threading; three of them are larger cone snail shells (*conidae*). Since
snails live in water, the shells were symbolically connected to the
underworld and, according to the chronicler Bernardino de Sahagún,
to fertility. Snail shells from both coasts found their way inland
through trade and as tribute and were valuable objects due to the
distance covered. Many were found in the sacrificial deposits of the
Templo Mayor in Mexico-Tenochtitlan. When threaded into chains,
the snail shells would jingle as they moved. Snail shells were cut to
size and polished for mosaics or used to create jewellery for people
and statues of gods, but also to make everyday objects such as
fishhooks. GvB

Cat. no. 56
Obsidian core

Obsidian
L: 16.5 cm
Mexico
Linden-Museum Stuttgart,
Inv. no. 034747
Photo: Dominik Drasdow

Cat. no. 57
Man dressed as a royal eagle

Ceramic, in the exhibition as replica
H: 150 cm
Templo Mayor, House of the Eagles
Mexico, Aztec, between 1450 and 1502 AD
Museo del Templo Mayor, Mexico City,
D.R. Secretaría de Cultura – INAH
Photo: Michel Zabé, Proyecto Templo Mayor,
D.R. Secretaria de Cultura – INAH

Ceramic figure in the shape of a man dressed as a royal eagle, representing the rising sun. Found in the "House of the Eagles", in the sacred district of Tenochtitlan. One of the warrior orders called itself the "Eagle Warriors". The warriors belonging to the order wore a similar costume. DK

Cat. no. 58
Atlas/Atlant, warrior sculpture

Basalt
H: 122 cm; W: 42 cm
Surroundings of the Templo Mayor, found in 1944
Mexico, Aztec, around 1500
Museo Nacional de Antropología, Mexico City,
D.R. Secretaría de Cultura – INAH, Inv. no. 10-81767
Photo: D.R. Archivo Digital de las Colecciones del Museo
Nacional de Antropología, Secretaria de Cultura – INAH

This warrior figure, worked in a style very close to the Toltec originals, bears a stylised butterfly pectoral. This refers to the monarch butterflies, which were thought to be the souls of deceased warriors. Since the sculpture was found with four others near the Templo Mayor, it is assumed that they represented the four cardinal points and the centre of the world, the world tree or *axis mundi* (see also Azteken 2003). DK

Cat. no. 59
Coyote or young wolf

Basalt
H: 39.8 cm; B: 21 cm; T: 23.3 cm
Mexico, Aztec, between ca. 1350 and 1521 AD
Museo Nacional de Antropología, Mexico City, D.R. Secretaría de Cultura – INAH, Inv. no. 10 47
Photo: D.R. Archivo Digital de las Colecciones del Museo Nacional de Antropología,
Secretaría de Cultura – INAH

This animal figure has so far been interpreted as a "feathered coyote" associated with Tezcatlipoca, the god of war and destruction. Recent research at the Templo Mayor revealed a sacrificial deposit containing 27 killed wolves, which suggests that the sculpture may show a young wolf (Ximena Chavez Balderas, personal communication). Wolves were the most frequently sacrificed mammals in the sacred district of Tenochtitlan, a fact attributed to the important function of the wolf in one of the sacrificial myths. One of the warrior orders of the Aztecs was known as the "Coyote Warriors". DK

Cat. no. 60
Stone sculpture, reclining jaguar

Basaltic lava
L: 10.2 cm; W: 28 cm; D: 18.5 cm
Central Mexico, Aztec, between ca. 1350 and 1521 AD
Museum der Kulturen Basel, Collection Lukas Vischer, Inv. no. IVb 644
Photo: Omar Lemke

This reclining jaguar is an excellent example of lifelike Aztec animal sculptures. It probably had a symbolic meaning associated with ruling power and the warrior cult. One of the warrior orders was called the "Jaguar Warriors". Jaguar skins were among the most coveted tributes. They decorated the ruler's palace and the throne of the ruler *hueitlatoani*. DK

Cat. no. 61
Miniature of an Eagle Warrior

Ceramic
H: 16 cm; W: 12 cm ; D: 5 cm
Mexico, Aztec, between ca. 1350 and 1521 AD
Royal Museum of Art and History Brussels,
Inv. no. AAM 2990

The "Eagle Warriors" were one of the Aztec warrior orders. Particularly meritorious warriors, who had taken numerous prisoners, could rise to join one of the orders and enjoyed privileges that were otherwise reserved only for nobles. DK

Cat. no. 62
Blades and points

Obsidian
L: 5.2–30.5 cm; W: 2.9–8.7 cm
Central Mexico, around 1500 AD
KHM-Museumsverband, Weltmuseum Wien,
Inv. nos. 12.427, 87.525, 87.527, 129.346
Photo: KHM-Museumsverband

Obsidian (*itztli*), or volcanic glass, was a material particularly appreciated in Meso-America because of its sharpness and brilliance. It was traded and processed everywhere. The control over deposits was of economic, political and religious importance. Either finished products were produced and offered directly on site or the core stones were traded as raw material. They were used to produce extremely sharp arrowheads, blades for cutting weapons (*macuahuitl*), scrapers and double-edged (sacrificial) knives with attached handles, needles, etc. using knock-off or pressing techniques. Obsidian objects have been found as offerings and burial objects. Obsidian was highly polished to create dark mirrors which enabled the mediators to look into parallel worlds, the past and the future during the rituals. The material was associated with the most important god of Central Mexico, Tezcatlipoca ("Smoking Mirror" or "Shining Mirror"). GvB

Cat. no. 63
Blade

Flint
L: 30.6 cm; B: 8.2 cm
Mexico, Aztec, around 1500 AD
KHM-Museumsverband, Weltmuseum Wien,
Inv. no. 14.695
Photo: KHM-Museumsverband

Sharp oval stone knives, *tecpatl*, often served as sacrificial instruments. Some of the known examples are painted with faces and decorated with mosaics. They thereby became sacrificial knives that were alive and could bite, drinking the blood of the sacrificed. Such knives were also found inserted into skulls – a picture that also appears in illuminated manuscripts and refers to Mictlantecuhtli, the god of the dead. In the Aztec calendar "flint" was a sign of the day; on the day "1 flint" the Mexican-Aztec patron god Huitzilopochtli was born. GvB

Cat. no. 64
Eagle's head

Stone
H: ca. 100 cm; W: ca. 120 cm
Mexico, from the area of Tehuacán, Puebla, Mexico; Aztec, between ca. 1350 and 1521 AD; Discovered at the foot of a mountain
Royal Museum of Art and History, Brussels, Inv. no. AAM 69.11

The eagle's head was probably carved out of a mountain to symbolise the rising sun. Eagles stood for the sun in Aztec culture. Rock temples with carved animal figures like the one at Malinalco were common in the Aztec Empire. DK

Cat. no. 65
Relief plate with eagle and snake, depicting the founding myth of Tenochtitlan

Olivine-Basalt
H: 59 cm; W: 27 cm; D: 12 cm
Central Mexico, Aztec, between
ca. 1350 and 1521 AD
Museum der Kulturen Basel,
Collection Lukas Vischer,
Inv. no. IVb 732
Photo: Peter Horner

The eagle clutches a rattlesnake, whose typical rattle is visible beside its tail-plumage, behind the other claw. To the left below the bird's beak there is a calendar sign which most probably represents the year "7 Reed" and thus refers to either 1447 or, 52 years later, 1499 (see also Bankmann and Baer 1990). DK

Cat. no. 67
Achitectural sculpture in the shape of a serpent's head

Andesite, red pigment
H: 56 cm; W: 54 cm; D: 56.5 cm; Length with pin: 105 cm
Mexico, Mexico City, Aztec, between ca. 1350 and 1521 AD;
found near San Lázaro, east of the sacred district of Tenochtitlan
Rautenstrauch-Joest-Museum, Donation Peter and Irene Ludwig, Inv. no. RJM 60381
Rheinisches Bildarchiv Köln, Photo: Wolfgang F. Meier, 2012

Serpent played an important role in the world view of Meso-American cultures. The serpent head shown here represents the Pan-Meso-American creator god, the "feathered serpent" Quetzalcoatl. Quetzalcoatl is the symbol of creation and fertility per se and the result of the fusion of two opposing and at the same time complementary fields. While his spiral body represents the earthly, his green quetzal feathers allude to the sky. This dual nature can be explained by the functions which the god fulfils for the origin of the universe and especially in the cosmogonic myths. In short, Quetzalcoatl is a being that unceasingly transcends temporal and spatial boundaries and provides the material cycle between the world of gods and the world of humans. As the wind, it is the precursor of rainfall; in the form of Venus, it enables the change between day and night; and as the Lord of the World Trees, it favours the calendar flow of the gods who are transformed into time. Accordingly, Quetzalcoatl, in his function as Creator, is the one who extracts the human race, its various groups and the newborn child from cave systems. Just as in the hereafter he receives light, fire and corn for the good of man. The great importance of Quetzalcoatl in the Aztec religion can be seen in the plastic arts, where his image was reproduced in a variety of ways using different types of stone. In general, Quetzalcoatl is represented as a serpent covered with quetzal feathers. The first depictions date from around 800 B.C. in Tlatilco. In addition, there are variants in the Basin of Mexico in which he carries the insignia of the wind god Ehecatl and in this form embodies especially the aspects of destruction and renewal associated with the wind as the precursor of rain and fertility of the land (see also cat. no. 140).

Sculpted serpent heads with cones like this were probably embedded in building walls or next to staircases. Apart from the Cologne sculpture, seven other monumental Mexican serpent heads in the "Neo-Xochicalca style" are still known today. Four of them have rounded forms; one was recently found at the corner of Mesones and 5 de Febrero streets in the historic centre of Mexico City. The other three were discovered in 1944 at the intersection of Cuba and Palma streets. These three bear the date "2 Reed" on the underside, which possibly refers to the new fire ceremony during the reign of Motecuhzoma II. Two other monumental heads, as well as that in the Rautenstrauch-Joest Museum, show the feathered serpent and have a geometric rectangular shape. One of them was discovered at the end of the eighteenth century in Calle Soledad, between Jesús María and Alhóndiga streets, and was described by the New Spain archaeologist Leon y Gama and the Luxembourg dragoon captain Guillaume Dupaix. The other one was found some years ago at the intersection of República de El Salvador and Correo Mayor streets.

The Cologne serpent's head was discovered in the middle of the twentieth century in the historical centre of Mexico City in Calle Alarcón 50. This site is located about 1,200 metres east of the main Aztec temple in Atzacualco, the northeastern of the four quadrants of the Aztec capital Tenochtitlan. It probably did not belong to the sacred district of the city, but could have decorated the wall of a district temple.

This monumental stone block depicts the mythical feathered serpent with laterally curved poison fangs and feathers running backwards on the sides. The remaining blue-green – also known as "Maya blue" – colour on the right refers to the splendid, intensely shimmering green tail feathers of the quetzal bird. The "Neo-Xochicalca" style of the sculpture proves that Aztec artists were also inspired by historical models: it has similarities with depictions of feathered serpents of Xochicalco of the epiclassical period between 650 and 900 AD., a ruin about three days' journey away from Tenochtitlan (see also Dyckerhoff 1999; López Austin and López Luján 2009; López Luján 2015b; López Luján 2016; López Luján and Fauvet-Berthelot 2016; Solís Olguín 2009; Solís Olguín and Velasco Alonso 2003; Teufel 2012a; Urcid and López Luján in print; Zanin 2003). AS/LLL

Cat. no. 66
**Stone sculpture
in the shape of a snake**

Stone
H: 20.5 cm; W: 29 cm; L: 28 cm
Central Mexico, Aztec, between ca. 1350 and
1521 AD
Royal Museum of Art and History, Brussels,
Inv. no. AAM 5857

Snakes were regarded as sacred animals of the various earth deities. Because of their moulting they also stood for constant renewal and were a symbol of fertility. It was on Coatepec, the "Snake Mountain", that the goddess Coatlicue became pregnant with Huitzilopochtli, the protective god of the Aztecs. DK

Cat. no. 68
**Codex Boturini or Tira
de la Peregrinación**

Facsimile, paper
H: 17.5 – 18.5 cm; L: 470.5 cm
Mexico City, unknown provenance;
Original created between 1530 and 1541 AD
Linden-Museum Stuttgart, gift of the INAH on
the occasion of the special exhibition "Azteken" /
"Aztecs"

The *Codex Boturini* is named after the Italian researcher Lorenzo Boturini de Benaducci (1702–1755), who made an intensive study of the pre-Columbian history of Mexico. The monochrome pictorial script shows the exodus of the Mexica from Aztlán, their mythical place of origin, their migration and finally their arrival in the Basin of Mexico. The modern name "Aztecs" goes back to Aztlán, the mythical place of origin. DK

Cat. no. 69
Obsidian mirror

Obsidian, wood
H: 50 cm; W: 40 cm
Museo Nacional de Ciencias Naturales – CSIC (Madrid), Inv. no. MNCN-LAP 18611
Photo: Servicio de fotografía – MNCN

Obsidian mirrors were a symbol of Aztec rule bestowed by the god
Tezcatlipoca ("Smoking Mirror"). Moctezuma is said to have seen a
group of warriors riding deer by looking in a mirror – a reference to the
Spanish conquerors. DK

This object is only on view in Stuttgart.

Cat. no. 70
Obsidian mirror

Obsidian, wood
H: 38.5 cm; W: 32 cm; D: 4 cm
Origin unknown, Aztec (?), late phase or early colonial period, 16th century AD
KHM-Museumsverband, Weltmuseum Wien, Inv. no. 12.510
Photo: KHM-Museumsverband

Obsidian mirrors enabled Mexican visionaries to look into the world beyond.
They were attributes of the omnipresent god Tezcatlipoca ("Smoking
Mirror", "Shining" Mirror), the patron saint of fortune-tellers. In Europe,
John Dee, a scholar and mystic at the English court of Queen Elizabeth I
and briefly at the imperial court of Rudolf II, used a similar obsidian mirror
from Meso-America for magical incantations. Ritual objects, jewellery and,
because of its sharpness, weapons and tools were made from the volcanic
glass obsidian. This mirror comes from the Viennese treasury, was previously
possibly in the treasury in Prague. It was initially thought to be Chinese. GvB

This object is only on view in Vienna.

Cat. no. 71
Bead

Jadeite
L: 3.4 cm; W: 1.7 cm
Mexico, probably Aztec, between ca. 1350 and 1521 AD
KHM-Museumsverband, Weltmuseum Wien, Inv. no. 12.510
Photo: KHM-Museumsverband

The bead is pierced lengthwise and bears an incised representation of
a mat. Woven mats were used everywhere, but they symbolised the
authority of the rulers. Thus the rhetorical stylistic figure in Nahuatl *in
petlatl in icpalli*, literally "the mat, the seat", refers to the government,
the authority. Jadeite (*chalchihuitl*) was the most valuable mineral of
Meso-America, which makes this bead with the mat engraving a
symbolic jewel. It was owned by Maximilian of Habsburg-Lorraine,
Emperor of Mexico from 1864 to 1867. GvB

Cat. no. 72
Stone box with lid owned by the Aztec ruler Moctezuma II

Granite
L: 33.5 cm; W: 15 cm; H: 21 cm
Mexico, Aztec, probably 1506 AD
Museum am Rothenbaum Hamburg, Inv. no. B.3767
Photo: Paul Schimweg

This stone box is an Aztec masterpiece. It is decorated on all sides with calendar signs, anthropomorphic and zoomorphic representations, which however do not all have to be attached to the piece at the same time. A date, the year sign "1 Reed", corresponds to 1519: the year in which Cortés reached Tenochtitlan. A name glyph containing the word "diadem" refers to Moctezuma II as the owner (see also McEwan and López Luján 2009). DK

Cat. no. 73
Stone box

Basalt
L: 40 cm; W: 28 cm; H: 37 cm
Mexico, Aztec, between ca. 1350 and 1521 AD
Museo Nacional de Antropología, Mexico City,
D.R. Secretaría de Cultura – INAH, Inv. no. 10-46504
Photo: D.R. Archivo Digital de las Colecciones del Museo
Nacional de Antropología, Secretaría de Cultura – INAH

Stone boxes with calendar glyphs or depictions of
gods are typical of Aztec culture. It is believed that
either agave or bone spines for blood sacrifices were
kept inside, or that they contained the ashes of
deceased rulers. DK

Cat. no. 74
Lip plug made of obsidian

Obsidian
L: 1.3 cm; W: 3 cm; H: 1.9 cm
Mexico, Post-classical Era, between ca. 1350 and 1521 AD
Collection Nationaal Museum van Wereldculturen. Coll.no. RV-4229-1
Photo: Irene de Groot

Lip plugs made of obsidian were worn on various occasions. In some,
different gemstones could be applied depending on the occasion. At
festivals for Tlaloc, for example, jade or turquoise was used. DK

Cat. no. 75
Duck head pendant

Amethyst, malachite
L: 3.1 cm; H: 1 cm; W: 1.2 cm
Mexico, Aztec, around 1500?
KHM-Museumsverband, Weltmuseum Wien, Inv. no. 10.407
Photo: KHM-Museumsverband

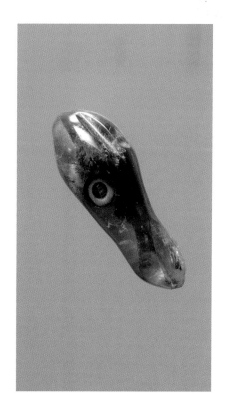

The head is made of amethyst; one eye is inlaid with malachite. Comparable
examples of the Aztec stonecutting art can be found in Florence and were formerly
part of the collection of Cosimo de Medici. Representations of ducks are known
from many Meso-American cultures. They were food and, of course, provided
feathers. But they also had symbolic meaning. According to the chronicler Diego
Durán, after their defeat in the civil war of 1473 against their relatives in Tenochtitlan, the Tlatelolca were forced to quack like ducks as proof of their submission.
Ducks thus seem to have had a connection with defeat and the underworld. Funeral
urns and sacrificial depots in the Templo Mayor contained duck head pendants.
The ability of the ducks to walk as well as to fly, swim and dive was interpreted
symbolically. Ducks appear as mediators between three – partly supernatural –
worlds and their inhabitants: the upper world, the earth and the underworld. GvB

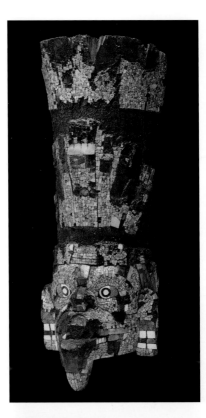

Cat. no. 76
Staff or statue attachment

Wood, turquoise, spondylus shell, resin, mother-of-pearl, malachite
H: 29 cm; W: 12 cm; D: 17 cm
Mexico, Aztec, between ca. 1350 and 1521 AD
National Museum of Denmark, Copenhagen, Inv. no. ODIh.41
Photo: National Museum of Denmark, Roberto Fortune

This turquoise mask was probably brought from Mexico to Southern Europe by Italian missionaries who began converting the indigenous population shortly after the conquest. In the nineteenth century it arrived in Denmark, where it was acquired by the National Museum.
Although this piece is usually referred to as a mask, it is actually clear that it could never be used as such. Much more likely, it was a staff attachment or the headdress of a statue. The pictorial language of the "mask" is unique, which has led researchers to several attempts at interpretation concerning the deity it depicts. In the past it was suspected that it shows a representation of the rain god Tlaloc. More recent research, on the other hand, interprets the piece as a representation of Xolotl, the twin brother of Quetzalcoatl, who always appears as a dog's head. Here the wrinkled muzzle, the canines and the tongue hanging out remind of this dog-like deity. MB

Cat. no. 77
Necklace consisting of nine links

Gold
H: 12.5 cm; W: 20 cm, D: 1.2 cm
Mexico, Mixtec-Aztec, between ca. 1350 and 1521 AD
Ministerie van de Vlaamse Gemeenschap, Collectie Paul en Dora Janssen-Arts, MAS, Antwerp, Inv. no. MAS. IB. 2010.017.329
Photo: Hugo Maertens, Bruges

These elements of a necklace show small, mask-like faces. All elements are made using the lost-wax technique and are therefore identical. The necklace is made in Mixtec style. DK

This object is only on view in Stuttgart.

Cat. no. 78
Pendant

Gold
Mexico, Mixtec-Aztec, between ca. 1350 and 1521 AD
L: 6 cm; W: 2.9 cm; H: 4 cm
Ministerie van de Vlaamse Gemeenschap, Collectie Paul en Dora Janssen-Arts, MAS, Antwerp, Inv. no. MAS. IB. 2010.017.065
Photo: Hugo Maertens, Bruges

Pendants in the Mixtec style were usually made using the lost-wax technique. This example shows a bird's head, probably that of an eagle, with a decorative element. The sun's rays are arranged around the eagle's head. DK

This object is only on view in Stuttgart.

Cat. no. 79
Lip plug with gold inlay

Gold; quartz; obsidian
L: 1.3 cm; W: 3 cm; H: 1.9 cm
Mexico, Mixtec-Aztec, between ca. 1350 and 1521 AD
Ministerie van de Vlaamse Gemeenschap,
Collectie Paul en Dora Janssen-Arts, MAS, Antwerp,
Inv. no. MAS. IB.2010.017.062.09-10
Photo: Hugo Maertens, Bruges

Wearing gold jewellery was a privilege of the nobles;
the selection of jewellery was extensive. Pendants, ear
plugs, bracelets, necklaces, lip plugs and ear jewellery
were among them. Most of the Aztec gold objects that
have survived were made by Mixtec goldsmiths or were
delivered directly from the Mixtec by tribute payments.
Mixtec goldsmiths lived in Tenochtitlan itself and
worked there. They obtained their raw materials from
the markets or from tributes. DK

This object is only on view in Stuttgart.

Cat. no. 80
Lip decoration

Gold; obsidian
L: 1.3 cm; W: 3 cm; H: 1.9 cm
Ministerie van de Vlaamse Gemeenschap,
Collectie Paul en Dora Janssen-Arts, MAS, Antwerp,
Inv. no. MAS. IB.2010.017.062.08-10
Photo: Hugo Maertens, Bruges

Lip and nose ornaments were considered decorations of
honour and were reserved exclusively for the nobility,
dignitaries, princes and honoured warriors. The
materials used, such as jade or gold, also served religious
purposes and were the privilege of the elite. Abuses
were severely punished. This ornament was used below
the lower lip. GvB

This object is only on view in Vienna.

Cat. no. 81
Lip ornament depicting a bird's head

Gold
H: 1.5 cm; W: 2 cm; D: 3 cm
Mexico, Mixtec-Aztec, between ca. 1350 and 1521 AD
Ministerie van de Vlaamse Gemeenschap, Collectie Paul en Dora Janssen-Arts, MAS,
Antwerp, Inv. no. MAS. IB.2010.017.067
Photo: Hugo Maertens, Bruges

The two lateral edges hold this ornament as if it were fixed into the
lower lip. The design is that of a bird's head. The over-eyebones and the
curvature of the beak make us think of an eagle's head. The crest at the
top of the head is sometimes interpreted as that of a *coxcoxtli* (Hokko
forest partridge) and is thus associated as an iconographic element with
the complex deity Xochipilli-Macuilxóchitl, one of the many aspects of
the sun. Gold and eagles were also closely associated with the sun in
Meso-American cultures. GvB

This object is only on view in Vienna.

Cat. no. 82
Ring with two bells and Tlaloc mask

Gold
H: 1.9 cm; D: 2 cm
Mexico, Mixtec-Aztec, between ca. 1350 and 1521 AD
Ministerie van de Vlaamse Gemeenschap, Collectie Paul en Dora
Janssen-Arts, MAS, Antwerp, Inv. no. MAS.IB.2010.017.068
Photo: Hugo Maertens, Bruges

Two bells and a figure are attached to the ring. The
figure shows rings around the eyes and is therefore
usually interpreted as an image of the god of rain or
storms. The Aztecs called this deity Tlaloc; among the
Zapotecs (Ben'zaa or 'People of the Clouds') his name
was Cocijo; and the Mixtecs (Ñuu Dzaui or 'People of
the Rain God') called him Dzaui. ^{GvB}

This object is only on view in Vienna.

Cat. no. 84
Ear decoration

Jadeite, greenstone
D: 3.8–10 cm; D: 0.7–2.8 cm
Mexico, Post-Classical Period
KHM-Museumsverband, Weltmuseum Wien, Inv. nos. 6.605,
59.518, 59.949
Photo: KHM-Museumsverband

The three jewellery discs are made of greenstones
(*chalchihuitl*, with the metaphorical meaning
"valuable"); they were inserted into dilated ear
holes. The green colour indicates growth, life and
fertility. A counterweight suspended on the back
was inserted through the middle to attach the
earrings. The wearing of such jewellery was a
privilege of the Aztec elite. ^{GvB}

Cat. no. 83
Bird head mask

Wood, turquoise, spondylus shell, resin, mother-of-pearl,
malachite
L: 29 cm; W: 15.5 cm; H: 13.5 cm
Mexico, Aztec, between ca. 1350 and 1521 AD
Stiftung Schloss Friedenstein Gotha. Inv. no. Eth7R

The art of making turquoise mosaics was highly
regarded in ancient Meso-America. Since its unique
shade of blue is very similar to the innermost and
hottest part of a blazing flame, turquoise was
associated with heat, fire and the sun. The most
important turquoise deposits were far outside the
Aztec Empire, in the southwest of what is today the
United States and in the northwest of Mexico. The
best and most important turquoise artists, however,
were Mixtecs from the southwest of the Aztec
Empire. They probably worked in Tenochtitlan itself,
in the ruler's workshops, where raw turquoise and
turquoise stones were processed into artistic mosaics.
The mask represents a bird, probably a raven. The
wind god Ehecatl always carries a bird's beak. Two
holes, probably used to fix the mask, suggest that it
was part of a priest's costume, worn by a priest
embodying the important deity Ehecatl during a
ceremony (Schwarz 2013). ^{MB}

Cat. no. 85
Jug

Ceramic, pigments
H: 19 cm; W: 15.5 cm; D: 11 cm
Mexico, Aztec, between ca. 1350 and 1521 AD
Royal Museum of Art and History, Brussels, Inv. no. AAM 1148

This jug was probably used to serve pulque, an alcoholic drink made from the fermented juice of the agave. The motifs depict snake heads, which suggests its use in a ceremonial context. DK

Cat. no. 87
Two tribrach bowls

Ceramic, pigment
L: 6.6 cm; W: 22 cm; H: 16.1 cm (each)
Mexico, Aztec, between ca. 1350 and 1521 AD
Museo Nacional de Antropología, Mexico City,
D.R. Secretaría de Cultura – INAH, Inv. no. 10-49998, 10-49989
Photo: D.R. Archivo Digital de las Colecciones del Museo Nacional de Antropología, Secretaría de Cultura – INAH

Tripod bowls with fine black painting. Black-orange ware like this was intended for everyday use. DK

Cat. no. 86
Tribrach plate

Ceramic, pigment
H: 12.8 cm; D: 29 cm
Mexico, Aztec, between ca. 1350 and 1521 AD
Museo Nacional de Antropología, Mexico City,
D.R. Secretaría de Cultura – INAH, Inv. no. 10-580953
Photo: D.R. Archivo Digital de las Colecciones del Museo Nacional de Antropología, Secretaría de Cultura – INAH

This plate is one of the most beautiful Aztec ceramics in existence. Food was served to the nobility on finely-worked plates like this one. They were found in places of sacrifice, as they were also used as offerings for the gods. DK

Cat. no. 88
Large vessel for food products

Ceramic, pigment
H: 38 cm; D: 40 cm
Mexico, probably Gulf coast, Aztec, around 1500 AD
Collection Nationaal Museum van Wereldculturen. Coll.no.TM-3502-4
Photo: Irene de Groot

With the growth of the Aztec empire, various ceramic shapes from the conquered provinces were also integrated into the range of pottery, and mixed forms developed. This vessel is typical of the Gulf Coast and was used at large festivals where rulers of the affiliated provinces were entertained on a lavish scale. The motif seems to depict a decorated nobleman holding a chalice or rattle in his hand. DK

Cat. no. 90
Plate

Ceramic, pigment
D: 17.3 cm; H: 2.5 cm
Mexico, Nahua-Mixteca, early
16th century
KHM-Museumsverband,
Weltmuseum Wien,
Inv. no. 59.490
Photo: KHM-Museumsverband

The mirror of the bowl shows a hand with white fingertips, crossed bones, a skull and a black disc with crossed ligaments, possibly with a severed eyeball. The hand refers to the Macuiltonaleque, five deities associated with the god Tezcatlipoca and invoked by diviners. These iconographic elements were widespread and should be seen as a visual language. They were associated with war, sacrifice, death and magical mirrors. The colouring of these symbols in yellow with red dots, and the ribbon which contains these symbols, convey brilliance or radiance. GvB

Cat. no. 89
Two chalice-shaped cups

Ceramic, pigment
H: 13 cm; D: 14.8 cm (each)
Mexico, Aztec, probably Late Period, early
16th century AD
Museo Nacional de Antropología, Mexico
City, D.R. Secretaría de Cultura – INAH,
Inv. no. 10-5256, 10-5260
Photo: D.R. Archivo Digital de las
Colecciones del Museo Nacional de
Antropología, Secretaría de Cultura – INAH

These cups come from the very heart of the Aztec Empire, the Basin of Mexico. Since they were found in large numbers, we can assume that they were in everyday use. DK

Cat. no. 91
Tribrach plate
Ceramic, pigment
H: 10 cm; D: 21.5 cm
Mexico, Aztec, between ca. 1350 and 1521 AD
Collection Nationaal Museum van Wereldculturen.
Coll.no. RV-2971-103
Photo: Irene de Groot

This typical Aztec plate represents the ceramic form most frequently found in the core zone. DK

Cat. no. 92
Tribrach plate
Ceramic, pigment
H: 9.5 cm; D: 21.5 cm
Mexico, Aztec, between ca. 1350 and 1521 AD
Collection Nationaal Museum van Wereldculturen.
Coll.no. RV-2971-104
Photo: Irene de Groot

This typical Aztec plate represents the ceramic form most frequently found in the core zone. DK

Cat. no. 93
Tribrach bowl, rattle bowl
Ceramic, pigment
H: 14.1 cm; W: 25 cm; D: 25 cm
Mexico, Aztec-Mixtec, between ca. 1350 and 1521 AD
Collection Nationaal Museum van Wereldculturen.
Coll.no. TM-3357-97
Photo: Irene de Groot

The three feet have clay beads inside which produce a rain-like noise when the bowl is moved. The staircase-wave motif, which is painted over the entire surface, suggests ritual use, as does its function as a rattle. The significance of the staircase-wave motif, which is frequently used in ancient America, is not known. It is also used on both feather shields. It may depict mountains as water dispensers or irrigation farming, to name just two possibilities. DK

317

Cat. no. 94
Goblet with stripe motif

Ceramic, pigment
H: 52 cm; D: 21 cm
Mexico, Aztec, Late Period, after
1506 AD, found in the former palace
of Moctezuma II.
Museo del Templo Mayor, Mexico City,
D.R. Secretaría de Cultura – INAH,
Inv. no. 10-646505
Photo: Gliserio Castañeda, D.R.
Secretaría de Cultura – INAH

A sacrificial site was found in the
present-day presidential palace
of Mexico City, which was built
above the palace of Moctezuma II,
It contained fifty such chalices,
three other ceramics and six
tribrach plates. DK

Cat. no. 95
Goblet with stripe motif

Ceramic, pigment
H: 45.7 cm; D: 22 cm
Mexico, Aztec, Late Period, after
1506 AD, found in the former palace
of Moctezuma II.
Museo del Templo Mayor, Mexico City,
D.R. Secretaría de Cultura – INAH,
Inv. no. 10-646506
Photo: Gliserio Castañeda, D.R.
Secretaría de Cultura – INAH

The use of these goblets is not
entirely clear. They may have
been used as pulque cups or as
incense vessels in which fragrant
resins were burned. Ceramics,
especially very high-quality
ones, were considered to be
living creatures and had a sacred
character. DK

Cat. no. 96
Goblet with stripe motif

Ceramic, pigment
H: 56 cm; D: 22 cm
Mexico, Aztec, Late Period, after
1506 AD, found in the former palace
of Moctezuma II.
Museo del Templo Mayor, Mexico City,
D.R. Secretaría de Cultura – INAH,
Inv. no. 10-646510
Photo: Gliserio Castañeda, D.R.
Secretaría de Cultura – INAH

The red and white stripes are
associated with the god Xipe
Totec, the god of war and the
renewal of nature. He wears the
skin of a slain human being and
often appears in the codices with
a white body adorned with red
dots or red stripes. The colours
red and white are interpreted as
the representation of decaying
skin. DK

Cat. no. 97
Two Aztec feather shields

Wood, cane, fleece, raw skin, feathers from the squirrel cuckoo and black-headed trogon,
probably black-throated tanager, azure cotinga, ridgeway cotinga, lovely cotinga, flame tangar
D: 75.5 cm; H: 2.5 cm (a); D: 71 cm; H: 5.8 cm (b)
Mexico, Aztec, around 1520 AD
Landesmuseum Württemberg Stuttgart, Inv. no. KK orange 6, E 1402
Photo: Hendrik Zwietasch [IdC]

These objects are only on view in **Stuttgart**.

Cat. no. 98
Quetzal-feather headdress

Feathers of the quetzal, cotinga,
roseate spoonbill, squirrel cuckoo,
kingfisher; wood, reed chips, fibres,
paper, cotton, leather, gold, brass
H: 130 cm, W: 178 cm
Mexico, Aztec, around 1520 AD
KHM-Museumsverband, Weltmuseum
Wien, Inv. no. 10.402
Photo: KHM-Museumsverband [GvB]

This object is only on view in **Vienna**.

Cat. no. 99
Badge or fan

Feathers, reed, colour
H: 119 cm
Mexico, Aztec,
16 century AD
KHM-Museumsver-
band, Weltmuseum
Wien, Inv. no. 43.381
Photo: KHM-Museums-
verband ᴳᵛᴮ

This object is only on
view in Vienna.

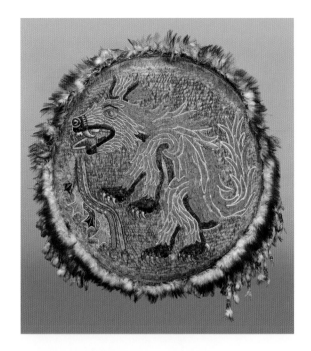

Cat. no. 100
Feather shield depicting a coyote

Feathers of the cotinga bird, roseate spoonbill ,
Venezuelan troupial, macaw and quetzal; gold plate, reed,
leather
D: 78 cm
Mexico, Aztec, around 1500 AD
KHM-Museumsverband, Weltmuseum Wien, Inv. no. 43.380
Photo: KHM-Museumsverband ᴳᵛᴮ

This object is only on view in Vienna.

Cat. no. 102
Sculpture in the shape of a feathered snake

Stone, polychrome paint
H: 20 cm; D: 28 cm
Mexico, Aztec, Late Period, after 1500 AD
Museum der Kulturen Basel, Collection Lukas Vischer, Inv. no. IVb 1359
Photo: Peter Horner

The god Quetzalcoatl took multiple forms. One of these was
that of a feathered serpent, as represented here. In this form he
was the Lord of Dawn, the creator of mankind and the bringer
of knowledge. In his other form he is Quetzalcoatl-Ehecatl, the
Wind God, recognisable by his red beak. ᴹᴮ

Cat. no. 101
Codex Borgia

Paper, complete facsimile edition of the Codex in original format;
Akademische Druck- und Verlagsanstalt Graz, n.a.
H: 24.4 – 26.6 cm; L: 1018.5cm
Mexico, Nahua, between ca. 1350 and 1521 AD
Linden-Museum Stuttgart, Inv. no. Gbc 361
Photo: Dominik Drasdow
Codex Borgia (renamed: Codex Yoalli Ehecatl, "the Book of Night and Wind"):
pre-colonial religious pictorial manuscript from Mexico, at present preserved in the Vatican Library
(https://digi.vatlib.it/view/MSS_Borg.mess.1; accessed on 7 July 2019).

Aspects of both style and content suggest that this is a Nahua document that originally came from the city of Cholula (Puebla-Tlaxcala Valley, Central Mexico). In the early colonial period it narrowly escaped being burnt at the stake (some pages still show fire damage). Friar Domingo de Betanzos may have brought it with him to Europe during his journey to Italy (1531–1533). It seems to have been subsequently in the possession of the Giustiniani family in Rome from the late sixteenth century until Cardinal Stefano Borgia (1731–1804) obtained the manuscript and transferred it to his private museum (Domenici and Laurencich Minelli 2014). After the Cardinal's death the codex was passed on to the Congregazione di Propaganda Fide, and from there to the Biblioteca Apostolica Vaticana.

The German Americanist Eduard Seler laid the foundation for the iconographical analysis of this spectacular painted book in his detailed commentary (1904/09). In accordance with the now outdated theories of his time he saw the religious images as elements of an occult astronomy. This "Astraldeutung" was corrected by the Austrian scholar Karl Anton Nowotny (1904–1978), who demonstrated that the codex had a divinatory (mantic) and ritual content (1961, 1976). His approach is followed by most modern studies (Anders, Jansen and Reyes García 1993; Boone 2007; Batalla Rosado 2008; Mikulska-Dąbrowska 2008; Jansen and Pérez Jiménez 2017).

According to this contemporary line of interpretation, the codex presents the ancient Mexican calendar of 260 days and shows how different days and periods are associated with deities and mantic symbols, indicating how certain times may be particularly inauspicious for specific activities and pointing out which deities are the ones to turn to for help and comfort or for the solution of problems. This symbolic system also predicted the character and destiny of those born on specific days, and prognosticated the relationships and fortunes of a married couple by adding up the numbers in their calendar names (their birthdays). A large section, known as the Temple Scenes, depicts the ritual activities and visionary experiences in the ceremonial centre (presumably of Cholula) during the agricultural year of 18 twenty-day months. [MJ]

Cat. no. 103
Teponatzli drum

Wood
L: 42 cm; H: 13.2 cm; D: 12.8 cm
Mexico, Mixtec, Post-Classical Period, 11th century before 1521
Museum der Kulturen Basel, Collection Lukas Vischer,
Inv. no. IVb 438
Photo: Markus Gruber

The Aztecs had two types of drums. One was the *teponatzli*, a long drum that was made of a hollowed-out log and was played horizontally. The other was the *huehuetl*, a large drum that was played vertically and was made of wood and animal skin. Both were used in festive and ritual music. Centuries-old *teponatzli* drums continue to be used in some indigenous communities today. MB

The carved motif of the two-tone drum is kept in the style of the codices. It shows two people in a bird costume singing and dancing around a central ceremonial object in which they have deposited spikes for blood sacrifices. On the side panels we see the sign for "flower" and "song": "*in xochitl, in cuicatl*", the Nahuatl expression for beautiful song or ceremonial discourse. MJ

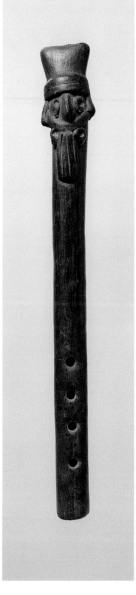

Cat. no. 104
Duct flute

Ceramic
L: 27 cm; W: 3 cm
Mexico, Colima,
200 BC to 300 AD
KHM-Museumsverband,
Weltmuseum Wien,
Inv. no. 158.936
Photo: KHM-Museums-
verband

A flute with the representation of a face on the mouthpiece. The face shows the iconographic features of the Meso-American rain god Tlaloc. GvB

Cat. no. 105
Double flute

Ceramic
L: 21.4 cm; W: 3.2 cm; D: 3 cm
Mexico, Aztec, between ca. 1350 and 1521 AD
Collection Nationaal Museum van Wereldculturen.
Coll.no. RV-2720-1
Photo: Irene de Groot

Music in Meso-America was based on the pentatonic scale, a sequence of just five tones per octave. Music was made with various flutes, trumpets, drums and rasps. Religious ceremonies were invariably accompanied by music. Musicians were extensively trained for the solemn responsibility of playing at festivals. MB

Cat. no. 106
Decorated bowl

Ceramic, pigment
H: 4.9 cm; D: 14.3 cm
Mexico, Aztec, between ca. 1350 and 1521 AD
Museo Nacional de Antropología, Mexico City,
D.R. Secretaría de Cultura – INAH, Inv. no. 10-50477
Photo: D.R. Archivo Digital de las Colecciones del Museo Nacional
de Antropología, Secretaría de Cultura – INAH

Food and drink were an important part of Aztec ritual,
since food was a gift from the gods to humankind. Ritual
food was served in special containers, which were
beautifully decorated. The skulls and bones on this bowl
may refer to the ancestors to whom this food was
offered. MB

Cat. no. 107
Incense burner

Ceramic, pigment
H: 28 cm; W: 37cm
Mexico, Aztec, between ca. 1350 and 1521 AD
Museo Nacional de Antropología, Mexico City, D.R. Secretaría de
Cultura – INAH, Inv. no. 10-220007
Photo: D.R. Archivo Digital de las Colecciones del Museo
Nacional de Antropología, Secretaría de Cultura – INAH

This incense burner has hollow feet, which contain
little ceramic balls. The vessel becomes a musical
instrument when shaken. Incense, made from a pine
resin called *copalli*, was essential in ceremonies.
During every important event, incense was burnt in
large quantities. MB

Cat. no. 108
Model of a ballcourt

Stone
L: 23.5 cm; W: 17.5 cm; H: 9.5 cm
Mexico, Aztec (?),between ca. 1350 and 1521 AD
Museum am Rothenbaum Hamburg, Inv. no. 56.49:2
Photo: Paul Schimweg

The ballgame *ollamaliztli* was played in the ballcourt. This game, played with a rubber ball, was both a regular pastime and a ritual ceremony. Players could only hit the ball with their hips. The ballcourt in the Sacred Precinct was primarily used for the re-enactment of creation stories. It was a place that gave access to the underworld, the place where the ancestors lived. MB

Cat. no. 109
Figure of the god Macuilxochitl

Volcanic stone
H: 50.5 cm; B: 16 cm; T: 17.5 cm
Mexico, Aztec, around 1500
KHM-Museumsverband, Weltmuseum Wien, Inv. no. 6.057
Photo: KHM-Museumsverband

Reddish Macuilxochitl ("Five Flower") has a feathered comb on his head, possibly referring to the *coxcoxtli*, a species of curassow. At the back of his head and on his temples there are the rosettes with hanging ribbons typical of Macuilxochitl-Xochipilli ("Flower Prince"). He wears a loincloth (*maxtlatl*) whose knot is visible at the front. Hints of a garment and ribbons are visible around his wrists and ankles. His arms rest on bent legs, a typical posture in similar sculptures. Macuilxochitl was the god of music and dance, pleasure and excesses and was considered to be another manifestation or name of the god Xochipilli. GvB

Cat. no. 111
Brazier

Ceramic, pigment
H: 9 cm; D: 20 cm
Mexico, Aztec, Late Period, early 16th century
Museo del Templo Mayor, Mexico City, D.R. Secretaría de Cultura – INAH, Inv. no. 10-252678
Photo: Gliserio Castañeda, D.R. Secretaría de Cultura – INAH

This brazier was found in the House of the Eagles, a large building next to the Templo Mayor. It depicts the rain god Tlaloc. It was in the House of the Eagles that new emperors performed the final rituals before ascending the throne. The brazier is decorated in Toltec style, like much of the art in the House of the Eagles. This way, the Aztec emperor associated himself with the glory of the Toltec ancestors. MB

Cat. no. 110
Chicahuaztli – sceptre

Travertine
L: 12.2 cm; B: 2.8 cm
Mexico, Aztec, Late Period, around 1500
AD; found in the Sacred District of
Tenochtitlan
Museo del Templo Mayor, Mexico City,
D.R. Secretaría de Cultura – INAH,
Inv. no. 10-213078
Photo: Gliserio Castañeda, D.R.
Secretaria de Cultura – INAH

This sceptre represents both the
rays of the sun and flashes of
lightning. It is mostly associated
with the god Xipe Totec, the god
of fertility. He used it to create
lightning and pierce the earth
so that the maize can grow. The
chicahuaztli, when not made
of stone, could also be used as a
rattle. MB

Cat. no. 112
Small bowl made of copal resin

Copal resin
Foto: Gliserio Castañeda,
D.R. Secretaría de Cultura – INAH

Copa incense continues to be widely
used in rituals today. These bowls of
copal were bought in contemporary
markets, but probably resemble the
ones that were sold in Tenochtitlan
500 years ago. MB

Cat. no. 113
Incense burner with long handle

Ceramic, pigment
L: 63 cm; W: 22.2 cm; H: 7.8 cm
Mexico, Aztec, between ca. 1350 and 1521 AD
Museo Nacional de Antropología, Mexico City, D.R. Secretaría de Cultura – INAH, Inv. no. 10-79894
Photo: D.R. Archivo Digital de las Colecciones del Museo Nacional de Antropología, Secretaría de Cultura – INAH

Copal incense was burnt during every ceremony in the Sacred Precinct. This took place in large
braziers that stood on the ground. At the same time, priests would hold incense burners like this
one in order to be able to direct the smoke in specific directions. MB

Cat. no. 115 a-q
Ritual deposit *ofrenda 78*

Various materials
Mexico, Aztec, between 1440 and 1499 AD; found
in the Sacred District, inside of the Templo Rojo Sur
Museo del Templo Mayor, Mexico City,
D.R. Secretaría de Cultura – INAH
All Photos: Gliserio Castañeda, D.R. Secretaría de
Cultura - INAH

During excavations in the Sacred District, archaeologists discovered four temples that were closely related to the architectural style of the Aztec precursor culture of Teotihuacan. They were all built between 1440 and 1502. In one of these temples, the Templo Rojo Sur, a sacrificial box made of volcanic stone, *tezontle*, was found. It was given the number 78. The four large stone slabs in the form of sacrificial knives were probably placed around it. Two of these slabs show the image of the deity Macuilxochitl-Xochipilli, which proves that the *ofrenda* was laid down for him. The contents of the sacrificial box were washed into a corner by a strong tidal wave, a clear indication that it was already there before 1499, the year of the great flooding of Tenochtitlan (Olmedo Vera 2002). Altogether there were 335 objects in the box. Most of them were miniatures of musical instruments, but also ritual objects, which were all related to rain and fertility as well as the associated ceremonies. In the exhibition we show a selection of 82 objects; in the catalogue there is a compilation of particularly meaningful objects that were laid down in the *ofrenda* as offerings. DK

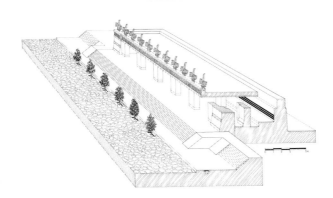

Cat. no. 114
Almena

Clay
H: 233 cm; W: 109 cm; D: 12.5 cm
Mexico, Aztec, Late Period, early 16th century;
found in the Sacred District
Museo del Templo Mayor, Mexico City,
D.R. Secretaría de Cultura – INAH, Inv. no. 10-650652
Photo: Gliserio Castañeda, D.R. Secretaría de Cultura – INAH

The roof of the *calmecac*, the priestly school, was decorated with many of these *almenas*. They represent the cross-section of a sea shell. The cut shell was one of the symbols of Quetzalcoatl, the patron god of knowledge and learning. MB

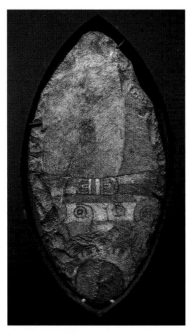

115c
Miniature of a drum

Volcanic stone *tezontle*, pigment
H: 18.8 cm; W: 21.6 cm; D: 16.8 cm
Museo del Templo Mayor, Mexico City, D.R.
Secretaría de Cultura – INAH, Inv. no. 10-252589

Typical drum of the Aztecs, used for rituals and processions. The drum membrane was often made of jaguar skin.

115a
Large stone slab in the shape of a sacrificial knife

Fine-grained basalt, pigment
H: 76.4 cm; W: 34.3 cm;
D: 4.6 cm
Museo del Templo Mayor, Mexico
City, D.R. Secretaría de Cultura
– INAH, Inv. no. 10-263096

115b
Large stone slab in the shape of a sacrificial knife

Fine-grained basalt, pigment
H: 83.5 cm; W: 43 cm; D: 5.3 cm
Museo Templo Mayor, Mexico
City, D.R. Secretaría de Cultura
– INAH, Inv. no. 10-220334

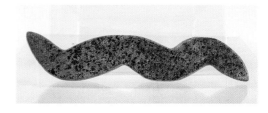

115e
Sceptre *chicahuaztli*

Basalt, pigment
H: 24.7 cm; W: 7.9 cm; D: 4.4 cm
Museo del Templo Mayor, Mexico City,
D.R. Secretaría de Cultura – INAH,
Inv. no. 10-252652

These sceptres, in Nahuatl *chicahuaztli*, were made of wood, with rattles of seeds or small stones to imitate the sound of falling rain. The sceptres represented the sun's rays that bring fertility to the earth. They were used in fertility rituals.

115d
Sceptre in the shape of a snake

Greenstone
L: 11.2 cm; W: 1.2 cm; D: 0.5 cm
Museo del Templo Mayor, Mexico City, D.R. Secretaría
de Cultura – INAH, Inv. no. 10-265743

The sceptre in the shape of a snake is a frequent attribute of the rain god Tlaloc. It is interpreted as a jet of water or lightning that the god sends to earth when the sky is full of rain. It is a symbol of the fertility that Tlaloc sends to earth as rain.

115f
Headdress of the god Xochipilli

Greenstone
H: 8.2 cm; W: 4.8 cm; D: 1.1 cm
Museo del Templo Mayor, Mexico City, D.R.
Secretaría de Cultura – INAH, Inv. no. 10-252573

This arrowhead-like headdress represents bird feathers. The bird's head is recognisable on the front of Xochipilli's headgear.

115h
Pendant made of sea snails

Sea snail oliva
L: 4.5 cm; W: 2.3 cm; D: 2 cm
Museo del Templo Mayor, Mexico City,
D.R. Secretaría de Cultura – INAH,
Inv. no. 10-253129 1/14

These pendants made of sea snails are associated with the waters of the underworld. This one was probably part of a necklace.

115g
Figure, rain god Tlaloc

Greenstone
H: 9.5 cm; W: 3.8 cm; D: 3 cm
Museo del Templo Mayor, Mexico City, D.R. Secretaría de Cultura – INAH, Inv. no. 10-252550

Small greenstone figures represent the rain god Tlaloc. Most of the objects, flowers and animals sacrificed in this *ofrenda* were dedicated to this deity.

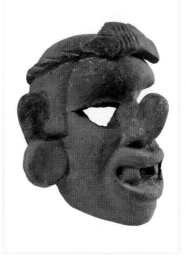

115i
Miniature mask

Clay
H: 11 cm; W: 7 cm; D: 1.1 cm
Museo del Templo Mayor, Mexico City, D.R. Secretaría de Cultura – INAH, Inv. no. 10-252598

The small mask represents a "ritual clown". He is often depicted in the codices with holders for feathers and fans used in rituals.

115j
Miniature mask, rain god Tlaloc

H: 5.7 cm; W: 5.6 cm; D: 1.4 cm
Museo del Templo Mayor, Mexico City, D.R. Secretaría de Cultura – INAH, Inv. no. 10-252570

The Mixtec-style mask shows a figure wearing a lot of jewellery. The many Mixtec objects of this *ofrenda* refer to the provenance of the god Xochipilli, whose origin is believed to lie in Oaxaca.

115k
Reproduction of a miniature turtle shell

Greenstone
L: 4.7 cm; W: 3 cm; D: 3.6 cm
Museo del Templo Mayor, Mexico City,
D.R. Secretaría de Cultura – INAH, Inv. no. 10-265588 2/5

This miniature turtle shell made of stone was a link in a necklace. The turtle is associated with the god of fire, the sun and music. All this is related to the god Xochipilli.

115m
Miniature of a pipe (*chichtli*) in Mixtec style

Greenstone
H: 3.5 cm; W: 3.5 cm; D: 2 cm
Museo del Templo Mayor, Mexico City,
D.R. Secretaría de Cultura – INAH,
Inv. no. 10-262947

115l
Miniature flute *tlapitzalli* in Mixtec style

Greenstone
L: 13.7 cm;
W: 2.1 cm;
D: 2.3 cm
Museo del
Templo Mayor,
Mexico City,
D.R. Secretaría
de Cultura –
INAH, Inv. no.
10-253049

115n
Miniature drum

Tezontle
L: 22.2 cm; W: 11.9 cm; D: 11.3 cm
Museo del Templo Mayor, Mexico City,
D.R. Secretaría de Cultura – INAH,
Inv. no. 10-252481

115p
Holder for feather fan, miniature
Volcanic stone
L: 22.9 cm; W: 6.8 cm; D: 5.7 cm
Museo del Templo Mayor, Mexico City,
D.R. Secretaría de Cultura – INAH,
Inv. no. 10-252581

Feather fans were used in ritual dances. The fans were made of feathers, which were put into a wooden holder. These fans were always used together with a musical instrument.

115o
Miniature rattle
Clay
L: 6.8 cm; D: 4.2 cm
Museo del Templo Mayor, Mexico City, D.R.
Secretaría de Cultura – INAH, Inv. no. 10-251293

The original instruments were made of pumpkin-like balls filled with seed shells. Or they were made of calabashes. They were indispensable instruments for ritual dancers.

115q
Guiro
Basalt
L: 14.6 cm; W: 8.7 cm; D: 5.3 cm
Museo del Templo Mayor, Mexico City, D.R. Secretaría de Cultura – INAH,
Inv. no. 10-EL.164; Ent.13405

This instrument was mostly made of human bone. Today it is made from calabash bowl and is called *guiro*. It is a rhythm instrument and widely used in Central America.

Cat. no. 116
Figure of the god Xochipilli-Macuilxochitl

Volcanic stone
H: 74.5 cm; W: 31 cm; D: 26 cm
Mexico, Aztec, Late Period, early 16th century; discovered in 1900
in the interior of the former Xochipolli-temple in the centre of Mexico City.
Reiss-Engelhorn-Museen Mannheim, Inv. no. V Am 1085
Photo: Reiss-Engelhorn-Museen, Jean Christen

Also known as the "Prince of Flowers", Xochipilli is the god of beauty, song, love and dance. He is also known as Macuilxochitl, the god of games and gambling. He presides over the offering dedicated to him, shown in the large showcase (see also Azteken 2003). MB

Cat. no. 117
Head of the god Xochipilli

Volcanic stone
H: 23.5 cm; W: 20 cm; D: 26.7 cm
Mexico, Aztec, around 1500 AD
KHM-Museumsverband, Weltmuseum Wien, Inv. no. 6.077
Photo: KHM-Museumsverband

This head has been broken off a sitting figure. It has a hairline visible from the side and is adorned with pearl necklaces, earrings and tubular nose jewellery. The eyes were originally inlaid with gemstones. It gazes out of the gaping beak of a bird. Parts of the beak are still present at the top and bottom. The feather comb has partly broken away. A rosette with three hanging ribbons is attached to each side of the bird's head. On the right side there is the representation of a heart, similar to the "Heart of the Copil" in the Museo Nacional de Antropología in Mexico City and referring to the heart sacrifices that nourished the gods and the sun. Xochipilli was a young sun god; in addition to music, dance and games, he was associated with the nobility, flowers and corn. GvB

Cat. no. 118
Figure of the god Xipe Totec

Volcanic tuff, pigment
H: 46 cm; W: 26.3 cm; D: 27.4 cm
Mexico, Aztec, between ca. 1350 and 1521 AD
Museum der Kulturen Basel, Collection Lukas Vischer, Inv. no. IVb 647
Photo: Peter Horner

This cult statue represents the Aztec God Xipe Totec, "Our Lord, the Owner of the Skin", shown as wearing the skin of a flayed man. Flaying was probably used as an agricultural metaphor for removing the vegetation from the Earth's surface (slash and burn) in spring as preparation for the planting of maize. Flaying was of course also practised on animals, for example for preparing codices. Colonial Spanish chronicles contain gory descriptions of humans being flayed alive during pre-colonial rituals, but these are not eye-witness accounts. We could speculate that flaying might have formed part of the ritual execution of enemy warriors and criminals (for example as a deterrent), but there is no proof for such a practice. MJ

Cat. no. 119
Sacrificial stone *temalacatl*

Basalt
H: 25 cm; D: 92 cm
Mexico, Aztec, between ca. 1350 and 1521 AD
Museo Nacional de Antropología, Mexico City,
D.R. Secretaría de Cultura – INAH,
Inv. no. 10-46485
Photo: D.R. Archivo Digital de las Colecciones del Museo Nacional de Antropología, Secretaría de Cultura – INAH

Some prisoners of war were killed in "gladiator fights". One foot was bound to a round stone, the *temalacatl*, which was decorated with representations of sunbeams. The prisoners were dressed in a feather costume and wore a sword in which the obsidian blades had been replaced by feathers. They faced an opponent with an obsidian sword wearing a jaguar skin costume. The outcome of the duel had therefore already been decided. MB

Cat. no. 120
Aztec "Chacmool" sculpture, depicting the Rain God Tlaloc

Basalt
L: 94 cm; H: 65.5 cm; D: 51.5 cm
Mexico, Aztec, between ca. 1350 and 1521 AD
Museo Nacional de Antropología, Mexico City,
D.R. Secretaría de Cultura – INAH, Inv. no. 10-10941
Photo: D.R. Archivo Digital de las Colecciones del Museo Nacional de Antropología,
Secretaría de Cultura – INAH

"Chacmool" sculptures were common throughout Meso-America as containers for offerings. This "chacmool" shows a person who is half reclining and holding a sacrificial bowl. He is wearing precious jewellery: earrings, a necklace, and bracelets on ankles and wrists. Sacred liquids and burnt offerings were presented to the gods in the sacrificial bowl. These offerings probably included human and animal blood as well as the hearts of humans and animals. MB

Cat. no. 121
Sacrificial altar

Basalt
L: 68 cm; W: 45 cm; D: 37 cm
Mexico, Aztec, Late Period, early 16th century
Museo Nacional de Antropología, Mexico City,
D.R. Secretaría de Cultura – INAH, Inv. no. 10-1080
Photo: D.R. Archivo Digital de las Colecciones del Museo
Nacional de Antropología, Secretaría de Cultura – INAH

This altar, which was probably used to present burnt offerings to the gods, is decorated with signs reminiscent of the antecedent city Teotihuacan. The human hearts depicted here, the most precious of all offerings, were sacrificed to the sun. Since Teotihuacan was the birthplace of the sun, it seems obvious that sacrificial vessels should have been decorated with this motif. MB

Cat. no. 122
Cuauhxicalli (Eagle Bowl), sacrificial bowl

Stone
H: 6.5 cm; D: 16 cm
Mexico, Aztec, around 1500 AD
KHM-Museumsverband, Weltmuseum Wien, Inv. no. 59.896
Photo: KHM-Museumsverband

After the Mexica-Aztecs had left Aztlan, their mythical country of origin, and arrived at Coatepec – the "Snake Mountain" – during the course of their journey, they built a temple for their god Huitzilopochtli and a ball playground. They made a so-called *cuauhxicalli*, a bowl in which the heart of a human sacrifice was placed after it had been removed from the chest and offered as food to the sun.

Eagle feathers are depicted on the outside of the bowl, referring to the name of this bowl. The discs below the feathers symbolise treasures. The sun inside the bowl is also surrounded by symbols for jade or treasures. On the underside there is a relief representation of the earth goddess Tlaltecuhtli, who could present herself in a double role as a life-giving and at the same time life-consuming god.

The mirror of the bowl shows the day sign Ollin ("movement"), the name of the present "Fifth Sun". The number 4, which belongs to the day name, is not shown. 4 Ollin is the name of the very last day of this creation, when an earthquake will destroy and sink everything and the Aztecs will lose their supremacy. GvB

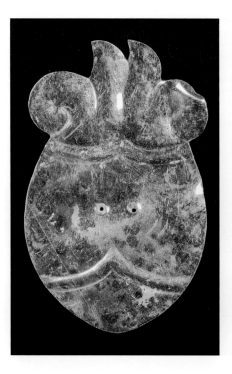

Cat. no. 123
Jewel in the shape of a heart

Gold
H: 4.1 cm; W: 2.6 cm; D: 0.1 cm
Mexico, Aztec, Late Period, early 16th century; discovered within an *ofrenda* at the Templo Mayor
Museo del Templo Mayor, Mexico City, D.R. Secretaría de Cultura – INAH, Inv. no. 10-654079
Photo: Jorge Pérez de Lara, D.R. Secretaría de Cultura – INAH

The most precious and sacred sacrifice was the human heart. Gold, called *teocuicatl*, "excrement of the gods", in Nahuatl, was the most valuable raw material. A golden heart thus represented an incredibly powerful and at the same time precious gift to the gods. The perforations in this piece show that it was once part of a necklace, bracelet or other kind of jewellery. Another special feature is the style in which the heart is worked. With the excavations at the Templo Mayor, gold objects which are worked in the Tenochtitlan style were recovered for the first time (see also López Luján 2017b). This differs clearly from the style of the Mixtec goldsmiths, also with regard to the technical production: while Mixtec gold objects were produced using the lost wax technique, Tenochtitlan objects are hammered and polished. MB/DK

Cat. no. 124 a,b,c
Three personified stone knives

Flint, sea shell, copal resin, obsidian, pigment
L: 15 cm, W: 6 cm, D: 2.3 cm (a); L: 23 cm, W: 6.7 cm, D: 2.1 cm (b); L: 17.5 cm, W: 6.7 cm, D: 1 cm (c)
Mexico, Aztec, Late Period, early 16th century; discovered within the Templo Mayor
Museo del Templo Mayor, Mexico City, D.R. Secretaría de Cultura – INAH, Inv. nos. 10-250230, 10-220280, 10-220291
Photo: Gliserio Castañeda, D.R. Secretaría de Cultura – INAH

These knives are often referred to as "sacrificial knives". However, their decoration and the fact that they are positioned upright in balls of copal resin, suggest that they were never used as such. It is more likely that they represent gods, other religious protagonists or animated creatures. The knives were painted, while the eyes are made of shell and obsidian. One of them has a speech bubble (c) coming out of his mouth, through which he sings or speaks. MB

Cat. no. 125
Heart

Jade
L: 3.5 cm; W: 2.7 cm; D: 2cm
Mexico, Aztec, between ca. 1350 and 1521 AD
Museum am Rothenbaum Hamburg, Inv. no. B3925
Photo: Paul Schimweg

This heart is made of jade, one of the most precious materials of the Aztecs and a symbol of young maize. Jade was mined far from Tenochtitlan and had to be transported hundreds of kilometres to be sacrificed in the Templo Mayor. Since the human heart was the supreme offering, it was replicated in many materials that were also considered very precious. MB

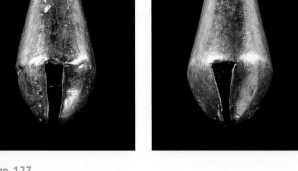

Cat. no. 126
Sculpture in the shape of a snake

Stone
H: 34 cm; W: 23 cm; D: 30 cm
Mexico, Aztec, between ca. 1350 and 1521 AD
Museum am Rothenbaum Hamburg,
Inv. no. B3637
Photo: Paul Schimweg

Snake sculptures were omnipresent in
the Templo Mayor. They were placed in
every imaginable place to commemorate Coatepec, the "Snake Mountain"
and birthplace of Huitzilopochtli. MB

Cat. no. 127
Golden bells

Gold
H: 2 cm; D: 0.9 cm (both)
Mexico, Aztec, Late Period, early 16th century; discovered within the Templo Mayor
Museo del Templo Mayor, Mexico City, D.R. Secretaría de Cultura – INAH,
Inv. no. 10-654077, 10-654078
Photo: Jorge Pérez de Lara, D.R. Secretaría de Cultura – INAH

According to the myth, Coyolxauhqui, the defeated sister of Huitzilopochtli, lay at the foot of the Templo Mayor. Her name means
"decorated with bells". These bells formed part of a sacrificial deposit
that had been placed to commemorate the birth of Huitzilopochtli. It
contained a total of 336 objects, among them 20 outstanding gold
objects. The sacrificial deposit also contained a sacrificed snake as a
reference to Huitzilopochtli's birthplace, the "Snake Mountain"
Coatepec. MB

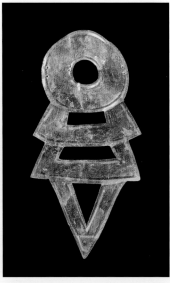

Cat. no. 128
Earrings of Coyolxauhqui

Gold
L: 8.3 cm; W: 4.2 cm; D: 0.2 cm (a); L: 8.9 cm;
W: 4.2 cm; D: 0.2 cm
Mexico, Aztec, Late Period, early 16th century;
discovered in the *ofrenda* 167 within the Templo Mayor
Museo del Templo Mayor, Mexico City, D.R. Secretaría de
Cultura – INAH, Inv. no. 10-654075, 10-654076
Photo: Jorge Pérez de Lara, D.R. Secretaría de Cultura
– INAH

One of the characteristic attributes of Coyolxauhqui are her earrings. On the stone sculpture
which depicts the goddess shattered at the foot
of the Templo Mayor, they are easily recognisable. Their original colour was reconstructed in
order to reproduce the original appearance of
the sculpture. MB

Cat. no. 129
Vessel depicting the rain god Tlaloc
Ceramic, pigment
H: 30 cm; W: 31.5 cm; D: 24.5 cm
Mexico, Aztec, Late Period, early 16th century; discovered within the Templo Mayor
Museo del Templo Mayor, Mexico City, D.R. Secretaría de Cultura – INAH, Inv. no. 10-168829
Photo: Gliserio Castañeda, D.R. Secretaría de Cultura – INAH

Tlaloc, the rain giver, is the god most frequently depicted in the Templo Mayor. His face can be found on ceramic vessels, stone sculptures and statuettes. On this vessel his eyes and eyebrows are represented by two intertwined snakes. Their mouths form the mouth of the deity. MB

Cat. no. 130
Head of the god Tlaloc
Metamorphic rock
H: 66 cm; W: 69 cm
Mexico, Aztec, Late Period, early 16th century
Museo Nacional de Antropología, Mexico City,
D.R. Secretaría de Cultura – INAH, Inv. no. 10-220843
Photo: D.R. Archivo Digital de las Colecciones del Museo Nacional de Antropología, Secretaría de Cultura – INAH

The rain god Tlaloc can be recognised by his "goggle eyes" and the long front teeth that protrude from his mouth. As a bringer of rain and fertility he was essential to survival. While Huitzilopochtli is an Aztec deity, Tlaloc has a long history in Meso-American cultures and has been revered by many people for centuries. MB

Cat. no. 131
Figurines, pendants
Stone
H: 4.8–6.4 cm; W: 1.7–2.3 cm
Mexico, Acatlán, Puebla, Mixtec?, around 1470 to 1515 AD
KHM-Museumsverband, Weltmuseum Wien, Inv. nos. 59.103, 59.209, 59.210
Photo: KHM-Museumsverband

Carvings like these are often found in the region of the Mixteca Baja in Puebla and in neighbouring Oaxaca. They are interpreted as protective beings, which is supported by their function as pendants. The specimens with closed eyes are interpreted as deceased ancestors. One figure shows the characteristic features of Tlaloc: rings around the eyes, a hook nose, rolled corners of the mouth and extended teeth. Figures like these are therefore called Tlaloques, small companions of the Aztec rain god Tlaloc. They helped him to distribute rain. These stone figures came to the Aztec centres as tributes, commodities or booty. A large number were housed in the sacrificial deposits of the Templo Mayor, half of which were dedicated to Tlaloc. GvB

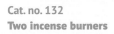

Cat. no. 132
Two incense burners

Ceramic
H: 31 cm, D: 31.7 cm (a); H: 29 cm, D: 24.6 cm (b)
Mexico, Aztec, Late Period, early 16th century
Museo Nacional de Antropología, Mexico City, D.R. Secretaría de Cultura – INAH,
Inv. no. 10-3885, 10-3883
Photo: D.R. Archivo Digital de las Colecciones del Museo Nacional de Antropología,
Secretaría de Cultura – INAH

These incense burners were used to burn copal resin. They were set up
everywhere in the Templo Mayor, and the copal resin was burned
continuously. These and all other fires in the Aztec Empire were extin-
guished only every 52 years at the New Fire ceremony. After a new fire
had been lit on a mountaintop outside Tenochtitlan, these incense
burners were the first to be rekindled inside the city. MB

Cat. no. 133
Incense burner in the form of a goddess of fertility

Ceramic, pigment
H: 14 cm; W: 17 cm
Mexico, Aztec, Late Period, early 16th century;
discovered within the Templo Mayor
Museo del Templo Mayor, Mexico City, D.R.
Secretaría de Cultura – INAH, Inv. no. 10-252247
Photo: Gliserio Castañeda, D.R. Secretaría de
Cultura – INAH

Some incense burners represented deities.
This one shows a fertility goddess
wearing a necklace of flowers and a paper
headdress. MB

Cat. no. 134
Mictlantecuhtli

Ceramic, pigment
H: 176 cm; W: 80 cm; D: 50 cm
Mexico, Aztec, Late Period, between 1430 and 1502;
found in the "House of Eagles" as one of two almost identical sculptures
Museo del Templo Mayor, Mexico City, D.R. Secretaría de Cultura – INAH, Inv. no. 10-264984
Photo: D.R. Archivo Digital de las Colecciones del Museo Nacional de Antropología,
Secretaría de Cultura – INAH

Mictlantecuhtli is the Lord of the Underworld, the Realm of the Dead, and the ancestors.
This sculpture was found in the Sacred District in the "House of the Eagles". Together
with another, almost identical figure, it flanked the northern entrance to the main room
of the building. The northern direction was associated with death and the ancestors.
Originally, one figure was painted blue and red, the other black, brown and red. A wig
with black curly hair was attached to the holes in the head. Mictlantecuhtli's liver and
gall bladder hang under his chest. *Ihiyotl*, "the sacred breath", dwelt within the liver. This
was one of the three souls that all humans possessed; the other two were located in the
heart and in the head.
The figure had shattered in hundreds of pieces when it was discovered. It took five
months to excavate it; the restoration work took almost a year. It weighs 128 kilograms
and is one of the most outstanding examples of the skill of Aztec artists. MB

Cat. no. 135
Skull mask

Human skull, flint, sea shell, pyrite
H: 19 cm; D: 13 cm
Mexico, Aztec, 15th century; discovered within
the Templo Mayor, *ofrenda* no. 11
Museo del Templo Mayor, Mexico City, D.R.
Secretaría de Cultura – INAH, Inv. no. 10-162934
Photo: Gliserio Castañeda, D.R. Secretaría de
Cultura – INAH

Skull masks were made from the skulls of
defeated elite warriors. They were buried as
grave goods of important Aztec rulers or
noblemen who were cremated and buried
in urns. Although these skulls are called
"masks", they were not worn as such, but
were probably part of a ceremonial
headdress or belt. MB

Cat. no. 136
Skull from the skull rack *tzompantli*

Human skull
H: 24 cm; D: 17 cm
Mexico, Aztec, 15th or 16th century; found during excavations
of the skull rack
Museo del Templo Mayor, Mexico City, D.R. Secretaría de
Cultura – INAH, Inv. no. 10-253311
Photo: Gliserio Castañeda, D.R. Secretaría de Cultura – INAH

The large openings on both sides of the skull show
that it was displayed on the skull rack *tzompantli*.
Hundreds of skulls, mounted on wooden beams,
were exhibited on a platform. In 2015 the "Great
tzompantli" of Tenochtitlan was discovered near the
Templo Mayor. So far about 500 skulls have been
found. Most of them come from young adults: a
possible indication that they are the heads of young
enemy warriors who had been executed. MB

Cat. no. 137
Pulque beaker

Phyllite
H: 37 cm; D: 18 cm; D: 26 cm
Mexico, Aztec, beginning of the 16th century
KHM-Museumsverband, Weltmuseum Wien, Inv. no. 6.069

The day sign "Grass" (*malinalli*) is prominent: it consists of a face with a fleshless lower jaw and tied-up hair. It is connected to Mayahuel, a pulque goddess. The patron of this day was the pulque god Patecatl.

In former times there were probably gemstones inlaid in the eyes. The large square ear jewellery is characteristic for pulque gods. Pulque is a traditional light alcoholic drink in Meso-America, made from the juice of the maguey agave. The drink was associated with the night and the souls of deceased – defeated and sacrificed – warriors. The calendar sign "8 Flint Sacrificial Knife" (*tecpatl*) engraved on the edge possibly refers to the catastrophic flooding in 1500 AD or gives the name of the maguey agave. Above the tied hair there is a half-darkened solar disc with the day sign "4 Movement" (*ollin*), the name of the present creation ("Sun"). It is being attacked by eight figures, which presumably represent threatening and militant *tzitzimime*. As dreaded death beings in the night sky, with whom the sun repeatedly has to fight, the *tzitzimime* threaten to destroy the Earth and creation. They attack in the darkness and at the end of a 52-year cycle. Some of the eight figures can be interpreted as gods: two pulque gods, the wind god Ehecatl-Quetzalcoatl, the fire god Xiuhtecuhtli and Tlahuizcalpantecuhtli, the god of the morning star (Venus). Across the entire back there is a goddess in a snake skirt with jaguar claws and two burning year bundles of 52 years. She holds sacrificial knives and is flanked by *atl tlachinolli*, war symbols. Streams of pulque flow from her breasts; a pulque vessel stands between her legs. She is interpreted as one of the *tzitzimime* and as the grandmother of the Mayahuel. Under the chin of the modelled head and – as in several Aztec stone sculptures – on the underside of the vessel, the earth deity Tlaltecuhtli is depicted with her throat and fangs open, skulls and crossed bones on her apron, as well as the calendar signs "1 Rabbit" (*tochtli*) and "Movement" (*ollin*). The day sign "Rabbit" was also identified with pulque. Mayahuel was the patron saint of this day. Tlaltecuhtli, the Earth, lies in the water, inhabited by snails. It is she who devours the sun at the end of every day. The complex symbolism of the vessel emphasises the pulque, the night and cosmic wars, the 52-year time cycles, sacrifices and the constant threat of destruction. GvB

Cat. no. 138
Goblet with applied clay skull

Ceramic, pigment
H: 29.2 cm; D: 15.5 cm
Mexico, Mixtec, around 1507; found during excavations at the Plaza del
Volador, in the immediate vicinity of today's Supreme Court of Mexico City
Museo Nacional de Antropologia, Mexico City, D.R. Secretaria de Cultura –
INAH, Inv. no. 10-3344
Photo: D.R. Archivo Digital de las Colecciones del Museo Nacional de
Antropología, Secretaria de Cultura – INAH

This goblet was part of a pair that probably belonged to an
extensive offering consisting of over 1,000 ceramics. The
archaeologist in charge suspects that the goblet was laid down
during the reign of Moctezuma II in 1507, at the time of the
New Fire ceremony. The painted red stripes form a symbolic
connection to Xipe Totec, the skull to the skull rack *tzompantli*.
The archaeologist further suspects that these goblets were filled
with the blood of sacrificed individuals. DK

Cat. no. 139
Figure of a god, aspect of Quetzalcoatl

Greenstone, coral or spondylus
H: 22.8 cm; W: 12 cm
Mexico, Aztec, Late Period, early 16th century
Landesmuseum Württemberg Stuttgart, Inv. no. E 1403

This unique figure made of greenstone probably embodies a nocturnal
aspect of the creator god Quetzalcoatl. The shell-shaped earrings and
the feathered snake on the back as well as the calendar signs on the
headstraps, hands and loincloth, associated with the Venus cycle,
indicate this legendary deity. However, Aztec gods often combined
several aspects or manifestations which make it difficult to identify
them unambiguously. It is also possible that this is the manifestation
of the God of Dawn, Tlahuizcalpantecuhtli.
There was a god with protective and at the same time harmful
qualities for all aspects of human life. The inner duct, which connects
the depression in the belly with the mouth suggests that the figure
was used in libation rituals. IdC

This object is only on view in Stuttgart.

Cat. no. 140
Sculpture of Ehecatl

Andesite
H: 195 cm; W: 40 cm; D: 55 cm
Location unknown, probably Central Mexico
Mexico, Aztec, Late Post-Classical Era, ca. 1480 to 1519 AD
Rautenstrauch-Joest-Museum Köln, donation Peter and Irene Ludwig. Inv. no. RJM 60382
Rheinisches Bildarchiv Köln, Photo: Wolfgang F. Meier, 2012

In Aztec times, the central figure of the creator god Quetzalcoatl ("feathered serpent") in large parts of Meso-America was worshipped especially in its appearance as the wind god Ehecatl. Ehecatl was generally regarded as the cause of winds from the four cardinal points, from the gentle breeze to destructive hurricanes. Since wind phenomena play a role in the plateaus of central Mexico, especially in the form of spiral-shaped tornados shortly before the onset of the rainy season, they were regarded as a harbinger of the rain gods that were indispensable for the fertility of the country. For this reason, their importance ranked second only to that of the rain god Tlaloc, especially among the rural population. The spiral shape of the tornados was taken up in architecture, but also in plastic art: temples with round forms were built in honour of Ehecatl, like the one in Calixtlahuaca in the valley of Toluca. The Cologne representation of Ehecatl with a spirally erected serpent body is unique: its head is clearly decorated with elements of the wind god. The columnar base in the form of a spiral-shaped serpent body with an animal or human head is also generally rare: Apart from two stone figures found between the third and fourth layers (around 1440 AD) of the main temple of the Aztecs on the stairs leading up to the Tlaloc sanctuary, no similar sculpture is known from the Aztec period. In pre-Classical and Classical times, the spirally screwed representation of the serpent's body can only be found in a clay pipe from Tlapacoya and a stone sculpture in Teotihuacan.

The Cologne Ehecatl probably stood on a cone embedded in the base on a temple platform or directly in front of the entrance to the sanctuary itself. With its height of almost two metres, it was visible from afar and emphasised the importance of the two deities united here. The body of a spiral winding serpent stands for the Quetzalcoatl aspect, but due to the missing feathers it probably emphasises more the shape of a whirlwind. The anthropomorphic head has iconographic elements with reference to some of Ehecatl's insignia, as they are also depicted in ethnohistorical sources, such as the Codex Borbonicus (sheet 22): with a cone-shaped hat made of jaguar skin, a jewel symbol, a red knot and earrings. There is also the typical sign of Ehecatl in many Aztec representations – the mouth mask in the shape of the duckbill. On the one hand it symbolises the blowing of the wind with its wide nostrils. On the other, the image of these birds falling through air and water also evokes an analogy to the deity Quetzalcoatl-Ehecatl, who often crossed the boundaries of the universe.

The origin of the Cologne Ehecatl cannot be clearly determined due to the lack of information and the uniqueness of this form of representation. So far, three possibilities have been discussed in the literature: the surroundings of the Huaxtecan village Castillo de Teayo in Northern Veracruz; the valley of Toluca (Calixtlahuaca); or also the Nahuatl-language area of the Basin of Mexico or alternatively of Puebla-Tlaxcala. However, an origin from the Aztec capital Tenochtitlan is most likely. The uniqueness of the sculpture could be explained by the fact that it was created in the course of the stylistic innovations that took effect there from around 1480. The monumental works of this period fell victim to the destruction caused by the Spanish conquest and mostly were not preserved.

Both Quetzalcoatl and Ehecatl play a central role in a version of the Aztec creation myth. In addition, Ehecatl played a prominent role in the Aztec calendar system: his symbol formed the second day of the 260-day calendar. The phenomenon of wind is still important today for some indigenous groups in Mexico – for example as an assumed cause of certain diseases ("*mal viento*", "*mal aire*")(see also Dyckerhoff 1999; Lopez Lujan 2015b; Lopez Lujan 2016; Lopez Lujan 2019; Solis Olguin 2009; Solis Olguin and Velasco Alonso 2003; Teufel 2012a; Urcid and Lopez Lujan in print; Zanin 2003). [AS]

Cat. No. 141
Bone flute

Human thigh bone
L: 26.5 cm; W: 4.2 cm; H: 3 cm
Mexico, Aztec, radiocarbon dating: between 1328 and 1415 AD
Linden-Museum Stuttgart, Inv. no. M 31956 L,
Acquired with fundings of the Zentralfonds Baden-Württemberg

This flute is made of a human thigh bone and has an incised decoration showing two dancers. One of them is an eagle warrior; the other embodies a deity who has not yet been identified.

The determination as a human thigh bone – for which we thank Dr. Michael Francken of the Institute of Scientific Archaeology, Dept. of Palaeoanthropology at the University of Tübingen – also revealed that the bone was deformed by lifelong, hard physical work.

Music was – and still is – an indispensable part of any ritual in Meso-America. Bone flutes, especially those made from the femurs of deer and humans, were played on important occasions as they were associated with continuity and fertility. Successful warriors kept the thighbones of their executed prisoners as a sign of their military skill. They were also used together with skulls to make ratchets. It was believed that this special sound made contact with the ancestors. MB

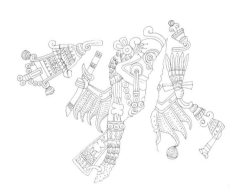

Cat. no. 142
Feather shield

Feathers of parrots, eagle and hummingbird;
fur from ocelot and jaguar
D: 67.5; H: 4 cm
Mexico, Aztec, around 1519 AD
Museo Nacional de Historia, Mexico City, D.R. Secretaría de Cultura – INAH
Photo: Omar Dumaine

This feather shield is preserved in the Museo Nacional de Historia in Chapultepec Castle, Mexico City. It was sent back to Mexico from Austria and belonged to Emperor Maximilian I of Mexico (reigned 1864–1867). It is one of four feather shields worldwide to have survived from the time of the Aztecs or very early colonial times. DK

This object is not on view in the exhibition.

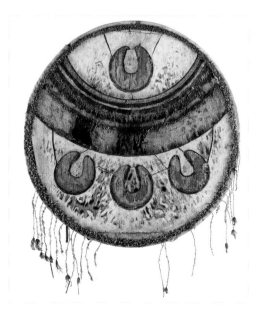

Appendix

Bibliography

Aguilar-Moreno, Manuel: Handbook to Life in the Aztec World, New York: Oxford University Press, 2007.

Alt-aztekische Gesänge. Nach einer in der Biblioteca Nacional von Mexiko aufbewahrten Handschrift [1536–1564], transl. by Leonhard Schultze Jena, ed. by Gerdt Kutscher, Stuttgart: Kohlhammer, 1957 (Quellenwerke zur Alten Geschichte Amerikas aufgezeichnet in den Sprachen der Eingeborenen 6).

Alvarado Tezozomoc, Hernando, Crónica Mexicana (Mexicayotl-1598), Mexico City: Edición Porrua, 1975.

Anales de Cuauhtitlan, in: History and Mythology of the Aztecs. The Codex Chimalpopoca, transl. and ed. by John Bierhorst, Tucson and London: The University of Arizona Press, 1992, pp. 23–138.

Anders, Ferdinand: Der altmexikanische Federmosaikschild in Wien, in: Archiv für Völkerkunde 32, 1978, pp. 67–88.

Anders, Ferdinand: Die Schätze des Montezuma. Utopie und Wirklichkeit, Vienna: Museum für Völkerkunde, 2001.

Anders, Ferdinand, Maarten E.R.G.N. Jansen and Luis Reyes García: Los Templos del cielo y de la oscuridad: oráculos y Liturgia. Libro explicativo del llamado Códice Borgia. Mexico City: Fondo de Cultura Económica, 1993.

Anders Ferdinand, Maarten E.R.G.N. Jansen and Gabina Aurora Pérez Jiménez (eds.): Códice Fejérváry-Mayer. El libro de Tezcatlipoca, Señor del tiempo. Libro explicativo del llamado Códice Fejérváry-Mayer, Graz, Mexico City: Akademische Druck- u. Verlagsanstalt, Fondo de Cultura Económica, 1994.

Anders Ferdinand and Maarten E.R.G.N. Jansen (eds.): Códice Vaticano-Latino 3738, Religión, costumbres e historia de los antiguos mexicanos. Libro explicativo del llamado Códice Vaticano A, Graz, Mexico City: Akademische Druck- u. Verlagsanstalt, Fondo de Cultura Económica, 1996.

Anders, Ferdinand and Maarten E.R.G.N. Jansen: Schrift und Buch im Alten Mexiko, Graz: Akademische Druck- u. Verlagsanstalt, 1988.

Anders, Ferdinand, Maarten E.R.G.N. Jansen and Gabina Aurora Pérez Jiménez: El Libro de Tezcatlipoca, Señor del Tiempo, libro explicativo del llamado Códice Fejérváry-Mayer, Mexico City: Fondo de Cultura Económica, 1994.

Anonymous Conqueror: The Chronicle of the Anonymous Conqueror. The Conquistadors, ed. by Patricia de Fuentes, Norman: University of Oklahoma Press, 1963, pp. 165–181.

Aparicio, Luis González: Plano reconstructivo de la región de Tenochtitlán, Mexico City: Instituto Nacional de Antropología e Historia, 1973.

Arens, William: The Man-Eating Myth. Anthropology and Anthropophagy, Oxford: Oxford University Press, 1979.

Atlas de Durán, Fray Diego Durán, Historia de las Indias de Nueva España e islas de Tierra Firme, 2 vols., ed. by José Rubén Romero and Rosa Camelo, Mexico City: Centro Nacional para la Cultura y las Artes, 1995.

Aveni, Anthony F., Edward Calnek and H. Hartung: Myth, Environment, and the Orientation of the Templo Mayor of Tenochtitlan, in: American Antiquity 53, no. 2, 1988, pp. 287–309.

Ayala Falcón, Maricela: La escritura, el calendario y la numeración, in: Historia Antigua de México, vol. 3, El Horizonte Posclásico, ed. by Linda Manzanilla and Leonardo López Luján, Mexico City: Miguel Ángel Porrúa, 1994, pp. 383–417.

Azteken, exh. cat. Martin Gropius-Bau Berlin and Kunst- und Ausstellungshalle der BRD Bonn, Cologne: DuMont Verlag, 2003.

Baer, Gerhard and Ulf Bankmann (eds.): Altmexikanische Skulpturen der Sammlung Lukas Vischer, Museum für Völkerkunde Basel, Basel: Wepf, 1990.

Barrera, Alan: Isotopía de estroncio aplicado a material óseo humano localizado en las ofrendas del Templo Mayor de Tenochtitlan. Tesis de licenciatura, Mexico City: Escuela Nacional de Antropología e Historia, 2014.

Barrera Rodríguez, Raúl: El Programa de Arqueología Urbana (2013–2014), in: Arqueología Mexicana, Edición Especial 56, 2014, p. 70.

Barrera Rodríguez, Raúl: El recinto sagrado de Tenochtitlan, Nuevos hallazgos, nuevas interpretaciones, in: Templo Mayor, Revolución y estabilidad, 40 aniversario del Proyecto Templo Mayor y 30 del museo, Secretaría de Cultura, Mexico City: Instituto Nacional de Antropología e Historia, 2018a, pp. 153–179.

Barrera Rodríguez, Raúl: Ventanas arqueológicas en el Centro Histórico de la Ciudad de México, Arqueología Mexicana, Edición Especial 79, 2018b, pp. 19–90.

Batres, Leopoldo: Exploraciones en la Calle de las Escalerillas, in: Eduardo Matos Moctezuma (ed.), Trabajos arqueológicos en el Centro de la Ciudad de México, Mexico City: Instituto Nacional de Antropología e Historia, 1990, pp. 109–167.

Batalla Rosado, Juan José: Codex Borgia, Madrid: Testimonio Compañía Editorial, 2008.

Baudez, Claude-François: La douleur rédemptrice. L'autosacrifice précolombien, Paris: Riveneuve, 2012.

Becker-Donner, Etta: Die Mexikanischen Sammlungen des Museums für Völkerkunde, Wien, Vienna: Museum für Völkerkunde, 1965.

Benavente, Toribio de (Motolinía): Historia de los indios de la Nueva España [1540], ed. by Giuseppe Bellini, Madrid: Alianza Ediciones, 1988.

Benavente, Toribio de (Motolinía), Memoriales o Libro de las Cosas de la Nueva España y de los Naturales de Ella [1555], ed. by Edmundo O'Gorman, Mexico City: UNAM, IIH, 1971.

Benavente, Toribio de (Motolinía): Memoriales: Manuscrito de la colección del señor Don Joaquín García Icazbalceta, Jalisco: Editorial Levy, 1967.

Benson, Elizabeth P. (ed.): Mesoamerican Sites and World-Views. A Conference at Dumbarton Oaks, October 16th and 17th, 1976, Washington, D.C.: Dumbarton Oaks Research Library and Collections, 1981.

Berdan, Frances F.: The Aztecs of Central Mexico: An Imperial Society, Fort Worth et al.: Holt, Rinehart and Winston, 2005.

Berdan, Frances F.: The Role of Provincial Elites in the Aztec Empire, in: Christina M. Elson and R. Alan Covey (eds.), Intermediate Elites in Pre-Columbian States and Empires, Tucson: The University of Arizona Press, 2006, pp. 154–165.

Berdan, Frances. F.: The technology of ancient Mesoamerican Mosaics: an experimental investigation of alternative super glues, FAMSI Report, 2007.

Berdan, Frances. F.: Aztec archaeology and ethnohistory, Cambridge: Cambridge University Press, 2014.

Berdan, Frances F. and Jacqueline de Durand-Forest (eds.): Matrícula de tributos (Códice de Moctezuma). Museo Nacional de Antropología, México (Cód. 35–52), Graz: Akademische Druck-u. Verlagsanstalt, 1980.

Berdan, Frances F.: The Codex Mendoza, 4 vols., Berkeley: University of California Press, 1992.

Berdan, Frances F. et al. (eds.): Aztec Imperial Strategies, Washington, D.C.: Dumbarton Oaks Research Library and Collection, 1996.

Berdan, Frances F. and Michael E. Smith: Imperial Strategies and Core-Periphery Relation, in: Frances F. Berdan et al. (eds.), Aztec Imperial Strategies, Washington, D.C.: Dumbarton Oaks Library and Collection, 1996, pp. 209–217.

Berdan, Frances. F. and Patricia R. Anawalt: The Essential Codex Mendoza, Berkeley: University of California Press, 1997.

Binnqüist, Citlalli López, Alejandra Quintanar-Isaías and Marie Vander Meeren: Mexican Bark Paper. Evidence of History of Tree Species Used and Their Fiber Characteristics, in: Economic Botany 66, no. 2, 2012, pp. 138–148.

Blanton, Richard and Gary M. Feinman: The Mesoamerican World System, in: American Anthropologist 86, 1984, pp. 673–682.

Blythin, Evan: Huei Tlatoani, the Mexican speaker, Lanham et al.: University Press of America, 1990.

Bonfil Batalla, Guillermo: México Profundo. Una civilización negada, Mexico City: Grijalbo, 1987.

Boone, Elizabeth Hill: Templo Mayor Research, 1521–1978, in: Elizabeth H. Boone (ed.), The Aztec Templo Mayor, A symposium at Dumbarton Oaks, 8th and 9th October 1983, Washington, D.C.: Dumbarton Oaks Research Library and Collection, 1987. pp. 5–69.

Boone, Elizabeth Hill: The Aztec World, Washington, Montreal: Smithsonian Books, St. Remy Press, 1994.

Boone, Elizabeth Hill: Cycles of Time and Meaning in the Mexican Books of Fate, Austin: University of Texas Press, 2007.

Bray, Warwick: Gold, Stone, and Ideology: Symbols of Power in the Tairona Tradition of Northern Colombia, in: Jeffrey Quilter and John W. Hoopes (eds.), Gold and Power in Ancient Costa Rica Panama, and Colombia, Washington, D.C.: Dumbarton Oaks Research Library and Collection, 2003, pp. 301–344.

Broda, Johanna, Davíd Carrasco and Eduardo Matos Moctezuma: The Great Temple of Tenochtitlan. Center and Periphery in the Aztec World, Berkeley: University of California Press, 1987.

Broda, Johanna: Calendarios, cosmovisión y observación de la naturaleza, in: Sonia Lombardo and Enrique Nalda (eds.), Temas mesoamericanos, Mexico City: Instituto Nacional de Antropología e Historia/CONACULTA, 1996, pp. 427–469.

Brumfiel, Elizabeth M. and Gary M. Feinman (eds.): The Aztec World, New York: Abrams, 2008.

Bujok, Elke: Der Aufzug der "Königin Amerika" in Stuttgart: Das "Mannliche unnd Ritterliche Thurnier unnd Ringrennen" zu Fastnacht 1599, in: Tribus, Jahrbuch des Linden-Museums N. F. 52, 2003, pp. 80–110.

Bussel, Gerard van: Der altmexikanische Federkopfschmuck. Aspekte seiner Rezeptionsgeschichte, in: Sabine Haag et al. (eds.), Der altmexikanische Federkopfschmuck, Vienna: KHM-Museumsverband 2012, pp. 115–133.

Bussel, Gerard van: Der Quetzalfeder-Kopfschmuck, Vienna: KHM-Museumsverband, 2017.

Bussel, Gerard van: Des Erzherzogs neues Federwerk, in: Christian Schicklgruber (ed.), Weltmuseum Wien, Vienna: KHM-Museumsverband, 2017, pp. 42–45.

Bussel, Gerard van: Abzeichen oder Fächer, in: Christian Schicklgruber (ed.), Weltmuseum Wien, Vienna: KHM-Museumsverband, 2017, p. 286.

Calnek, Edward: The Internal Structure of Tenochtitlan, in: Eric Wolf (ed.), The Valley of Mexico. Studies of Pre-Hispanic Ecology and Society, Albuquerque: University of New Mexico Press, 1976, pp. 287–324.

Carballal Staedtler, Margarita and María Flores Hernández: Hydraulic Features of the Mexico-Texcoco Lakes during the Postclassic Period, in: Barbara Fash and Lisa Lucero (eds.), Precolumbian Water Management. Ideology, Ritual and Power, Tucson: University of Arizona Press, 2006, pp. 155–170.

Carballal Staedtler, Margarita and María Flores Hernández: Las Calzadas Prehispánicas de La Isla de México, in: Arqueología 1, 1989, pp. 71–80.

Carrasco, Davíd: Religions of Mesoamerica. Religious Traditions of the World, San Francisco et al.: Harper and Row, 1990.

Carrasco, Davíd: Quetzalcoatl and the Irony of Empire. Myths and Prophecies in the Aztec Tradition, Chicago, London: Chicago University Press, 1992.

Carrasco, Davíd (ed.): The Oxford Encyclopedia of Mesoamerican Cultures. The Civilizations of Mexico and Central America, Oxford: Oxford University Press, 2001.

Carrasco, Davíd: Religions of Mesoamerica, 2. ed. Long Grove: Waveland Press Inc., 2014.

Carrasco, Davíd and Eduardo Matos Moctezuma: Moctezuma's Mexico. Visions of the Aztec World, Niwot: University of Colorado Press, 1992.

Carrasco, Pedro: The Political Economy of the Aztec and Inca States, in: George A. Collier, Renato I. Rosaldo and John D. Wirth (eds.), The Inca and Aztec States 1400–1800, New York et al.: Academic Press, 1982, pp. 23–40.

Carrasco, Pedro: Estructura politico-territorial del Imperio tenochca. La Triple Allianza de Tenochtitlan, Texcoco y Tlacopan, Mexico City: Fondo de Cultura Económica, 1996.

Carter, Jeffrey: Understanding Religious Sacrifice: a Reader, London: Continuum, 2003.

Casas, Bartolomé de las: Apologética Historia Sumaria, Mexico City: Instituto de Investigaciones Históricas, UNAM, 1967.

Caso, Alfonso: Los calendarios prehispánicos, Mexico City: UNAM, IIH, 1967.

Chávez Balderas, Ximena: Los rituales funerarios en el Templo Mayor de Tenochtitlan, Mexico City: Instituto Nacional de Antropología e Historia, 2007.

Chávez Balderas, Ximena: Fire, Transformation, and Bone Relics: Cremated Remains at the Templo Mayor of Tenochtitlan, in: Vera Tiesler and Andrew K. Scherer (eds.), Smoke, Flames and Body in Mesoamerican Ritual Practice, Washington, D.C.: Dumbarton Oaks Research Library and Collection, 2017.

Chimalpahin Quuauhtlehuanitzin, Domingo Francisco de San Antón Muñón, in: Arthur J. O. Anderson and Susan Schroeder (eds.), Codex Chimalpahin: Annals of the history of Central Mexico (1285–1612), 2 vols., Norman: University of Oklahoma Press, 1997.

Clavigero, Francesco Saverio: Geschichte von Mexico aus spanischen und mexicanischen Geschichtsschreibern, Handschriften und Gemälden der Indianer zusammengetragen, vol. 1, Leipzig: Schwickertscher Verlag, 1789.

Codex Aubin. Geschichte der Azteken, Codex Aubin [16. Jh.] und verwandte Dokumente, Aztec text transl. and explained by Walter Lehmann and Gerdt Kutscher, Berlin: Gebr. Mann, 1981 (Quellenwerke zur Alten Geschichte Amerikas aufgezeichnet in den Sprachen der Eingeborenen 13).

Códice Florentino, El manuscrito 218–220 de la colección Palatina de la Biblioteca Medicea Laurenziana, 3 vols., Florence, Mexico City: Giunti Barbéra, Archivo General de la Nación, 1979.

Códice Matritense del Real Palacio, El origen del nuevo sol en Teotihuacán, Textos de los informantes de Sahagún, in: Miguel León-Portilla (ed.), Antología. De Teotihuacán a los

Aztecas, Fuentes e Interpretaciones Históricas, Mexico City: UNAM, 1983, pp. 57–61.

Coltman, Jeremy: The Aztec Stuttgart Statuette. An Iconographic Analysis, in: Mexicon 29, no. 3, 2007, pp. 70–77.

Conway, Richard: Lakes, Canoes, and the Aquatic Communities of Xochimilco and Chalco, New Spain, in: Ethnohistory 59, no. 3, 2012, pp. 541–568.

Cortés, Hernán: Die Eroberung Mexikos. Eigenhändige Berichte an Kaiser Karl V., 1520–1524, Frankfurt: Insel-Verlag, 1980.

Day, Jane: Aztec. The World of Moctezuma, Niwot: Denver Museum of Natural History, Roberts Rinehart Publishers, 1992.

Delgado Gómez, Ángel (ed.): Hernán Cortés, Cartas de relación [1519–1526], Barcelona: Castalia Ediciones, 2016.

Deutsche Dahlien-, Fuchsien- Gladiolen- Gesellschaft e. V.: Heimat der Dahlien, URL: <http://www.dahlienzentrum.de/PDF-Dateien/1-Arten-Tafel1.pdf> [gelesen am 29.6.2019].

De Rojas, José Luis: Tenochtitlan – Capital of the Aztec Empire, Gainesville: University Press of Florida, 2012.

Díaz del Castillo, Bernal: The Memoirs of the Conquistador Bernal Diaz del Castillo, written by himself containing a true and full account of the discovery and conquest of Mexico and New Spain, London: J. Hatchard and Son, 1844.

Díaz del Castillo, Bernal: Historia verdadera de la conquista de la Nueva España, 2 vols., Mexico City: Editorial Nuevo Mundo 1943.

Díaz del Castillo, Bernal: The Conquest of New Spain, Baltimore: Penguin, 1963.

Díaz del Castillo, Bernal: Historia verdadera de la conquista de la Nueva España, ed. by Sáenz de Santa María, Mexico City: Patria, 1988.

Díaz del Castillo, Bernal: Die Eroberung von Mexiko, ed. and revised by Georg A. Narciß, Frankfurt am Main: Insel-Verlag, 2017, in: Estudios de Cultura Nahutal 47. 2014, pp. 169–209.

Díaz del Castillo, Bernal: Historia verdadera de la conquista de la Nueva España [1568]: manuscrito Guatemala [before 1575], ed. by José Antonio Barbón Rodríguez, Mexico City: El Colegio de México, 2005.

Die Geschichte der Königreiche von Colhuacan und Mexico [1536–1570], transl. by Walter Lehmann, ed. by Gerdt Kutscher, Stuttgart: Kohlhammer, 1974 (Quellenwerke zur Alten Geschichte Amerikas aufgezeichnet in den Sprachen der Eingeborenen 1).

Domenici, Davide and Laura Laurencich Minelli: Domingo de Betanzos' Gifts to Pope Clement VII in 1532–1533: Tracking the Early History of Some Mexican Objects and codices in Italy, in: Estudios de Cultura Náhuatl 47, 2014, pp. 169–209.

Durán, Fray Diego: Historia de las Indias de Nueva España y islas de tierra firme, Mexico City: N.N., 1880.

Durán, Fray Diego: The Aztecs. The history of the Indies of New Spain, New York: Orion Press, 1964.

Durán, Fray Diego: Libro de ritos y ceremonías en las fiestas de los dioses y celebración de ellas [1570], vol. 1, Mexico City: Editorial Porrúa 1967.

Durán, Fray Diego: Historia de las Indias de Nueva España e islas de la tierra firme [1570–1581], 2 vols., Mexico City: Editorial Porrúa, 1967.

Durán, Fray Diego: Historia de las Indias de la Nueva España e islas de la tierra firme, 2 vols., Mexico City: Editorial Porrúa, 1984.

Durán, Fray Diego: The History of the Indies of New Spain, Norman: University of Oklahoma Press, 1994.

Durán, Fray Diego: Historia de las Indias de Nueva España e islas de la tierra firme, 2 vols., ed. by José Rubén Romero and Rosa Carmelo, Mexico City: CONACULTA,1995.

Durand-Forest, Jacqueline de: The native sources and the history of the Valley of Mexico, Oxford: Oxford University Press, 1984.

Duverger, Christian: Crónica de la eternidad. ¿Quién escribió la Historia verdadera de la conquista de la Nueva España?, Mexico City: Taurus, 2015.

Dyckerhoff, Ursula: Statue des Windgottes Ehecatl (Objekttext Katalog-Nr. 12, RJM Nr. 60382), in: Michael Eissenhauer (ed.), Ludwigs Lust. Die Sammlung Irene and Peter Ludwig, exh. cat. Germanisches Nationalmuseum Nürnberg, Munich: Prestel, 1993, p. 11.

Dyckerhoff, Ursula: Monumentaler Schlangenkopf (Objekttext Katalog-Nr. 85, RJM 60381), in: Gisela Völger (ed.), Kunst der Welt im Rautenstrauch-Joest-Museum in Köln, exh. cat. Munich: Prestel 1999, p. 188.

Dyckerhoff, Ursula: Quetzalcoatl-Ehecatl (Objekttext Katalog-Nr. 84, RJM 60382), in: Gisela Völger (ed.), Kunst der Welt im Rautenstrauch-Joest-Museum in Köln, exh. cat. Munich: Prestel 1999, p. 186.

Edmonson, Munro S. (ed.): Sixteenth-century Mexico. The work of Sahagún, Albuquerque: University of New Mexico Press, 1974.

Eggebrecht, Arne: Glanz und Untergang des Alten Mexiko. Die Azteken und ihre Vorläufer, Mainz: Philipp von Zabern, 1987.

Evans, Susan Toby: Aztec royal pleasure parks. Conspicuous consumption and elite status rivalry, in: Studies in the History of Gardens and Designed Landscapes 20, 2000, pp. 206–228.

Evans, Susan Toby: Aztec palaces, in: Susan Toby Evans and Joanne Pillsbury (eds.), Palaces of the Ancient New World, A symposium at Dumbarton Oaks, 10th and 11th October, 1998, Washington, D.C.: Dumbarton Oaks Research Library and Collection, 2004, pp. 7–58.

Evans, Susan Toby: The Aztec palace under Spanish rule. Disk motifs in the Mapa de México de 1550 (Uppsala Map or Mapa de Santa Cruz), in: Susan Kepecs and Rani T. Alexander (eds.), The Postclassic to Spanish-Era Transition in Mesoamerica, Albuquerque: University of New Mexico Press, 2005, pp. 13–34.

Evans, Susan Toby: Ancient Mexico and Central America. Archaeology and Culture History, 3rd edition London, New York: Thames and Hudson, 2013.

Feest, Christian F.: Vienna's Mexican Treasures. Aztec, Mixtec, and Tarascan Works from 16th Century Austrian Collections, in: Archiv für Völkerkunde 44, 1990, pp. 1–64.

Feest, Christian F.: Der altmexikanische Federkopfschmuck in Europa, in: Sabine Haag et al. (eds.), Der altmexikanische Federkopfschmuck, Vienna: KHM-Museumsverband, 2012, pp. 5–28.

Ferino-Pagden, Sylvia (ed.): Wir sind Maske, exh. cat. Kunsthistorisches Museum Wien, Vienna: KHM-Museumsverband, 2009.

Fields, Virginia M., John M. D. Pohl and Victoria I. Lyall: Children of the Plumed Serpent. The Legacy of Quetzalcoatl in Ancient Mexico, London: Scala Publishers, 2012.

Filloy Nadal, L. and María Olvido Moreno Guzmán: From "Rich Plumes" to War Accoutrements. Feathered Objects in the Codex Mendoza and Their Extant Representatives, in: Maarten E. R. G. N. Jansen, Virginia M. Lladó-Buisán and Ludo Snijders (eds.), Mesoamerican Manuscripts, New Scientific Approaches and Interpretations, Brill: Leiden, 2012.

Filloy Nadal, Laura and María Olvido Moreno Guzmán: Precious Feathers and Fancy Fifteenth-Century Feathered Shields, in: Deborah L. Nichols et al. (eds.), Rethinking Aztec Economy, Tucson: University of Arizona Press, 2017, pp. 156–194.

Frankl, Viktor: Die Cartas de Relación des Hernán Cortés und der Mythos der Wiederkehr des Quetzalcoatl, in: Adeva Mitteilungen 10, 1966, pp. 7–17.

García, Élodie D.: The materiality of color in pre-Columbian codices: Insights from cultural history, in: Ancient Mesoamerica 28, no. 1, 2017, pp. 21–40.

Gentry, Howard Scott: Agaves of Continental North America, Tucson: The University of Arizona Press, 1982.

Gibson, Charles: The Aztecs under Spanish Rule. A History of the Indians of the Valley of Mexico, 1519–1810, Stanford: Stanford University Press, 1964.

Gierloff-Emden, Hans-Günter: Mexico. Eine Landeskunde, Berlin: De Gruyter, 1970.

Gillespie, Susan D.: The Aztec Kings. The Construction of Rulership in Mexica History, Tucson, London: University of Arizona Press, 1989.

Graham, Elizabeth: This Means War!, in: Shawn G. Morton and Meaghan Peuramaki-Brown (eds.), Seeking Conflict. Approaches and Interpretations in Maya and Mesoamerican Studies, Boulder: University Press of Colorado, in the press.

Graham, Elizabeth and Eric Golson: The Faces of Tribute. Paper presented at the 71st Meeting of the Society for American Archaeology Meetings, San Juan (Puerto Rico), 2006.

Graulich, Michel: Montezuma ou l'apogée et la chute de l'empire aztèque, Paris: Fayard, 1994.

Graulich, Michel: Myths of Ancient Mexico, Norman, London: University of Oklahoma Press, 1997.

Graulich, Michel: Le Sacrifice humain chez les Aztèques, Paris: Fayard, 2005a.

Graulich, Michel: Autosacrifice in Ancient Mexico, in: Estudios de Cultura Náhuatl 36, 2005b, pp. 301–329.

Grube, Nikolai: Unterkiefer einer Seekuh, in: Wilfried Seipel (ed.), Der Turmbau zu Babel. Ursprung und Vielfalt von Sprache und Schrift, vol. 3b, Writing, exh. cat. Kunsthistorisches Museum Wien, Milan: Skira, 2003, pp. 350–351.

Grube, Nikolai: Bilimeksches Pulquegefäß, in: Wilfried Seipel (ed.), Der Turmbau zu Babel. Ursprung und Vielfalt von Sprache und Schrift, vol. 3b, Writing, exh. cat. Kunsthistorisches Museum Wien, Milan: Skira, 2003, pp. 352–354.

Grube, Nikolai: Lippe einer Meeresschnecke, in: Wilfried Seipel (ed.), Der Turmbau zu Babel. Ursprung und Vielfalt von Sprache und Schrift, vol. 3b, Writing, exh. cat. Kunsthistorisches Museum Wien, Milan: Skira, 2003, pp. 356–357.

Guilliem Arroyo, Salvador: El templo calendárico de México-Tlatelolco, in: Arqueología Mexicana 6, no. 34, 1998, pp. 46–53.

Gunsenheimer, Antje: The Study of Human Sacrifice in Pre-Columbian Cultures: A Challenge for Ethnohistorical and Archaeological Research, in: Trutz von Trotha and Jakob Rösel (eds.), On Cruelty, Cologne: Köppe, 2011, pp. 255–284.

Haag, Sabine et al.: El Penacho del México Antiguo, Altenstadt: ZKF Publishers, 2012.

Hassig, Ross: Trade, Tribute, and Transportation. The sixteenth-century political economy of the Valley of Mexico, Norman: University of Oklahoma Press, 1985.

Hassig, Ross: Aztec Warfare. Imperial Expansion and Political Control, Norman, London: University of Oklahoma Press, 1988.

Hassler, Peter: Menschenopfer bei den Azteken? Eine quellen- und ideologiekritische Studie, Bern et al.: Lang, 1992.

Heikamp, Detlef: Mexico und die Medici-Herzöge, in: Karl-Heinz Kohl (ed.), Mythen der Neuen Welt. Zur Entdeckungsgeschichte Lateinamerikas, Berlin: Frölich und Kaufmann, 1982, pp. 126–146.

Heyden, Doris: Azteken. Gartenkünstler in der neuen Welt, in: Spektrum der Wissenschaft 10, 2003.

Hinz, Eike: Sozialisation in aztekischsprachigen Gesellschaften im 16. Jahrhundert, Hamburg: Public lecture, 1982, URL: <https://www.researchgate.net/publication/279806914_Sozialisation_aztekischsprach_Gesellschaften_EHinz [accessed on 29.6.2019].

Hinz, Felix: "Hispanisierung" in Neu-Spanien 1519–1568, Hamburg: Kovac, 2005.

Hinz, Felix: Der aztekische Dreibund – ein Tributimperium, in: Michael Gehler and Robert Rollinger (eds.), Imperien und Reiche in der Weltgeschichte. Epochenübergreifende und globalhistorische Vergleiche, Teil 1, Imperien des Altertums, Mittelalterliche und frühneuzeitliche Imperien, Wiesbaden: Harrassowitz Verlag, 2014, pp. 777–815.

Hirth, Kenneth G.: The Aztec Economic World. Merchants and Markets in Ancient Mesoamerica, Cambridge et al.: Cambridge University Press, 2017.

Hirth, Kenneth G., Sarah Imfeld and Colon Hirth: The Sixteenth-Century Merchant Community of Santa María Acxotla, Puebla, in: Deborah L. Nichols et al. (eds.), Rethinking Aztec Economy, Tucson: The University of Arizona Press, 2017, pp. 68–101.

Historia de los mexicanos por sus pinturas, in: Joaquín García Icazbalceta (ed.), Nueva colección de documentos para la historia de México, Mexico City: Salvador Chavez Hayhoe, 1941, pp. 209–240.

Hochstetter, Ferdinand von: Ueber mexikanische Reliquien aus der Zeit Montezuma's in der k. k. Ambraser Sammlung, Vienna: K. Gerolds Sohn, 1884.

Hodge, Mary G.: Aztec City-States, Ann Arbor: Museum of Anthropology, University of Michigan, 1984.

Homburg, Kirsten and Arne Homburg: theobroma-cacao.de, URL: <https://www.theobroma-cacao.de/wissen/geschichte/1500vchr-bis-1492nchr/azteken-und-schokolade/> [accessed on 29.6.2019].

Horcacitas, Fernando: The Aztecs Then and Now. Mexico City: Editorial Minutiae Mexicana, 1979.

Isaac, Barry L.: Cannibalism among Aztecs and their neighbors. Analysis of the 1577–1586 Relaciones Geográficas for Nueva España and Nueva Galicia Provinces, in: Journal of Anthropological Research 58, 2002, pp. 203–224.

Jansen, Maarten E.R.G.N.: Lord 8 Deer and Nacxitl Topiltzin, in: Mexicon 18, Nr. 2, April 1996, pp. 25–29.

Jansen, Maarten E. R. G. N. and Gabina Aurora Pérez Jiménez: Encounter with the Plumed Serpent. Drama and Power in the Heart of Mesoamerica, Boulder: University Press of Colorado, 2007.

Jansen, Maarten E. R. G. N. and Gabina Aurora Pérez Jiménez: Time and the Ancestors: Aztec and Mixtec Ritual Art. Series The Early Americas: History and Cultures, vol. 5, Leiden; Boston: Brill, 2017.

Jansen, Maarten E. R. G. N., Virginia M. Lladó-Buisán and Ludo Snijders (eds.): Mesoamerican manuscripts. New scientific approaches and interpretations, Leiden: Brill, 2018.

Jansen, Maarten E. R.G.N. and Gabina Aurora Pérez Jiménez: Time and the Ancestors. Aztec and Mixtec Ritual Art, Leiden, Boston: Brill, 2017.

Joyce, Rosemary A.: Mesoamerica. A Working Model for Archaeology, in: Julia A. Hendon and Rosemary A. Joyce (eds.), Mesoamerican Archaeology. Theory and Practice, Oxford: Blackwell Publishing, 2003, pp. 1–42.

Kirchhoff, Paul: Mesoamérica. Sus límites geográficos, composición étnica y caracteres culturales, in: Acta Americana 1, no. 1, 1943, pp. 92–107.

Kistler, Logan et al.: Gourds and squashes (Cucurbita ssp.) adapted to megafaunal extinction and ecological anachronism through domestication, in: Proceedings of the National Academy of Sciences, 2015.

León-Portilla, Miguel: La filosofía náhuatl estudiada en sus fuentes, Mexico City: Instituto Indigenista Interamericano, 1956.

León-Portilla, Miguel (ed.): Rückkehr der Götter. Die Aufzeichnungen der Azteken über den Untergang ihres Reiches, Zurich: Unionsverlag 1997.

Levine, Marc N. and David M. Carballo: Obsidian Reflections. Symbolic Dimensions of Obsidian in Mesoamerica, Boulder: University Press of Colorado, 2014.

Leyenda de los Soles, in: History and Mythology of the Aztecs. The Codex Chimalpopoca, transl. and ed. by John Bierhorst, Tucson, London: The University of Arizona Press, 1992, pp. 139–162.

Lienzo de Tlaxcala, ed. by Alfredo Chavero, Mexico City: editorial cosmos, 1979 (Reprint of the first edition of 1892).

Lockhart, James: Nahuas and Spaniards. Postconquest Central Mexican history and philology, UCLA Latin American Studies 76, Stanford: Stanford University Press, 1991.

Lockhart, James: The Nahuas After the conquest. A Social and Cultural History of the Indians of Central Mexico, Sixteenth through Eighteenth Centuries, Stanford: Stanford University Press, 1992.

Lockhart, James (ed.): We people here. Nahuatl accounts of the conquest of Mexico, Berkeley, London: University of California Press, 1993.

López, John F.: "In the Art of My Profession". Adrian Boot and Dutch Water Management in Colonial Mexico City, in: Journal of Latin American Geography 11, 2012, pp. 35–60.

López Binnqüist, Rosaura Citlalli: The Endurance of Mexican Amate Paper. Exploring Additional Dimensions to the Sustainable Development Concept, ITC Dissertation no. 97, University of Twente, 2003.

López Austin, Alfredo: Cuerpo humano e ideología, 2 vols., Serie Antropológica 39, 2nd edition Mexico City: UNAM, 1980

López Austin, Alfredo: Los mitos del tlacuache, Mexico City: Alianza Editorial, 1990.

López Austin, Alfredo: La religión, la magia y la cosmovisión, in: Linda Manzanilla and Leonardo López Luján (eds.), Historia Antigua de México, vol. 3, Mexico City: Miguel Ángel Porrúa, 1994, pp. 419–458.

López Austin, Alfredo: La cosmovisión de la tradición mesoamericana, 3 vols., Mexico City: Editorial Raíces, 2016.

López Austin, Alfredo and Leonardo López Luján: Mexico's Indigenous Past, Norman: University of Oklahoma Press, 2001.

López Austin, Alfredo and Leonardo López Luján: Aztec Human Sacrifice, in: Elizabeth M. Brumfiel and Gary M. Feinman (eds.), The Aztec World, New York: Abrams/The Field Museum, 2008, pp. 137–152.

López Austin, Alfredo and Leonardo López Luján: Monte Sagrado –Templo Mayor. El templo y la pirámide en la tradición religiosa mesoamericana, Mexico City: Instituto Nacional de Antropología e Historia, 2009.

López Austin, Alfredo and Leonardo López Luján: State Ritual and Religion in the Sacred Precinct of Tenochtitlan, in: Deborah L. Nichols and Enrique Rodríguez-Alegría (eds.), The Oxford Handbook of the Aztecs, New York: Oxford University Press, 2017, pp. 605–621.

López Luján, Leonardo: Las ofrendas del Templo Mayor de Tenochtitlán, Mexico City: Instituto Nacional de Antropología e Historia, 1993.

López Luján, Leonardo: The Offerings of the Templo Mayor of Tenochtitlan, Albuquerque: University of New Mexico Press, 2005.

López Luján, Leonardo: La Casa de las Águilas. Un ejemplo de la arquitectura religiosa de Tenochtitlan, 2 vols., Mexico-Stadt: Fondo de Cultura Económica, 2006.

López Luján, Leonardo: Echoes of a Glorious Past. Mexica Antiquarianism, in: World Antiquarianism. Comparative Perspectives, Alain Schnapp et al. (eds.), Los Angeles: The Getty Research Institute, 2013, pp. 273–294.

López Luján, Leonardo: El capitán Guillermo Dupaix y su álbum arqueológico de 1794, Mexico City: Museo Nacional de Antropología, Instituto Nacional de Antropología e Historia, 2015.

López Luján, Leonardo: The Great Temple Project. In Search of the Sacred Precinct of Mexico-Tenochtitlan, in: 2015 Shanghai Archaeology Forum, Awarded Projects, Shanghai: Research Center for World Archaeology, Shanghai Academy, Chinese Academy of Social Sciences, 2015, pp. 296–313.

López Luján, Leonardo: El Proyecto Templo Mayor (1991–2017). Recuento de cinco lustros de actividades, in: Eduardo Matos Moctezuma and P. Ledesma Bouchan (eds.), Templo Mayor: Revolución y estabilidad, Mexico City: Instituto Nacional de Antropología e Historia, 2017a, pp. 35–57.

López Luján, Leonardo: El oro de las ofrendas y las sepulturas del recinto sagrado de Tenochtitlan, in: Arqueología Mexicana, 24, no. 144, March/April 2017b, pp. 58–63.

López Luján, Leonardo: Cuando la gente "se uno-aconejó". La gran sequía de 1454 en la Cuenca de México, in: Arqueología Mexicana 25, no. 149, January/February 2018, pp. 36–45.

López Luján, Leonardo: Ruinas sobre ruinas: el subsuelo del centro histórico de la ciudad de México, in: Ventanas arqueológicas en el Centro Histórico de la Ciudad de México, Arqueología Mexicana, Edición Especial 79, 2018, pp. 10–18.

López Luján, Leonardo: Pretérito, Pluscuamperfecto, visiones mesoamericanas de los vestigios arqueológicos, inaugural lecture, 15 March 2019, Mexico City: El Colegio Nacional, 2019.

López Luján, Leonardo, Jaime Torres and Aurora Montúfar: Los materiales constructivos del Templo Mayor de Tenochtitlan, Estudios de Cultura Náhuatl 34, 2003, pp. 137–166.

López Luján, Leonardo and Judy Levin: Tenochtitlan, New York: Oxford University Press, 2006.

López Luján, Leonardo and Marie-France Fauvet-Berthelot: Spiegel mit einem Relief von Quetzalcoatl-Ehecatl (Objekttext zu Katalog-Nr. 127, Laboratoire d'Ethnologie, Musée de l'Homme, Paris, M.H. 78.1.61), in: Azteken, exh. cat. Martin Gropius-Bau Berlin and Kunst- und Ausstellungshalle der BRD Bonn, Cologne: DuMont Verlag, 2003, p. 430.

López Luján, Leonardo and Marie-France Fauvet-Berthelot: Aztèques. La collection de sculptures du Musée du quai Branly, Paris: Musée du quai Branly, 2005.

López Luján, Leonardo and Marie-France Fauvet-Berthelot: Antonio de León y Gama y los dibujos extraviados de la Descripción histórica y cronológica de las dos piedras …, in: Arqueología Mexicana 24, no. 142, 2016, pp. 18–28.

López Luján, Leonardo and Guilhem Olivier (eds.): El sacrificio humano en la tradición religiosa meso-americana, Mexico City: Instituto Nacional de Antropología e Historia, 2009.

López Luján, Leonardo and José Luis Ruvalcaba Sil: El oro de Tenochtitlan. La colección arqueológica del Proyecto Templo Mayor, in: Estudios de Cultura Náhuatl 49, 2015, pp. 7–57.

López Luján, Leonardo and Ximena Chávez Balderas (eds.): Al pie del Templo Mayor de Tenochtitlan. Estudios en honor a Eduardo Matos Moctezuma, Mexico City: El Colegio Nacional, 2019.

Lupo, Alessandro, Leonardo López Luján and Luisa Migliorati (eds.): Gli Aztechi tra passato e presente. Grandezza e vitalità di una civiltà messicana, Rome: Università degli Studi di Roma "La Sapienza" – Carocci Editore, 2006.

Marcus, Joyce: Mesoamerican Writing. Propaganda, Myth, and History in Four Ancient Civilizations, Princeton: Princeton University Press, 1992.

Marquina, Ignacio: El Templo Mayor de México, Mexico City: Instituto Nacional de Antropología e Historia, 1960.

Martínez de Cuervo, Consuelo: La tira de la peregrinación. Códice Boturini, Tepic: Gobierno del estado de Nayarit, 1975.

Matos Moctezuma, Eduardo: The Great Temple of the Aztecs. Treasures of Tenochtitlan, London: Thames and Hudson, 1988.

Matos Moctezuma, Eduardo and Felipe Solis Olguín: Aztecs, London: Royal Academy of Arts, 2002.

Matos Moctezuma, Eduardo (ed.): Excavaciones del Programa de Arqueología Urbana, Mexico City: Instituto Nacional de Antropología e Historia, 2003.

Matos Moctezuma, Eduardo: La muerte entre los mexicas, Mexico City: Tusquets Editores, 2010.

Matos Moctezuma, Eduardo: Vida y muerte en el templo mayor, Mexico City: Fondo de Cultura Económica, 2014.

Matos Moctezuma, Eduardo and Raúl Barrera Rodríguez: El Templo de Ehécatl-Quetzalcóatl del recinto sagrado de México-Tenochtitlán, in: Arqueología Mexicana 18, no. 108, 2011, pp. 72–77.

Matos Moctezuma, Eduardo and Leonardo López Luján: Escultura monumental mexica, Mexico City: Fondo de Cultura Económica, 2012.

Matos Moctezuma, Eduardo, Raúl Barrera Rodríguez and Lorena Vázquez Vallin: El Huei Tzompantli de Tenochtitlan, in: Arqueología Mexicana 25, no. 148, 2017, pp. 52–57.

McEwan, Colin, Andrew Middleton, Caroline Cartwright and Rebecca Stacey: Turquoise Mosaics from Mexico. Durham: Duke University Press, 2006.

McEwan, Colin and Leonardo López Luján: Moctezuma, Aztec Ruler, London: British Museum Press, 2009.

Márquez Morfín, Lourdes and Rebecca Storey: Population history in pre-Columbian and colonial times, in: Deborah L. Nichols and Enrique Rodríguez-Alegría (eds.), The Oxford Handbook of the Aztecs, New York: Oxford University Press, 2017, pp. 193–194.

Mendieta, Gerónimo de: Historia eclesiástica indiana [1870], ed. by Joaquín García Icazbalceta, Mexico City: Editorial Porrúa 1980.

Mikulska-Dabrowska, Katarzyna: El lenguaje Enmascarado. Un acercamiento a las representaciones gráficas de deidades nahuas, Mexico City: Instituto de Investigaciones Antroploógicas, Universidad Nacional Autónoma de México; Warsaw: Sociedad Polaca de Estudios Latinoamericanos, Instituto de Estudios Ibéricos e Iberoamericanos, University of Warsaw, 2008.

Mikulska, Katarzyna: On Numbers, Tables, and Calendars: When Writing Appeared, in: Contributions in New World Archaeology 7, 2014, pp. 47–72.

Miller, Mary and Karl Taube: The Gods and Symbols of Ancient Mexico and the Maya. An Illustrated Dictionary of Mesoamerican Religion, London: Thames and Hudson, 1993.

Miriello, Domenico et al.: Characterization and Provenance of Lime Plasters from the Templo Mayor of Tenochtitlan (Mexico City), in: Archaeometry 53, no. 6, 2011, pp. 1119–1141.

Moreiras, Diana K. and Fred. J. Longstaffe: Human Bone Enamel Phosphate Oxygen Istope Results from Multiple Templo Mayor Offerings (unpublished report), London: The University of Western Ontario, 2018.

Moreno de los Arcos, Roberto: Los territorios parroquiales de la ciudad arzobispal, Mexico City: Arzobispado de México, 1982.

Mundy, Barbara E.: Mapping the Aztec Capital. The 1524 Nuremberg Map of Tenochtitlan, Its Sources and Meanings, in: Imago Mundi 50, 1998, pp. 1–22.

Mundy, Barbara E.: The Death of Aztec Tenochtitlan, the Life of Mexico City, Austin: University of Texas Press, 2015.

Museum für Völkerkunde, Vienna (eds.): Das Altertum der Neuen Welt. Voreuropäische Kulturen Amerikas, Berlin: Reimer, 1992.

Nichols, Deborah L.: Merchants and Merchandise. The Archaeology of Aztec Commerce at Otumba, Mexico, in: Kenneth G. Hirth and Joanne Pillsbury (eds.), Merchants, Markets, and Exchange in the Pre-Columbian World, Washington, D.C.: Dumbarton Oaks Research Library and Collection, 2013, pp. 49–83.

Nichols, Deborah L.: Farm to Market in the Aztec Imperial Economy, in: Deborah L. Nichols et al. (eds.), Rethinking Aztec Economy, Tucson: The University of Arizona Press, 2017, pp. 19–43.

Nichols, Deborah L. and Enrique Rodríguez-Alegría (eds.): The Oxford Handbook of the Aztecs, New York: Oxford University Press, 2017.

Nicholson, Henry B.: Topiltzin Quetzalcoatl. The Once and Future Lord of the Toltecs, Boulder: University Press of Colorado, 2001.

Nicholson, Henry B. and Eloise Quiñones Keber: Art of Aztec Mexico. Treasures of Tenochtitlan, Washington, D.C.: National Gallery of Art, 1983.

Nicholson, Henry B.: The "Return of Quetzalcoatl". Did it Play a Role in the Conquest of Mexico?, Lancaster: Labyrinthos, 2001.

Nielsen, Jesper and Helmke, Christophe: Crowning Rulers and Years: Interpreting the Year Sign Headdress at Teotihuacan, in: Ancient Mesoamerica, p. 1–16, URL: <https://doi.org/10.1017/S0956536118000585> [accessed on 3.9.2019].

Nowotny, Karl A.: Cassis-Lippe mit mexikanischen Tageszeichen, in: Archiv für Völkerkunde 14, 1959, pp. 132–135.

Nowotny, Karl A.: Mexikanische Kostbarkeiten aus Kunstkammern der Renaissance im Museum für Völkerkunde Wien und in der Nationalbibliothek Wien, Vienna: Museum für Völkerkunde, 1960.

Nowotny, Karl A.: Tlacuilolli, die mexikanischen Bilderhandschriften, Stil und Inhalt, mit einem Katalog der Codex Borgia Gruppe, Berlin: Gebrüder Mann, 1961.

Nowotny, Karl A.: Unterkiefer einer Sirene mit Ritzungen, in: Archiv für Völkerkunde 14, 1961, pp. 113–116.

Nowotny, Karl A.: Codex Borgia, Graz: Akademische Druck- u. Verlagsanstalt, 1976.

Nowotny, Karl A., Tlacuilolli. Style and contents of the Mexican pictorial manuscripts with a catalog of the Borgia Group, Norman: University of Oklahoma Press, 2005.

Offner, Jerome: Law and Politics in Aztec Texcoco, Cambridge: Cambridge University Press, 1983.

Olivier, Guilhem: Mockeries and Metamorphoses of an Aztec God. Tezcatlipoca, "Lord of the Smoking Mirror", Boulder: University Press of Colorado, 2003.

Olivier, Guillem: The Sacred Bundles and the Coronation of the Aztec King in Mexico-Tenochtitlan, in: Julia Guernsey and F. Kent Reilly (eds.), Sacred Bundles. Ritual Acts of Wrapping and Binding in Mesoamerica, Barnardsville: Boundary End Archaeology Research Center, 2006, pp. 199–225.

Olivier, Guillem: Cacería, sacrificio y poder en Mesoamérica. Tras las huellas de Mixcóatl, "Serpiente de Nube", Mexico City: Fondo de Cultura Económica, 2015.

Olko, Justyna: The Insignia of Rank in the Nahua World. From the Fifteenth to Seventeenth Centuries. Boulder: University Press of Colorado, 2014.

Olmedo Vera, Bertina: Los templos rojos del recinto sagrado de Tenochtitlan, Mexico City: Colección Científica; Serie arqueológía Instituto Nacional de Atnropología e Historia, 2002.

Pagden, Anthony (ed.): Hernán Cortés. Letters from Mexico [1519–1526], New Haven: Yale University Press, 1986.

Palerm, Angel: Obras hidráulicas prehispánicas en el sistema lacustre del Valle de México, Mexico City: Instituto Nacional de Antropología e Historia, Seminario de Etnohistoria del Valle de México, 1973.

Parsons, Jeffrey R.: The Aquatic Component of Aztec Subsistence. Hunters, Fishers, and Collectors in an Urbanized Society, in: Subsistence and Sustenance. Michigan Discussions in Anthropology 5, no. 1, 2005, pp. 49–89.

Pasztory, Esther: Aztec Art, Norman: University Press of Oklahoma, 1998.

Pohl, John M. D.: Sorcerers of the Fifth Heaven. Nahua Art and Ritual of Ancient Southern Mexico, PLAS Cuadernos 9, Princeton: Princeton University, 2007.

Pohl, John M. D. and Claire L. Lyons: The Aztec Pantheon and the Art of Empire, Los Angeles: J. Paul Getty Museum, 2010.

Pohl, Mary E. D., Kevin O. Pope and Christopher von Nagy: Olmec Origins of Mesoamerican Writing, in: Science 298, no. 5600, 2003, pp. 1984–1987.

Prem, Hanns J.: Die Azteken. Geschichte, Kultur, Religion, Munich: C. H. Beck, 1995.

Prescott, William: The World of the Aztecs, Geneva: Editions Minerva, 1970.

Prescott, William H.: Die Eroberung von Mexiko. Der Untergang des Aztekenreiches, Cologne : Parkland-Verlag, 2000.

Quiñones Queber, Eloise (ed.): Códice Telleriano-Remensis. Ritual, Divination, and History in a Pictorial Aztec Manuscript, Austin: University of Texas Press, 1995.

Riese, Berthold: Das Reich der Azteken. Geschichte und Kultur, Munich: C. H. Beck, 2011.

Rojas, Araceli: El tiempo y la sabiduría. Un calendario sagrado entre los ayöök de Oaxaca, Oaxaca: CONACULTA, 2014.

Román Berrelleza, Juan: El sacrificio de niños en el Templo Mayor, Mexico City: Instituto Nacional de Antropología e Historia, 1990.

Román Berrelleza, Juan and Leonardo López Luján: El funeral de un dignatario mexica, in: Arqueología Mexicana 7, no. 40, 1999, pp. 36–39.

Rozat Dupeyron, Guy: Indios imaginarios y indios reales en los relatos de la conquista de México, Mexico City: TAVA ediciones, 1993.

Ruíz de Alarcón, Br. D. Hernando: Tratado de las Supersticiones de los Naturales de Esta Nueva España, Tratado de las Supersticiones, Dioses, Ritos, Hechicerías y Otras Costumbres Gentilicias de las Razas Aborígenes de México [1629], vol. 2, ed. by Francisco del Paso y Troncoso, Mexico City: Fuente Cultural Navarro 1953, pp. 17–180.

Rzedowski, Jerzy and Graciela Calderón de Rzedowski: Flora fanerogámica del Valle de México, 2 vols., Pátzcuarao: Instituto de Ecología A.C. y Comisión Nacional para el Conocimiento y Uso de la Biodiversidad, 2000.

Sahagún, Fray Bernardino de: Historia general de las cosas de Nueva España, Book IX: The Merchants, Florentine Codex (9), Florence: Biblioteca Medicea Laurenziana, 1577a.

Sahagún, Fray Bernardino de: Historia general de las cosas de Nueva España, Book XI: Natural Things, Florentine Codex (3), Florence: Biblioteca Medicea Laurenziana, 1577b.

Sahagún, Fray Bernardino de: Colloquios y doctrina christiana – Sterbende Götter und christliche Heilsbotschaft. Wechselreden indianischer Vornehmer und spanischer Glaubensapostel in Mexiko 1524, "Colloquios y doctrina christiana" des Fray Bernardino de Sahagún aus dem Jahre 1564, ed. by Walter Lehmann and Gerdt Kutscher, Stuttgart: Kohlhammer, 1949 (Quellenwerke zur Alten Geschichte Amerikas aufgezeichnet in den Sprachen der Eingeborenen 3).

Sahagún, Fray Bernardino de: General History of the Things of New Spain (Florentine Codex) [1569], transl. and ed. by Arthur Anderson and Charles E. Dibble, Santa Fe: The School of American Research and the University of Utah, 1950–1982.

Sahagún, Fray Bernardino de: Aus der Welt der Azteken. Die Chronik des Fray Bernardino de Sahagún, Frankfurt am Main: Insel-Verlag, 1989.

Sahagún, Fray Bernardino de: Historia general de las cosas de Nueva España [1569], Mexico City: Editorial Porrúa, 1999.

Sahagún, Fray Bernardino de: Historia general de las cosas de Nueva España [1569], Mexico City: Consejo Nacional para la Cultura y las Artes, 2000.

Sahagún, Fray Bernardino de: Historia general de las cosas de Nueva España [1569], Mexico City: Editorial Porrúa, 2006.

Schwartz, Stuart B. (ed.): Victors and Vanquished: Spanish and Nahua Views of the Conquest of Mexico, Boston et al.: Bedford et al., 2000.

Schwarz, Hansjörg: Die "Vogelkopfmaske" in Gotha, in. Gothaisches Museumsjahrbuch 15, 2012 [publ. 2013], pp. 29–42.

Schweppe, Helmut: Handbuch der Naturfarbstoffe. Vorkommen, Verwendung, Nachweis, Landsberg/Lech: ecomed, 1992.

Seler, Eduard: Die achtzehn Jahresfeste der Mexikaner (Erste Hälfte), in: Veröffentlichungen aus dem Königlichen Museum für Völkerkunde 6, no. 2/4, Königliche Museen zu Berlin, 1899, pp. 67–209.

Seler, Eduard: Codex Borgia. Eine altmexikanische Bilderschrift der Bibliothek der Congregatio de Propaganda Fide (3 vols.), Berlin: Gebrüder Unger, 1904–1909.

Seler, Eduard (ed.): Códice Borgia, Mexico City: Fondo de Cultura Económica 1963.

Seler, Eduard: Das Pulquegefäß der Bilimek'schen Sammlung im k. k. naturhistorischen Hofmuseum, in: Annalen des k. k. Naturhistorischen Hofmuseums 17, 1902, pp. 323–349.

Seler, Eduard: Uitzilopochtli, der sprechende Kolibri, in: Gesammelte Abhandlungen zur Amerikanischen Sprach- und Altertumskunde 4, Berlin: A. Asher, 1902–1923, pp. 157–167.

Seler, Eduard: Das Grünsteinidol des Stuttgarter Museums, in: Gesammelte Abhandlungen zur Amerikanischen Sprach- und Altertumskunde 3, Berlin: A. Asher, 1908, pp. 392–409.

Seler-Sachs, Caecilie, Walter Lehmann and Walter Krickeberg (eds.): Einige Kapitel aus dem Geschichtswerk des Fray Bernardino de Sahagún [1540–1585] aus dem Aztekischen übersetzt, Stuttgart: Kohlhammer, 1927.

Serna, Jacinto de la: Manual de ministros de indios para el conocimiento de sus idolatrías y extirpación de ellas, Tratado de las Supersticiones, Dioses, Ritos, Hechicerías y Otras Costumbres Gentilicias de las Razas Aborígenes de México [1653], vol. 1, ed. by Francisco del Paso y Troncoso, Mexico City: Fuente Cultural Navarro, 1953.

Smith, Michael E.: The Aztecs. The Peoples of America, Oxford, Cambridge: Oxford University Press, 1996.

Smith, Michael E.: Aztec City-States, in: Mogens Herman Hansen (ed.), A Comparative Study of Thirty City-State Cultures. An Investigation Conducted by the Copenhagen Polis Centre, Historisk-filosofiske Skrifter 21, The Royal Danish Academy of Sciences and Letters, Copenhagen: C. A. Reitzels Forlag, 2000, pp. 581–595.

Smith, Michael E.: The Aztecs, 3rd edition, New Jersey: Wiley-Blackwell, 2011.

Snijders, Ludo: The Mesoamerican codex re-entangled. Production use and re-use of precolonial documents, Leiden: Leiden University Press, 2016 (Archaeological Studies Leiden University 31).

Solís Olguín, Felipe: Head of a feathered serpent (Object text catalogue no. 18, Museo Nacional de Antropología, Mexico City, inv. no. 10-81558), in: Colin McEwan and Leonardo López Luján (eds.), Moctezuma: Aztec Ruler, exh. cat. British Museum London, London: British Museum Press, 2009, p. 74.

Solís Olguín, Felipe and Roberto Velasco Alonso: Gefiederte Schlange (Object text catalogue no. 78, Fundación Televisa Mexico City Reg. 21 pj.8), in: Azteken, exh. cat. Martin Gropius-Bau Berlin and Kunst- und Ausstellungshalle der BRD Bonn, Cologne: DuMont Verlag, 2003, p. 418.

Soustelle, Jacques: The Daily Life of the Aztecs on the Eve of the Spanish Conquest, Stanford: Stanford University Press 1970.

Staller, John E. and Michael Carrasco: Pre-Columbian Foodways in Mesoamerica, in: John E. Staller and Michael Carrasco (eds.), Pre-Columbian Foodways – Interdisciplinary Approaches to Food, Culture, and Markets in Ancient Mesoamerica, New York et al.: Springer-Verlag, 2010.

Staller, John E.: Maize cobs and cultures. History of Zea mays, Berlin, Heidelberg: Springer Verlag, 2010.

Stenzel, Werner: Quetzalcoatl von Tula. Die Mythogenese einer postkortesischen Legende. Vienna: Österreichisches Lateinamerika-Institut, 1980.

Stitzer, Michelle C. and Jeffrey Ross-Ibarra: Maize domestication and gene interaction, in: New Phytologist 220, no. 2, 2018, pp. 395–405.

Sued Badillo, J.: Los caribes: realidad o fábula. Ensayo de rectificación histórica, Río Piedras: Editorial Antillana 1978.

Tapia, Andrés de: Relación de la Conquista de México, Mexico City: Axial, 2008.

Taube, Karl A.: The Bilimek Pulque Vessel. Starlore, calendrics, and cosmology of Late Postclassic central Mexico, in: Ancient Mesoamerica 4, no. 1, Spring 1993, pp. 1–15.

Teufel, Stefanie: Quetzalcoatl-Ehecatl (object text catalogue no. RJM 60382), in: Azteken, exh. cat. Martin-Gropius-Bau Berlin and Kunst- und Ausstellungshalle der BRD Bonn, Cologne: DuMont Verlag, 2003, pp. 424.

Teufel, Stefanie: Fassadenskulptur in Schlangenkopfform (Object text catalogue no. RJM 60381), in: Christiane Clados and Stefanie Teufel (eds.), The Divine Heart of Things. Pre-Columbian Art from the Ludwig Collection, exh. cat. Rautenstrauch-Joest-Museum Köln, Cologne: Buchhandlung Walther König, 2012a, pp. 98.

Teufel, Stefanie: Skulptur des Ehecatl (Object text catalogue no. RJM 60382), in: Christiane Clados and Stefanie Teufel (eds.), The Divine Heart of Things. Pre-Columbian Art from the Ludwig Collection, exh. cat. Rautenstrauch-Joest-Museum Köln, Cologne: Buchhandlung Walther König, 2012b, p. 99.

Tezozomoc, Alvarado H.: Crónica mexicana, Madrid: Editorial Dastin, 2001.

Thévet, André: Histoyre du Mechique, manuscrit français inédit du XVIe siècle, Edouard de Jonghe (editor), in: Journal de la Société des Américanistes 2, 1905, pp. 1–41.

Thurston, Tina and Christopher T. Fisher; Seeking a Richer Harvest. The Archaeology of Subsistence Intensification, Innovation and Change. Studies in Human Ecology and Adaptation, vol. 3, New York: Springer Science and Business Media, 2006.

Torquemada, Juan de: Monarquía indiana, vol. 2, Mexico City: Editorial Porrúa, 1986.

Townsend, Richard F.: The Aztecs, London: Thames and Hudson, 1992.

Umberger, Emily: The Metaphorical Underpinnings of Aztec History. The case of the 1473 civil war, in: Ancient Mesoamerica 18, no. 1, 2007, pp. 11–29.

Unos annales históricos de la nación Mexicana. Die Manuscrits Mexicains Nr. 22 und 22bis der Bibliothèque nationale de Paris [Annalen von Tlatelolco, ca. 1528–1540], transl. by Ernst Mengin, part 1, Manuscript with translation with 30 illustrations in the text, Berlin: Reimer, 1939 (Baessler Archiv, vol. 22/nos. 2–3).

Urcid, Javier: Zapotec Hieroglyphic Writing, Studies in Pre-Columbian Art and Archaeology 34, Washington, D.C.: Dumbarton Oaks Library and Collection, 2001.

Urcid, Javier and Leonardo López Luján: Xochicalco en Mexico-Tenochtitlan. Apropiaciones gráficas en la tradición escrita tardía de la Cuenca de México, in: Estudios de Cultura Náhuatl, im Druck.

Velasco Piña, Antonio: Tlacaelel, Mexico City: JUS, 2001.

Viola, Herman J. and Carolyn Margolis (eds.), Seeds of Change. A Quincentennial Commemoration, Washington: Smithsonian Institution Press, 1991.

Von Oechelhäuser, Adolf: Philipp Hainhofers Bericht über die Stuttgarter Kindtaufe im Jahre 1616, in: Neue Heidelberger Jahrbücher 1, 1891, pp. 254–335.

Yetman, David A.: The Cactus Metaphor, in: William H. Beezley (ed.), A Companion to Mexican History and Culture, Chichester: Wiley-Blackwell, 2011.

Zanin, Daniela: Schlange (Object text catalogue no. 114, Musei Vaticani, Vatican City, AM 3296), in: Azteken, exh. cat. Martin Gropius-Bau Berlin and Kunst- und Ausstellungshalle der BRD Bonn, Cologne: DuMont Verlag, 2003, p. 427.

Zantwijk, Rudolf van: Handel en wandel van de Azteken. De sociale geschiedenis van voor-Spaans Mexico, Assen: Van Gorcum, 1977.

Zantwijk, Rudolf van: Zegevierend met de Zon. Duizend jaar Azteekse gedichten en gedachten, Amsterdam: Prometheus, 1994.

Zimmerman, Günter (ed.), Briefe der indianischen Nobilität aus Neuspanien an Karl V. und Philipp II. um die Mitte des 16. Jahrhunderts, Hamburg: Museum für Völkerkunde, 1970 (Beiträge zur mittelamerikanischen Völkerkunde 10).

Zorita, Alonso de: Breve y sumaria relación de los señores de la Nueva España, ed. by Joaquin Ramirez Cabañas, Mexico City: Universidad Nacional Autónoma, 1963.

List of Authors

Aguilar-Moreno, Manuel, Prof. Dr.: Professor of Art History at California State University in Los Angeles. Renowned expert on pre-Columbian civilisations, the colonial history of Mexico and Latin America and Mexican Muralism. Research: Meso-American art and history, colonial art and history of Mexico with emphasis in the Indian-Christian art of the transculturation process, funerary art and the pre-Columbian ballgame.

maguila2@calstatela.edu

Athie Islas, Ivonne: Student attending the Archaeology Master's course at Leiden University. Research: Obsidian sources, properties and technology; Obsidian collection from the Templo Mayor of Tenochtitlan.

ivonne.athie@wereldculturen.nl

Bayer, Ehrentraud, Dr. habil.: Vice-Director at the Botanical Garden, Munich-Nymphenburg, Curator of Crop Plants, Succulents, Coldhouse Plants; responsible for Public Relations. Research: Flora of Chile.

bayer@snsb.de

Barrera Rodríguez, Raúl: Senior Researcher at Instituto Nacional de Antropología e Historia (Dirección de Salvamento Arqueológico) in Mexico City and Head of the Programa de Arqueología Urbana of the Templo Mayor Museum. Research: The sacred district of Tenochtitlan.

Berdan, Frances, Prof. Dr.: Professor Emerita of Anthropology, California State University, San Bernardino, USA. Prof. Berdan has published numerous books on the Aztecs. Research: Aztec culture, economy and society; Colonial Mexico.

fberdan@csusb.edu

Berger, Martin, Dr.: Curator of the Middle and South America Department at the National Museum of World Cultures, Leiden. Curator of the exhibition "Aztecs". Research: Global flows of people and objects, indigenous forms of representation, (ethnographic) museums and histories of collections, and popular culture.

martin.berger@wereldculturen.nl

Bussel, Gerard van: Curator of the North and Central America Department at the Weltmuseum Wien, Vienna. Historical and iconographical research.

Chávez Balderas, Ximena .: Forensic expert at Fiscalía General del Estado de Quintana Roo in Cancún. Bioarchaeologist at the Templo Mayor Project; Research: Aztec bioarchaeology and archaeozoology; forensic anthropology.

xchavezb@tulane.edu

de Castro, Inés, Prof. Dr.: Since 2010 director of the Linden-Museum Stuttgart, State Museum of Ethnology of the State of Baden-Württemberg, Germany. Former research field: Meso-American archaeology and ethnohistory.

deCastro@lindenmuseum.de

Evans, Susan Toby, Prof. Dr.: Editor for Anthropology, Pennsylvania State University, University Park, State College, USA. Research: Aztec culture, settlement patterns, palaces; Teotihuacan plan, orientation and processions; Meso-American culture history and evolution.

ste@psu.edu

Hinz, Felix, Prof. Dr.: Professor for Contemporary History and its didactics, University of Education Freiburg. Research: transculturation, colonialism, popular historical culture.

felix.hinz@ph-freiburg.de

Jansen, Maarten E.R.G.N., Prof. Dr.: Emeritus Professor, "Heritage of Indigenous Peoples" at Leiden University. Research: Meso-American heritage, memory and symbolism, with focus on Nahua and Mixtec pictorial manuscripts, colonial texts and cultural continuity.

m.e.r.g.n.jansen@arch.leidenuniv.nl

Kurella, Doris, Dr.: Curator of the Latin- and North America Department at the Linden-Museum Stuttgart. Curator of the exhibition "Aztecs". Research: Linden-Museum collections; ethnohistory and archaeology of Colombia; history of Empires; Southern Andes, Amazonia.

kurella@lindenmuseum.de

López Luján, Leonardo, Prof. Dr.: Senior professor at the National Institute of Anthropology and History in Mexico City. Director of the Templo Mayor Project. Research: Religion, politics, and art of pre-Hispanic societies in Central Mexico.

www.mesoweb.com/about/leonardo.html

Macuil Martínez, Raul, Dr.: Researcher at the historical and cultural research center of the Ministry of Culture of the Government of the State of Hidalgo at Pachuca de Soto, Mexico. Speaker of the Nahuatl language and researcher on the history of indigenous peoples, colonial and contemporary times.

macuil2@gmail.com

Matos Moctezuma, Eduardo, Dr.: Expert in Aztec culture, Templo Mayor Museum, Mexico City. Member Emeritus of National Institute of Anthropology and History, Mexico City.

ematosm4@gmail.com

Mundy, Barbara E., Prof. Dr.: Professor of Art History, Fordham University, New York. Author of *The Death of Aztec Tenochtitlan, the Life of Mexico City*. Research: Mesoamerican manuscripts and cartography.

mundy@fordham.edu

Olivier, Guilhem, Dr.: Research professor at the Instituto de Investigaciones Históricas de la Universidad Nacional Autónoma de México in Mexico City. Research: Mesoamerican gods (Tezcatlipoca, Quetzalcoatl, Itzpapalotl, Mixcoatl, etc.), human sacrifice, symbols of power, the foretelling and presages of the Conquest.

olivier@unam.mx

Olko, Justyna, Dr. habil.: Associate Professor at the Faculty of "Artes Liberales", University of Warsaw; director of the Center for Research and Practice in Cultural Continuity; Research: Meso-American ethnohistory, anthropology and sociolinguistics with a special focus on Nahua language and culture.

jolko@al.uw.edu.pl

Pérez Jiménez, Gabina Aurora: Retired teacher of Mixtec language and culture at Leiden University. Research: Mixtec society and oral traditions; ancient Mexican codices; rights of Indigenous Peoples; decolonizing methodology.

aurora.perez.oax@gmail.com

Rojas, Araceli, Dr.: Postdoctoral researcher at the Institute of Iberian and Iberoamerican Studies, University of Warsaw. Grantee of a Marie Skłodowska-Curie fellowship, European Union's Framework Program for Research and Innovation "Horizon 2020", Agreement no. 800253. Research: Central Mexican and Oaxacan codices; archaeology and decolonial practices.

araceli.rojas@wn.uw.edu.pl

Slenczka, Anne, Dr.: Curator of the American Collections at the Rautenstrauch-Joest-Museum – Cultures of the World in Cologne, Germany. Research: Pre-Columbian history and ethnohistory of Meso-America, Mexican culture of death (Día de los Muertos), Mexican museology.

anne.slenczka@stadt-koeln.de

Snijders, Ludo, Dr.: Independent Researcher. Research: Precolonial Meso-American codices; materiality of Meso-American artefacts.

l.snijders.87@gmail.com

Authors of the object texts

DK – Doris Kurella
MB – Martin Berger
IdC – Inés de Castro
LLL – Leonardo López Luján
AS – Anne Slenczka
GvB – Gerard van Bussel
MJ – Maarten E.R.G.N. Jansen

AZTECS

An exhibition of the Linden-Museum Stuttgart
in collaboration with Nationaal Museum van Wereldculturen

Baden-Württemberg State Exhibition at the Linden-Museum Stuttgart	Special Exhibition at the Weltmuseum Wien	Special Exhibition at the Museum Volkenkunde, Leiden
12 October 2019 to 3 May 2020	24 June 2020 to 6 January 2021	21 Februar 2021 to 29 August 2021

Edited by Doris Kurella, Martin Berger and Inés de Castro
in cooperation with the Instituto Nacional de Antropología e Historia (INAH), Mexico

Project Management, Hirmer Publishers: Jutta Allekotte
Copy-editing German Edition: Ute Rummel, Cairo
Copy-editing English Edition: Jane Michael, Munich
Translations into English: Karsa Capacitación Empresarial, Mexico City; Marcus Berendsen
Layout, Typesetting and Production: Lucia Ott
Cover Design: Lucia Ott after the poster design by OPERA Amsterdam
Pre-Press: Reproline Mediateam, Munich
Printing and Binding: Passavia Druckservice GmbH & Co.KG, Passau
Paper: Magno Satin, 150 g/m2
Typeface: PT Sans Pro, DTL Documenta

Printed in Germany

Bibliographic information published by the Deutsche National-bibliothek
The Deutsche Nationalbibliothek lists this publication in the Deutsche Nationalbibliografie; detailed bibliographic data are available in the Internet at http://www.dnb.de.

ISBN 978-3-7774-3378-3 (English trade edition)
ISBN 978-3-7774-3483-4 (English museum edition)
www.hirmerpublishers.com
www.hirmerpublishers.co.uk

www.lindenmuseum.de
www.volkenkunde.nl
www.weltmuseumwien.at

PATRON EXHIBITION STUTTGART:
Federal President Frank-Walter Steinmeier

IN COOPERATION WITH

BADEN-WÜRTTEMBERG STATE EXHIBITION AT THE LINDEN-MUSEUM STUTTGART HAS BEEN MADE POSSIBLE BY:

Baden-Württemberg

MINISTRY OF SCIENCE, RESEARCH AND ARTS

FOR THE KIND SUPPORT OF THE BADEN-WÜRTTEM-BERG STATE EXHIBITION AT THE LINDEN-MUSEUM STUTTGART WE WOULD LIKE TO THANK:

FOR THE KIND SUPPORT OF THE SPECIAL EXHIBITION AT THE MUSEUM VOLKENKUNDE WE WOULD LIKE TO THANK:

Exhibition Organisation

IN COOPERATION WITH

Secretaría de Cultura, Mexico:
Alejandra Frausto Guerrero, Secretaría

Instituto Nacional de Antropología e Historia (INAH):
Diego Prieto Hernández, Director General

Aída Castilleja González, Secretaría Técnica

Juan Manuel Garibay López, Coordinador Nacional de Museos y Exposiciones

Alejandra Barajas Moreno, Directora de Exposiciones

Itzia Villicaña Gerónimo, Coordinadora de Proyecto

Antonio Saborit, Director del Museo Nacional de Antropología

Patricia Ledesma Bouchan, Directora del Museo del Templo Mayor

EXHIBITION DESIGN:

OPERA Amsterdam

LENDERS

Collectie Paul en Dora Janssen-Arts,
Museum aan den Stroom, Antwerp

Landesmuseum Württemberg, Stuttgart

Linden-Museum Stuttgart

Museo Ciencias Naturales, Madrid

Museo Nacional de Antropología, Mexico City

Museo Templo Mayor, Mexico City

Museum am Rothenbaum, Hamburg

Museum der Kulturen Basel

Nationaal Museum van Wereldculturen,
Amsterdam and Leiden

National Museum of Denmark, Copenhagen

Rautenstrauch-Joest-Museum, Cologne

Reiss-Engelhorn-Museen, Mannheim

Royal Museum of Art and History, Brussels

Stiftung Schloss Friedenstein Gotha

Weltmuseum Wien, Vienna